The very word "restricted" reflects the self assumed monopoly of the West over certain branches of science and, especially, its efforts to curtail the development the Muslim World which the Western powers unjustifiably see as potential threat to their monopoly. Development made by certain Muslim states in the "restricted" technologies does not trickle down to others because of international pressures and lack of coordination and cooperation among the Muslim countries. The achievements of the Muslim scientists working in their own countries do not create a cumulative effect on the Muslim world because of the absence of an efficient and coherent mechanism of transfer of technologies developed by them. The scientific and technological development in the Muslim world is visible in patches, not in the form of a continuous, cumulative pattern.

Dr. A.Q. Khan

DR. A.Q. KHAN
ON
Science and Education

Editors
S. Shabbir Hussain
Mujahid Kamran

SANG-E-MEEL PUBLICATIONS
25-LOWER MALL LAHORE.

507 Dr. A.Q. Khan on Science and
Education / edited by S. Shabir
Hussain and Mujahid Kamran.
Lahore; Sang-e-Meel Publications,
1997.
267p.
Index included.
1. Science 2. Education.
I. Shabir Hussain, S. II. Mujahid
Kamran. III. Title.

1997

Published by :
NIAZ AHMAD
Sang-e-Meel Publications
Lahore

Rs.400.00

ISBN = 969-35-0821-1

Pinted at : ***PRINTING PROFESSIONAL LAHORE.***

CONTENTS

ACKNOWLEDGMENTS

The editors wish to thank Dr. A.Q. Khan (N.I., H.I) for his kind cooperation throughout the writing of this book. The editors also wish to thank Dr. Nazeer Ahmad, Director, Technical and Scientific Cooperation Division, A.Q. Khan Research Laboratories, for his constant availability and kind help regarding various questions that arose in connection with different aspects of the book. The editors are most thankful to Syed Shamoon Hashmi for having assisted them in material gathering, proof reading and other aspects of this compilation. Without the efforts of Dr. Nazeer Ahmad and Syed Shamoon Hashmi the publication of the book would have taken much longer. It is a great pleasure to acknowledge the patient cooperation of Mr. Niaz Ahmad of Sang-e-Meel Publications and his sons Afzal Ahmad and Ijaz Ahmad in this venture. One of the editors (MK) would like to thank his wife Dr. Najma Najam for help with proof reading.

DR. ABDUL QUADEER KHAN

Award: **Hilal-i-Imtiaz**

Field: **Science**

The name of Dr. Abdul Quadeer Khan will be inscribed in golden letters in the annals of the national history of Pakistan for his singular and monumental contribution in the field of nuclear science. Dr. Khan has published more than 72 scientific research papers in the field of nuclear energy, besides a well-known book on Physical Metallurgy.

In 1976, imbued with the supreme spirit of patriotism, he returned to Pakistan to serve his motherland and gave up a most lucrative job in the West. In the face of all sorts of threats he stoically remained steadfast in his resolve to work for the strength and solidarity of Pakistan.

His contribution in the field of nuclear physics has received national and international recognition by various agencies and organizations all over the world.

In recognition of his epoch-making contributions in the field of science, the President of the Islamic Republic of Pakistan has been pleased to confer on Dr. Abdul Quadeer Khan, the award of "Hilal-i-Imtiaz'.

March 23,1989

DR. ABDUL QUADEER KHAN, H.I.

Award: **Nishan-i-Imtiaz**

Field: **Science**

Dr. Abdul Quadeer Khan has carved out an enviable place in the national history of Pakistan for his outstanding achievements in the field of peaceful application of nuclear energy. He is already a legend in his lifetime. Dr. Khan has published more than 139 scientific papers in the fields of nuclear science and physical metallurgy in reputed international journals, besides four well-known books on Physical Metallurgy and Advanced Materials. Some international patents are also registered in his name.

Imbued with a high spirit of patriotism Dr. Khan returned to Pakistan in 1976 to serve his motherland. His unflinching resolve to work for the progress, strength and solidarity of the country could not be shaken by many adverse circumstances and obstacles he had to face in his endeavours. His untiring efforts spread scientific and technological education in the country and are a beacon for others to follow.

Dr. Khan is a member of many national and international professional organizations and has received wide recognition from within the country as well as by international agencies. He was awarded `Hilal-i-Imtiaz' in 1989.

In recognition of his enduring contributions in the field of science, the President of the Islamic Republic of Pakistan has been pleased to confer on Dr. Abdul Quadeer Khan, the award of "Nishan-i-Imtiaz".

March 23, 1997

PREFACE

It is impossible to over-emphasise Dr.A.Q.Khan's achievement. Within a brief span of time, working in the most difficult and hostile conditions, Dr.A.Q.Khan has managed to place Pakistan on the global nuclear map. The far-reaching implications of his achievement for the security and development of our country are now abundantly clear to everybody. He has, throughout these years, displayed a remarkable combination of scientific and technological creativity and leadership qualities.

In the words of a Nobel Laureate, science and technology depend for their advancement, on "towering individuals". Dr.A.Q.Khan belongs to this rare breed. One may further elaborate this point by an incisive observation of late Prof. Abdul Baqi Beg who divided scientists into two categories, "Greeks" and "Romans" as he called them. The "Greeks" are the ones who are preoccupied with their own creative efforts without any interest in organisation and establishment of research centres. The "Romans", on the other hand, are able to combine creativity with organisation. Dr.A.Q.Khan is both, a creator and a builder.

Dr.A.Q.Khan's achievements and the direction his research has taken, were not born out of a vacuum. They reflect his world view and his deep and passionate concern regarding the survival of his countrymen and their kith and kin in the adjoining regions. It may also reflect an inherent sense of profound self-respect. What Dr.A.Q.Khan has achieved could not be done without bringing about a transformation of the ethos of those who have been, and continue to be, the main hurdles in the development of science and technology — the bureaucrats, the rulers, and the science publicists.

Besides successfully facing the ignorant, and hence arrogant, bureaucrats, he has also exposed the hollowness of non-science publicists who are afraid of every genuine voice. He did not utter a single word unless he had achieved the objective, that of evolving indigenous capability to enrich uranium. A major problem could be posed if one or the other national leader had succumbed to pressures of global powers or been swayed away by the virulent propaganda of the so-called international media. Each one of the country's rulers had to be kept alive to the possibility of the achievement 'and then to its efficacy. No lesser person or one with less strong nerves could have made it possible for the rulers, of whatever category, to remain firm in the face of the crudest pressure from the world's pre-eminent powers.

Viewed thus, Dr.A.Q.Khan stands at an entirely different plane. He is not merely an active scientist, he has also set up an organisation which represents our only hope of reversing scientific brain drain. He has given his scientists adequate facilities and salaries and provided them with definite targets to achieve. Also, he has given them a sense of pride. Thus, in a nation, where very little sustained positive work is done, he has achieved the most remarkable feat of setting up an island of sustained creative scientific activity. One may add the observation that scientific creativity is perhaps the most difficult kind of creativity, particularly in countries where the tradition of scientific research either does not exist or has ceased to exist. In the words of the Nobel Laureate Abdus Salam, "To create science at the highest level, one has to eat one's heart out."

"Dr.A.Q.Khan on Science and Education" is the first of the series of compilations which the Editors propose to produce to project the achievements of towering Muslims in the realm of contemporary science. The present compilation comprises various articles written and addresses delivered by

Dr.A.Q.Khan since 1984, and provides an insight into the sweep of ideas and intentions of the man who has been acknowledged all over the world as the protector of Pakistan against India's nuclear blackmail.

How did Dr.A.Q.Khan become available to Pakistan and how was he able to initiate the project, which in less than five years made him a "marked man" in the eyes of the Western World? The story is as fascinating as the achievements that will ever remain linked with the name Dr.A.Q.Khan. In spite of having been created in the name of Islam, Pakistan would not become science-oriented because none of the leaders was aware what science actually meant in the contemporary world. It was precisely for this reason that while Pandit Nehru, with his links with Cambridge as a student, had planned at the very outset to develop nuclear and other scientific capabilities of his country, none in Pakistan thought of utilising even the opportunity of Atoms for Peace. All that we did was to set up an Atomic Energy Committee under the Ministry of Industries eight years after winning independence. The only leader to raise the issue of scientific development was Allama Mashriqi, a record holder at Cambridge as Nehru's contemporary. On the conclusion of Kashmir Conference in September, 1955, he called upon the moneyed people of Karachi to donate initially Rs. 10 million for the establishment of a scientific institute in the country. He himself announced a donation of Rs.30,000/-. With the country's elite and its snobbish politico-bureaucratic set-up, nobody listened to what Mashriqi said. All that was done was to raise the status of Atomic Energy Committee, three years later, to that of a Commission.

It was, however, in 1960 that Ayub Khan took a somewhat serious view of the situation and brought a nuclear scientist, Dr.I.H.Usmani, to head the PAEC. Full of energy and confidence, Usmani laid firm foundations of Atomic Energy Commission, and made the scientists a respectable community. He utilised the services of an international architect, Edward Durrel Store, to plan a complex for research, development and training facilities, which resulted in the first national atomic research institute called PINSTECH.

When Z.A.Bhutto assumed power, he appeared to be anxious to make his country a nuclear power, and appointed Mr. Munir Ahmad Khan as PAEC Chief. It seems that Dr.A.Q.Khan was equally alive to the dangers that lay ahead for Pakistan. He visited Pakistan in 1972-73, soon after Pakistan's break up, and felt that the nation needed something to raise its spirits. In the middle of 1974, he wrote to Mr. Bhutto what the nation required and what, after the detonation by India of a nuclear device, he (Dr.A.Q.Khan) could do in this behalf. Mr. Bhutto asked Dr.A.Q.Khan to meet him in Karachi in December, 1974. It was during this meeting that Dr. Khan told Mr. Bhutto that instead of going for the ill-advised purchase of a very costly reprocessing plant, Pakistan should manufacture her own centrifuge plant. Dr. Khan was asked to join PAEC as an Advisor.

What Dr.A.Q.Khan saw was intolerable and one day in the middle of 1976 he told Mr. Bhutto everything. Bhutto too was in a hurry as was Dr.A.Q.Khan and, therefore, he separated the project from the PAEC and asked Dr. Khan to take everything in his own hands. The plunge was taken instantly, but without making the slightest noise. The Engineering Research Laboratories (currently known as Dr.A.Q.Khan Research Laboratories), established in July, 1976, were shifted to the new premises. As has been stated by General Arif, "Its previous location comprising old, dingy, leaking huts, resembling junk shops had served the purpose. The tiny centrifuge project of Sihala was conceived and fabricated here". Kahuta followed the success of the Sihala Pilot Plant.

Things could not remain secret for long and Pakistan's own newspapers aroused the "curiosity, surprise, and ire of the Western World." The whole world was stunned; a country unable to produce needles and ball bearings had fabricated, through its own efforts, centrifuges which required extremely sensitive technology and material. The noise by the West continued with an unabated venom, and so did Pakistan's efforts under the strict guidance of Dr.A.Q.Khan till the President Ziaul Haq announced in December 1982; "We have the capability to enrich uranium". The miracle was brought about in a period of six years after Dr.A.Q.Khan took over the project.

The PAEC, meanwhile, remained in shambles. The people at the helm could not create a team to be able to produce light water power reactors out of ignorance, lethargy or venom to minimise the benefits of Dr. A. Q. Khan's rare achievement.

Apart from making Pakistan immune to India's nuclear blackmail, there are two very important revolutions that Dr. Khan has envisioned before mankind. He has demonstrated that science and technology cannot be monopolised by a single race or community for all times to come. Nature is as generous to a searching soul in the Third World countries as it is to a similar longing by a Westerner. He has thus removed the dread of perpetual domination of the West in the field of science and technology. The second revolution in the thought process of the world community of scientists is that the partisan and war-mongering politician must not be left alone to run the affairs of mankind or of his or her country. In fact, both these revolutions are interlinked and who knows that identical movements in every country will soon start to replace the partisan politician with the Scientist who will at once be a humanist on account of being generator of power, and, hence international in outlook, and a true guarantor of peace.

Every genuine scientist is a child of Nature. In the present day divided mankind, he may belong to one or the other community but his main concern is the survival of man as a single species. He is not materialistic. In spite of dealing with the physical world, he is, in fact, in search of the spiritual. The more is his background spiritual, the more is he worried about man as a species. If he devotes his energies to uplift a community, he does so to enable his own community to play a worthwhile role in the survival struggle of mankind as a whole, and not to wage war against another people. This applies to Dr.A.Q.Khan more than most of his Western colleagues in the profession. An ample proof of this is available in the present collection of his articles in which he warns mankind against accumulation of nuclear arsenal.

Unlike the image which the West has been trying to create of Dr.A.Q.Khan – a monster with nuclear weapons capabilities of his own – he is more worried about the future of mankind than any Indian scientist has so far been able to appear. In one of his articles, he recalls how the advice given by "that genius Neils Bohr that temporary advantage (from using nuclear weapons against Japan) would result in perpetual menace to human security", was ignored. The advice given subsequently by Szilard, Frank, Einstein, etc., was also ignored. Dr. Khan says, "Scientists and engineers think rationally and their advice can play a positive role, but unfortunately because of their dedication to work and isolation, they have not been able to influence the course of politics".

The articles included in the present compilation are both general and specific, wide-ranging as well as of immediate concern to his nation. They explain the state of affairs in his country's education efforts, rather effortlessness, in various sectors, and has sought to awaken those who would realize the urgency of evolving a new outlook on the shape of things to come.

The Editors

CHAPTER - 1

NUCLEAR WAR, NUCLEAR PROLIFERATION AND THEIR CONSEQUENCES*

The present colloquium organized by Prince Sadruddin Aga Khan, which is being attended by world-ranking civil servants, politicians, nuclear physicists, political scientists, writers, philosophers, theologians and professors, is going to provide a unique opportunity to draw world attention to the menace of nuclear proliferation. It will allow the 121 nations who have signed the Non Proliferation Treaty to encourage and press the super powers, at the Third Review Conference to be held in Geneva in September 1985, to take concrete and sincere steps for nuclear disarmament, as required and agreed upon earlier by them under Article VI of the Treaty. It will also provide an opportunity to scrutinize the effectiveness and future of this whole non proliferation regime. To remind us all of the commitments made under Article VI of the NPT, I reproduce the said Article:

> "Each of the parties to the Treaty undertakes to pursue negotiations in good faith on effective measures relating to cessation of the nuclear arms race at an early date and to nuclear disarmament, and on a Treaty in general and complete disarmament under strict and effective international control."

Article VI, is certainly the most important by product of the NPT and one of its most important provisions.

---

* This paper was read at the 4th International Colloquium organised by the GROUPE DE BELLERIVE at Geneva on 27-29 June, 1985

.ch has been written and published, and so much has id, about the need to control the spread of nuclear .s that one hesitates to say anything more on this subjeci. But the matter is serious, and the threat is so real that there should not be any slackening of attention towards this most dangerous threat faced by mankind.

Even though only five states have so far openly admitted that they have nuclear devices, India is the sixth country which has tested a nuclear device, and it has unfortunately been engaged in the rhetoric of the peaceful nuclear explosion, which is no more than a blatant insult to the intelligence of educated people all over the world. We all know that there is no such thing as a peaceful nuclear explosion. All nuclear explosions generate shock waves, heat, fire and radiation, tools of destruction and it is only an academic question whether a nuclear test is dubbed as peaceful or non peaceful. How can firearm be classified as peaceful? Although no other nation has exploded its first nuclear weapon since 1974 and none of the nuclear weapon threshold countries have accumulated for the first time the fission materials required for the manufacture of nuclear weapons, unfortunately all of the threshold countries have refused either to sign the NPT or to allow their unsafeguarded facilities to be inspected. It is, therefore, high time to debate rationally the coming nuclear threat that is already overhanging everybody. One can only hope that good sense and sanity will prevail and that both the nuclear and near nuclear states will see the grave danger to humanity and to this beautiful world of ours, and will get down to serious thinking and negotiations to avoid a nuclear holocaust or the predicted nuclear winter.

For those who have been working relentlessly and are dedicated to stopping the spread of nuclear weapons the last few years have been nerve-wrecking and bad. They could have been much worse. However, it is not all that black and there have been some positive developments, which I will discuss later.

History has shown us that most technologies have acted as

double edged sword, double edged because advances that promised to better the lot of some human beings often not only threatened, but actually harmed others in the process. When the threat got rather serious, drastic action on the part of the threatened was the result. Following Murphy's classical law that a thing will happen if it can happen, the proliferation of nuclear weapons has taken place and is going to continue to take place if good sense and intelligence do not prevail on those involved in this mad race towards global destruction. This has put great strain on the entire non proliferation regime and many challenges to the NPT are to be expected at the NPT Review Conference. The last decade has not been very successful in containing the potential threat of proliferation of nuclear weapons.

Throughout history, humanity has always concentrated all its efforts on developing new technologies and their special applications. Even though all these technologies were initially developed for peaceful purposes, all ended up being used for killing fellow human beings. The work on fission by Hahn and Strassman and related work by Fermi, Bohr, etc., was of a purely academic nature, but the sudden terror of war and butchery unleashed by the Nazis forced the scientists (Oppenheimer, Szilard, Teller, Frisch, Peierls, etc.) to use this technology, which offered so much to humanity, for the destruction of that same humanity. Never in the history of mankind were such talented manpower and so many resources used for such a terrible weapon of destruction as the atom bomb. Victory in World War II was won by an alliance of the United States, the USSR and the United Kingdom and its contribution to the defeat of Fascism was crucial and essential. Even though differing technologies and interests were involved, the allies succeeded in hammering out a real framework for future international security in the form of the United Nations Organization.

The end of the war made increasingly evident the inherent differences between the allies. The use of the bomb had fundamentally changed the nature of the military conflict and the balance of power. It gave the United States the unrivalled position of a prime arbiter of international affairs. The USSR, having suffered so much initially at the hands of the Nazis, got down to safeguarding its interests and to breaking this monopoly, and developed its own nuclear weapons. The Berlin blockade, the detonation of a nuclear bomb by Russia and the Korean War started a trail of mistrust and the nuclear arms race, which is still going on and has engulfed more states. The mistrust was not confined to the United States and the USSR, it has also played a big role in the development of nuclear weapons by the United Kingdom and France. These two countries did not want to accept the role of second rate powers and be ignored in international politics. The same mistrust forced the People's Republic of China to go all out for nuclear weapons. Chairman Mao had earlier described the philosophy of politics that "political power grows out of the barrel of gun" and Marshall Chen Yi, feeling rather ineffective as a Foreign Minister without the weight of a nuclear force, lamented that as Foreign Minister, he could not straighten his back. The Marshall said that "even if we have to pawn our pants, China should develop a nuclear arsenal so it can start on equal terms with other nuclear powers". A country of 700 million people (now over 1 billion) had to exert itself and not be treated as a second rate power.

Moreover, the industrial fall out of the nuclear weapons programme was so attractive that even President De Gaulle was forced to say, "A weapons programme gives a technical rub off that makes you compete on the world market in a thousand other ways".

2. NUCLEAR WEAPONS PROMOTION AND PROLIFERATION

The first nuclear bombs produced by the United States were manufactured as a noble cause. All those involved worked with a sense of duty and as a means of safeguarding humanity from

Fascism. The development of these awful weapons by the Soviet Union was to protect its security after the bitter experience of Nazi invasion and the butchery of millions of its citizens. The production of nuclear weapons by the United Kingdom and France was not based on reasons of danger to their security but more to gain status and weight in international affairs. The same reasons can be attributed to the development of the Chinese and Indian nuclear devices.

In the past 40 years since the first nuclear bomb was dropped on Japan by the United States, five additional states, mentioned above, have detonated nuclear devices and all have developed and deployed (India has not deployed so far) very sophisticated and costly nuclear weapons delivery systems. Lack of technological and financial resources has stopped many nations from acquiring this capability and many nations have chosen to refrain from doing so despite having all the necessary facilities at their disposal. Even though the arsenal of nuclear weapons has become awesome (vertical proliferation) the record shows that at least for those countries which were in a position to develop or acquire nuclear weapons, either the motivations to do so were not very strong or the disincentives have been even stronger. What are these incentives and disincentives which can lead to, or dissuade from, nuclear weapons?

2.1 Motivation To Manufacture Nuclear Weapons

The dominant nuclear incentive for many states is the requirement to enhance their prestige and status at regional as well as at the international levels followed by the requirement to protect their security. Every country considers that its first and foremost duty is to protect its territory from outside aggression, its interest from foreign powers. There is a great incentive to become a nuclear power as it can increase a country's influence on regional security arrangements as well as in the United Nations agencies, including the Security Council and the IAEA.

2.2 Lack Of Motivation To Manufacture Nuclear Weapons

A number of incentives can be given to those countries which are in a position to make or feel compelled to undertake the production of nuclear weapons, to refrain from going nuclear. Security Council Resolution 255 is meant to deter the use of nuclear weapons and thus, indirectly, to deter their manufacture and possession. Unfortunately, this has not been very successful. The Security Council should undertake to come to a general consensus on a modified Resolution 255 to prohibit the acquisition of nuclear weapons as such. In this matter, the United States and the USSR could play a major and consensus role, as most of the countries of the world are directly or indirectly under their spheres of influence. In virtually all cases, these two super-powers are in a position to influence the policies of these countries. In principle, India, Iraq and Libya can be persuaded by the Soviet Union, while Pakistan, Israel, South Africa, Argentina, Brazil, South Korea and Taiwan could easily be influenced by the United States. A sort of security umbrella and some form of mutual security pact with one of the super powers could easily provide incentives to most of these nations to refrain from acquiring nuclear weapons and to concentrate on national development projects. Super power security guarantees, NATO, Warsaw Pact, etc., have provided a sense of security to these countries, and the industrial progress of the countries concerned is exemplary. Even though the super powers will be inclined to pursue conflicting objectives, it is high time that they realize that acquisition of nuclear weapons by developing non nuclear nations will result in serious risks for their own security. One can appreciate that such a mutually acceptable system is extremely difficult to chart out because of their differences and priorities, but it is in the interest of humanity that such a system should be evolved. Another incentive to reduce or eliminate incentives for nuclear weapon acquisition is to encourage regional security or friendship treaties to avoid confrontation and the quest for more powerful weapons, including atomic bombs.

3. PROLIFERATION SOURCES

The biggest and most potential source of nuclear weapons material is the civil nuclear power industry, which also provides the necessary training and experience for the technical personnel. Any country engaged in a well founded nuclear power programme would need much less time to switch over to a weapon programme, if ever it decided to do so. Naturally, the time required to do it would depend on the facilities (uranium enrichment, fuel reprocessing) the country has in operation. All of us are fully aware of the close connection between a nuclear power industry and weapons proliferation. The example of India's switch over from a civil to a weapon oriented programme is the biggest eye opener. The development of the civil power programme is making huge quantities of plutonium available for potential risk of misuse or diversion for the manufacture of nuclear weapons. In the last decade the risk has increased considerably due to large quantities of plutonium produced in these facilities.

Since the early 1960s' the successful manufacturing and operation of gas centrifuges has further enhanced the danger of proliferation. It has qualitative advantage over the gaseous diffusion plant used by the United States, the USSR, the United Kingdom, France and China and has great potential. Even though no nation has so far claimed to have enriched uranium to weapon grade concentration, the theoretical possibility is there. Moreover, the next generation of enrichment processes such as laser and plasma techniques are undergoing intense development effort. If one succeeds in mastering them, the danger of nuclear proliferation will be enhanced greatly. Uranium enrichment technology has become very important for countries which are interested in keeping their options open on nuclear and uranium enrichment facilities. It has also failed to safeguard the proliferation of this technology as it is outside the scope of the NPT.

4. THE FAILURE OF THE NPT

After World War II, the undiminished nuclear arms race between the United States and the USSR, the resulting radiation contamination and the enhanced danger of nuclear proliferation, resulted in a large number of countries taking an initiative that culminated in 1968 in the NPT, which took effect in 1970. By this time, concern about nuclear proliferation had decreased considerably. However, because no universal consensus was reached on the NPT, its scope was seriously limited. As the NPT is highly discriminatory with regard to the application of safeguards and discriminates in its privileges and obligations between nuclear weapon and non nuclear weapon states, it has brought no diminution of nuclear weapons proliferation and the arms race. It has failed to prohibit the possession of nuclear weapons by those countries which have stockpiled large nuclear arsenals. In addition, the NPT does not contain any provision on security guarantees to non nuclear weapon states against violators of the Treaty. The fundamental hope that the NPT would be able to create an adequate barrier between peaceful and non peaceful uses of nuclear energy through the IAEA has failed due to the absence of an international consensus. Of the several non nuclear weapon states with substantial nuclear programmes which have not signed the NPT, India is the only country which exploded a nuclear device in 1974 based on plutonium produced in a Canadian supplied reactor for peaceful purpose and using heavy water supplied by the United States. India thus became the first manifest proliferation case after the NPT entered into force in 1970. It shattered a very tender and delicate status quo and encouraged a dangerous precedent.

The First Review Conference of the NPT in 1975 made it evident to non nuclear weapon states that the weapon possessing member states of the treaty (the United States, USSR, the United Kingdom, France and China are members) had not taken any substantial and serious measures to halt vertical proliferation, nor were they prepared to make definite commitments to specific measures to that effect, such as the Comprehensive Test Ban Treaty prepared by the non aligned states. The failure of the NPT was further manifested by the Second Review Conference held in September 1980, which demonstrated the failure of the nuclear weapon states to fulfil their obligations to good faith negotiations and to stopping the nuclear arms race as soon as possible. No measurable progress was made between the First and Second Review Conferences, no Comprehensive Test Ban Treaty had been agreed upon and the SALT II agreement had not been ratified. On the contrary, vertical proliferation by the nuclear weapon states continued unabated with more powerful and sophisticated nuclear and thermonuclear weapons. It was in this atmosphere that the Second NPT Review Conference was not even able to produce a Final Declaration. The present colloquium is meant as a sincere effort to urge the nuclear weapon possessing powers, especially the United States and the USSR, to do their utmost to make the Third Review Conference a success.

4.1 Vertical Proliferation

In spite of all the vocal preaching and rhetoric to the contrary, the nuclear weapon states have expressed their confidence in the value and usefulness of nuclear weapons in the most unambiguous manner by investing billions of dollars in enhancing the already massive stock and in new generations of all kinds of usable nuclear weapons. This way they have shown the hypocrisy of their own commitments to NPT and have made a mockery of efforts at nuclear disarmament based on good faith. Their actions have made nuclear weapons more attractive (and less expensive compared to the large regular requirements of conventional weapons) to many nations which face potential threats to their sovereignty and security. Thus, vertical proliferation by the nuclear weapon states continues unabated and provides incentives to near nuclear and non nuclear states to press for acquisition of these awesome and monstrous tools of destruction. There is a great danger that if the United States and the USSR show no progress in limiting their own nuclear arms race major non nuclear threshold powers may quit NPT and go nuclear in the near future. That would mean the death of the NPT. If there is continued nuclear stockpiling by the super powers and observance of the Treaty by non nuclear powers, the latter see the strong getting stronger and the weak getting weaker. This is the main reason why the non nuclear weapon states have insisted upon a Review Conference every five years to keep up the pressure on the super powers to reach agreement. The Third Review Conference is for this purpose and this colloquium is a serious and sincere attempt to make the super powers aware of their duties towards humanity.

4.2 Horizontal Proliferation And Its Relation To Vertical Proliferation

In the past 30 years, since nuclear technology first became available for peaceful purposes, most advanced and semi advanced countries of the world have gained access to at least some of this technology. This access, together with the trained manpower and the seemingly attractive advantages in prestige, status and security, have made the task of non proliferation of nuclear technology and materials very difficult and important. Only very few countries with the ability and incentive, to manufacture a nuclear bomb have not signed, but even this proves a great danger for horizontal proliferation. If one of these countries goes nuclear, others are bound to follow. The appreciation by the threshold countries that nuclear weapons confer enormous advantages upon the countries to keep all options open. India's persistence and continuing quest for international recognition as more than a pawn on a global chessboard forced it to detonate a nuclear device in 1974. Pakistan's future policy is to remain closely tied to Indian actions. If India openly starts a weapons programme, the deep rooted Pakistani fears of India, especially after its active role in the dismemberment of Pakistan in 1971, would put tremendous pressure on Pakistan to take appropriate measures to avoid a nuclear Munich at India's hands in the event of an actual conflict, which many Pakistanis think very real.

4.3 How To Contain Horizontal Proliferation

I have already described the various incentives a nation might have for producing nuclear weapons. Below are some of the main points which can contribute towards containing horizontal proliferation:

a) The super-powers must make good their commitment to Article VI of the NPT. Unabated production and testing of nuclear weapons discredit this in the eyes of the non nuclear states and accentuate the discriminatory nature of the NPT. A voluntary complete ban on the testing of nuclear weapons would be a good initial step. It would be a positive act and would save them from the hypocrisy of preaching one thing while practising something different.

b) Super power guarantees to non nuclear states against threat or use of nuclear weapons could make a positive contribution to the containment of nuclear weapons. It would take away the incentive to go nuclear at the huge cost of industrial development and the people's welfare.

c) The industrialized countries must honour commitments made to the developing countries. The unilateral cancellation of all assistance and nuclear fuel to Pakistan by Canada after the Indian nuclear test through no fault of Pakistan's has directly led to the efforts by Pakistan to set up a complete nuclear fuel cycle and not to be subjected to such humiliation in future. The cancellation by France of the reprocessing plant (though it was approved by the IAEA) added fuel to the fire and forced Pakistan to work on an enrichment plan to ensure domestic nuclear fuel for all future nuclear power plants. India has recently been subjected to the same treatment by the United States with regard to the fuel for the Tarapur reactor, and though France has made good the American refusal, there are good reasons to believe that India will do all in its power to avoid this humiliation in the future.

d) Regional cooperative and non aggression or friendship agreements must be actively encouraged by the super powers with the support of the United Nations. A lot of regional conflicts or disagreements are creating security problems for many nations and they fear for their survival. United Nations resolutions and mutually agreed pacts as in the case of Kashmir by India have been blatantly flouted creating a situation where super power persuasion and help could avoid a nuclear race and contribute to peace and stability.

e) The super powers must behave as super powers and must not interfere in the internal affairs of non nuclear nations. Aggression or interference is bound to be counter productive and the non nuclear nations will have great incentives, and good reasons to go nuclear to safeguard their independence and sovereignty. With their backs to the wall, they will not hesitate to use these weapons, even against a formidable adversary.

f) Developing countries should not be indiscriminately, denied the benefits of nuclear power, but proper and adequate safeguards must be made to ensure proper functioning of their facilities and handling of nuclear materials. Denial or refusal of such facilities will be counter productive and these countries will go all out to create domestic facilities with all the inherent dangers of misuse and proliferation.

g) One of the best means of containing nuclear proliferation is agreement by regional regimes to mutual inspection of facilities. Pakistan has all along proposed to India to open nuclear facilities for mutual inspections. Both countries are claiming that their nuclear programmes are solely for peaceful purposes and they are not engaged in the manufacture of nuclear weapons. The main difference, however, lies in the fact that, irrespective of the discriminatory nature of the NPT, Pakistan has time and again offered to open nuclear facilities for mutual inspection, which India has always refused under one pretext or another, even to the extent of using arguments insulting the intelligentsia of the world. An agreement between the two countries would serve as an example for other nations to follow. The sub-continent could be free from the dangers of a mad nuclear race. In the absence of India signing the NPT or a bilateral agreement with Pakistan, Pakistan cannot sign the NPT and cannot allow itself to be subjected to nuclear blackmail. The Indian military intervention in East Pakistan in 1971, the inability of China and the unwillingness of the United States to assist Pakistan against an Indian attack and, above all, the Indo-Soviet defence agreement of 1971 that is aimed at Pakistan, has put Pakistan in a special perspective and unless and until watertight safeguards for its sovereignty and security are forthcoming, no government can take unilateral action and jeopardize the existence and security of the country. India's unsafeguarded huge plutonium stock is enough to give nightmares to any neighboring country.

h) The establishment of a regional nuclear weapon free zone on the same lines as the Treaty for the Prohibition of Nuclear Weapons in Latin America of 1968, commonly known as the Tlatelolco Treaty, can contribute substantially to the non proliferation of nuclear weapons. The Treaty can work as a model for all other regions including the Indo-Pakistan sub-continent and South-East Asia. In the absence of NPT commitments, such zones can be a valuable source of reduction of horizontal proliferation. Both the United States and the USSR support this Treaty, and all the nuclear weapon processing countries have pledged that the statute of denuclearization of Latin America will be respected. Pakistan has also been the champion of a similar proposal to declare South Asia a nuclear weapon free zone. The proposal has been adopted by the United Nations a number of times, but unfortunately, as in the case of mutual inspection, India is the biggest opponent of this proposal. Pakistan sincerely believes that the signing of such an agreement would usher in an era of peace and trust in the sub-continent and would make practical and valuable contributions to containment of horizontal proliferation. As in the case of the Tlatelolco Treaty, the super-powers and other nuclear weapon states can guarantee the sanctity of such a treaty. In this connection, the recent news that Brazil and Argentina have reportedly agreed in principle to develop a mutual inspection regime for their nuclear facilities is very heart warming and can serve as an example for India and Pakistan.

5. RISKS OF NUCLEAR WAR BY ACCIDENT

Irrespective of vertical or horizontal proliferation, there is a real danger of nuclear war by accident due to technical failure or malfunctioning, or due to accidental detonation or launching of a nuclear weapon. Nuclear war can also be started by unauthorized action, human error or sheer madness. There is, moreover, a very great danger of a person, or a group of persons, responsible for launching nuclear weapons going insane and deciding to launch a nuclear attack on the enemy, eliciting immediate retaliation and causing a real holocaust. In the presence of these dangers the ideal solution is not to minimize war, but to stop such a horrible and devastating war altogether by completely eliminating nuclear stockpiles.

6. MILITARIZATION OR DEVELOPMENT

Any nation that decides to establish a weapon industry especially nuclear weapons must commit huge resources to the programme. The requirements depend on the sophistication and quantity of the weapons, but a major weapons programme has a direct relation to nuclear proliferation as it provides a sound engineering basis for it.

Total world military expenditure has gone to about $500 billion. Weapons production is widespread and advances in military technology are being made at a very fast rate. Total world military expenditure is more than total world wide government expenditure on education. Weapons development and production programmes in all countries show remarkable resilience to the economic difficulties of the people ($20-30 million is considered peanuts to buy a fighter aircraft). In spite of poverty, hunger and lack of medical facilities, defence industries (and with them the threat of nuclear proliferation) continue to mature and spread. The arms race in conventional weapons and especially the capacity of more and more countries to develop and manufacture their own major weapons is creating a dangerous situation. The financial and technical resources devoted to the development and production of conventional nuclear weapons are awesome. The development programmes in all those countries which are directly or indirectly involved in conventional and/or nuclear weapons production are suffering badly. This is not limited to the developing countries. Conditions in the United States, the United Kingdom, the USSR and France, and more so in China and India, are far from satisfactory. Large numbers of people live in shameful conditions, cannot afford two proper meals and have no roof over their heads. The starvation in Ethiopia, Chad, Sudan and India should serve as a clear pointer and eye opener for all. Unless good sense prevails and some positive steps are made towards universal disarmament, the horizontal and vertical proliferation of conventional (and ultimately nuclear) weapons will almost certainly continue. If the super powers can come to an agreement on mutual disarmament and can create an atmosphere of mutual trust, industrial and social development at reasonable pace can be undertaken by non nuclear weapon states for the welfare of humanity.

7. CONCLUSION

Nuclear proliferation is running only in one direction. It is almost impossible that the world will ever see the end of proliferation. However, as time goes on, the serious shortcomings of nuclear deterrents are becoming widely understood and appreciated as inhuman, irrational and barbarous. The problem of nuclear weapon proliferation will not be solved until the incentives, discussed earlier, are removed and until nuclear weapons are outlawed by a universal international consensus as morally unacceptable. Fortunately for all of us, the awareness of the threat posed by nuclear and non nuclear weapons today has been appreciated enough by all those who matter-scientists, writers, philosophers, theologians, politicians, civil servants, and even armed forces personnel and they have realized that there is no choice but to halt this mad arms race and to do everything humanly possible for disarmament or face that ultimate absurdity, total annihilation. The consciousness of people all over the world has been awakened and a consensus has emerged today that proliferation or accumulation of these tools of destruction must be banned, must be eliminated. The greatest shock and damage to the NPT was done by India's detonation of a nuclear device in May 1974. A country that was proclaiming all along that it was the champion of non violence shattered a highly precarious and delicate balance of nuclear power.

In short, it can be said that although the NPT has fallen far short of what is essential to ensure only the peaceful use of nuclear technology, it still represents a genuinely positive development in the efforts by the super powers and others to establish a peaceful international nuclear energy regime. The late President Lyndon Johnson had hoped of the NPT that "It will be for all the world the brightest light at the end of the tunnel since 1945" and former United Nations Ambassador

Arthur Goldberg said: "The NPT will assure that control over nuclear weapons, with their catastrophic power of destruction, shall spread no further among the nations of the earth." The Soviet Deputy Foreign Minister Kuzenetzov asked the United Nations General Assembly: "Who profits, more from the Treaty on the Non-proliferation of Nuclear Weapons". More than 15 years have passed since the NPT was signed with such hopes and although all has not been as ideal as one would have liked, the situation is not so hopeless either. All forecasts of wide proliferation have failed and dates given repeatedly for impending Pakistani, Israeli, South African, Libyan and Iraqi nuclear bombs have not come true. There is still hope that good sense and intelligence will prevail over madness and that we will not devastate our beautiful world. The following acts strengthen this hope and optimism:

a) The Tlatelolco Treaty (February 1967)

b) The Treaty on the Non Proliferation of Nuclear Weapons (1968)

c) The Threshold Test Ban Treaty (July 1974);

d) The Supplies Agreements (London Club, 1976);

e) The Nuclear Non Proliferation Act (1978);

f) Large anti-nuclear demonstration in Bonn;

g) Simultaneous anti-nuclear weapon rallies throughout European capitals (October 1981);

h) Very large anti-nuclear weapon demonstrations against President Reagan in Europe (June 1982);

i) Call by Catholic Bishops for nuclear freeze (May 1983);

j) United States House of Representatives, approval of resolution calling on administration to negotiate an immediate and verifiable mutual nuclear weapon freeze;

k) Huge anti nuclear demonstrations in European capitals;

l) United States film **The Day After** seen by record audience of 100 million, etc;

Further more, the Antarctic Treaty of 1959 declaring it a nuclear-weapon free zone, the Treaty on the Prohibition of the Emplacement of Nuclear Weapons on the Sea Bed and the Ocean Floor and in Sub Soil Thereof of 1971, the Treaty to Ban Nuclear Weapons in Outer Space (1967), the Second Bilateral Agreement between the United States and the USSR and the United Kingdom (1977), the agreement between the United States and the USSR on the Prevention of Incidents on the High Seas (1972), SALT I (1972), the ABM Treaty between the United States and the USSR (1972) the Standing Consolation Commission of 1972 between the United States and USSR, the Prevention of Nuclear War Agreement of 1973 between the USSR, and the United States, and the SALT II Agreement of 1979 (still to be ratified by the United States) are big concrete steps towards reducing the risk of nuclear war and making this world safer. The real possibility of an unintentional nuclear war has aroused great concern among large sections of the public. People from all walks of life are increasingly alarmed and conscious of the prospects of a sudden doomsday. As a result of this, sensible people all over the world are insisting on total disarmament and stringent measures on nuclear proliferation. They are carrying out demonstrations, holding conferences and publishing literature to force the super powers and other nuclear and near nuclear weapon countries, to face up to the fact that they are no longer the prime arbiters and that others could also call the shots. In the light of the above mentioned positive actions taken by the super powers and other nuclear weapon states, we hope that the Third Review Conference will be more constructive, especially now that there is universal international consensus on nuclear disarmament, and that concrete and positive steps will be taken towards reduction and eventual disarmament of nuclear weapons. I hope that this colloquium will be able to make positive contributions towards that noble cause.

Before I conclude my observations, I would like to remind the distinguished audience of the statements made by three public figures;

> "In present day conditions there is no way out. Indeed, there are only two ways; either peaceful coexistence or the most destructive war in history. There is no third way" (Mr. N. Khrushchev, 14 February 1956).

> "It may be possible to have a just war but there can be no such thing as just mutual obliteration. It is vital that we see modern weapons of war for what they are – evidence of madness. (The Archbishop of Canterbury, 1981).

> "Our fine great buildings, our homes will exist no more. The thousands of years it took to develop our civilization will have been in vain... there will be no help, there will be no hope". (Earl Mountabatten)

In this respect I would also like to draw attention the advice given by the great Danish physicist, Professor Niels Bohr, to President Roosevelt and Prime Minister Churchill in a memorandum dated 3 July 1944:

> "The fact of immediate preponderance is that a weapon of unparalleled power is being created which will completely change all future conditions of warfare. Quite apart from the question of how soon the weapon will be ready for use and what role it may play in the present war, this situation raises a number of problems which call for most urgent attention. Unless, indeed, some urgent agreement about the control of the use of the new active material can be obtained in due time a temporary advantage, however great, may be outweighed by a perpetual menace to human security".

Both Roosevelt and Churchill failed to understand the advice given by this genius and 40 years after it there is precious little evidence that the six nuclear power States are willing to give up the temporary advantage obtained through nuclear weapons. What Professor Bohr failed to grasp was the overwhelming importance and prestige the `temporary advantages' gave to the politicians of many countries. Let us hope that the super powers do not forget this when they sit down in September 1985 to review Article VI of the NPT and that they listen to all for the safety and betterment of our beautiful world.

CHAPTER - 2

THE NUCLEAR NON PROLIFERATION TREATY AT CROSS ROADS*

Among the most significant historical events of this century hardly any surpass in dramatic impact and long range importance the testing of the first nuclear bomb at Almogordo, New Mexico in July 1945, and the subsequent dropping of the two atomic bombs on Japan in August 1945. Since that time nuclear proliferation has been a feature of the international political system. It was not until the 1960s, however, that an East-West consensus that the acquisition of nuclear weapons by more states, i.e. nuclear proliferation, would result in a serious threat to world security, was created. This consensus was formalized in the Non Proliferation Treaty, NPT, which was signed in 1968 and came into force in 1970. However, some states felt that a treaty did not ensure actual nuclear disarmament was not desirable and could even be counter productive. The main objection was that a treaty which prohibited non nuclear weapon states from acquiring nuclear weapons, while allowing the nuclear weapon states to retain and to improve their nuclear stocks, would contain such unbalanced obligations that it would become impracticable in the long run. Therefore, in order to meet the objection of these states and to pacify them, Article VI, of the NPT which obliges the nuclear weapon states to "pursue negotiations in good faith on effective measures relating to cessation of the nuclear arms

---

* This article was published in daily `The Muslim' Islamabad, Pakistan on September 13, 1985.

race at an early date and to nuclear disarmament" was included in the treaty.

As a result of further insistence by a number of non nuclear weapon states that the nuclear weapon states commit themselves not to use nuclear weapons against them, UN Security Council Resolution No. 255 of 19th June 1968 was adopted.

Art VIII.3 of the NPT states that "Five years after the entry into force of this Treaty a conference of Parties to the Treaty be held in order to review the operation of this treaty with a view to assuring that the purposes of Preamble and the provisions of the Treaty are being realized". Since then there have been two conferences to review the operation of the NPT, one in 1975, and the other in 1980. The Third Review Conference is now underway in Geneva. In 1995 the Treaty will cease to exist unless all the parties choose to extend its life. There are serious doubters and grave fears that the non nuclear weapon states disenchantment with the working of the Treaty will lead to its tragic demise as a new universal instrument for preventing nuclear proliferation.

All over the world a general consensus has evolved that the mad race for the acquisition of more and more powerful nuclear weapons must he halted. This has led to a large number of publications conferences seminars, protests and appeals; the latest being an international conference arranged by H.H Prince Sadruddin Agha Khan at Geneva from 27-29 July 1985. In this conference world renowned scientists, clergymen, civil servants, politicians, etc., participated and warned the nuclear weapon states that if they did not show sanity and were not engaged in real disarmament and non proliferation, the world was bound to meet her doomsday soon. Let us hope that the Third Review Conference now underway at Geneva is different from the first two Review Conferences which failed.

HISTORICAL BACKGROUND

"My God! what have we done?"..... were the words uttered in awesome surprise by Capt. Robert Lewis, co-pilot of the craft Enola Gay that dropped the first atom bomb on Hiroshima on August 6, 1945. He was horrified to see the devastation brought on the city and its inhabitants by this new horrible weapon of unimaginable destructive power.

"My hands are covered with blood... I have become death, the shatterer of worlds?".... were the words spoken by a shocked Oppenheimer, father of the American Atom Bomb, when he saw the destruction brought about by the scientific and engineering masterpiece he had created.

All this happened 40 years ago when the Japanese cities of Hiroshima and Nagasaki were pulverized by the `Little Boy' and the `Fat Man'. Now the world is shuddering at the very thought of a nuclear holocaust, as the nuclear race begun on August 6, 1945 has progressed unabated and has resulted in stockpiles enough to give the equivalent of many tonnes of explosive to each and every inhabitant of our beautiful world. The uncontrolled spread of nuclear weapons poses one of the greatest threats of our time and is among the probable source of a future nuclear Armageddon.

The use of atomic weapons by America in 1945 had brought a qualitative change in the balance of power and had fundamentally changed the nature of the military conflict. It had given the USA the unrivalled position of a prime arbiter of international affairs. This was naturally unacceptable to Russia and it laid the foundation of the nuclear arms race in which the UK, France and China joined for various international and domestic reasons. While one can understand and appreciate the reasons of universal acquisition of nuclear weapons by the USSR and China there was no reason or compulsion for India to go nuclear and to shatter a scared trust put in her by America and Canada to use a nuclear reactor and the heavy water supplied by them for peaceful purposes.

The undiminished nuclear arms race between the USA and USSR, the production of nuclear weapons by the UK, France and China, and the resulting radiation contamination and enhanced danger of nuclear proliferation forced a large number of non nuclear developed and developing countries to take an initiative to put pressure on the nuclear weapon states to agree to a treaty to control the nuclear arms race and eventually to total disarmament. The efforts were crowned with partial success when in 1968 the USA, USSR and UK agreed to frame a treaty, and opened it to signature on July 1st of that year the Nuclear Non Proliferation Treaty went into force on March 5, 1970.

THE NPT

What is the NPT? In short the NPT provides that nations possessing nuclear weapons would not transfer their weapons to any non nuclear country. Each non nuclear nation agreed not to acquire nuclear weapons and the nuclear weapons possessing states agreed to continue efforts to limit their nuclear weapons. Moreover the non nuclear countries agreed to arrange with the International Atomic Energy Agency, IAEA, means to prevent the diversion of nuclear material from peaceful to military purpose. 134 countries, including the USA, the USSR and the UK, have signed the Treaty. West Germany, Japan, Israel, South Africa, India and Pakistan have not signed it. Pakistan is more than willing to sign it, provided India agrees to do the same. Time has proved Pakistan to be right in not trusting India and refraining from taking unilateral action. I will come back to this later. However, for the sake of convenience for a layman who does not get down to consulting a library or has no literature at hand the whole Nuclear Non Proliferation Treaty is reproduced here:

"The States concluding this Treaty, herein after referred to as the "Parties to Treaty"

Considering the devastation that would be visited upon all mankind by a nuclear war and the consequent need to make every effort to avert the danger of such a war and to take measures to safeguard the security of peoples,

Believing that the proliferation of nuclear weapons would seriously enhance the danger of nuclear war,

In conformity with resolution of the United Nations General Assembly calling for the conclusion of an agreement on the prevention of wide dissemination of nuclear weapons,

Undertaking to cooperate in facilitating the application of International Atomic Energy Agency safeguards on peaceful nuclear activities ,

Expressing their support for research, development and other efforts to further the application, within the framework of the International Atomic Energy Agency safeguards system, of the principle of safeguarding effectively the flow of source and special fissionable materials by use of instruments and other techniques at certain strategic points,

Affirming the principle that the benefits of peaceful application of nuclear technology including any technological by product which may be derived by nuclear-weapon states from the development of nuclear explosive devices, should be available for peaceful purpose to all parties to the Treaty, whether nuclear weapon or non nuclear weapon states.

Convinced that, in furtherance of this principle, all parties to the Treaty are entitled to participate in the fullest possible exchange of scientific information for, and to contribute alone or in cooperation with other States, to the further development of the application of atomic energy for peaceful purposes,

Declaring their intention to achieve at the earliest possible date the cessation of the nuclear arms race and to undertake effective measures in the direction of nuclear disarmament,

Urging the cooperation of all states in the attainment of this objective,

Recalling the determination expressed by the Parties to the 1963 Treaty banning nuclear weapon tests in the atmosphere, in outer space and under water in its preamble to seek to achieve the discontinuance of all test explosions of nuclear weapons for all times and to continue negotiations to this end,

Desiring to further the easing of international tension and the strengthening of trust between states in order to facilitate the cessation of the manufacture of nuclear weapons, the liquidation of all their existing stockpiles, and the means of their delivery pursuant to Treaty on general and complete disarmament under strict and effective international control,

Recalling that, in accordance with the Charter of the United Nations, States must refrain in their international relations from the threat or use of force against the territorial integrity or political independence of any State, or in any other manner inconsistent with the purposes of the United Nations, and that the establishment and maintenance of international peace and security are to be promoted with the least diversion for armaments of the world's human and economic resources, have agreed as follows;

Article 1 :

Each nuclear-weapon State Party to the Treaty undertakes not to transfer to any recipient whatsoever nuclear weapons or explosive devices or control over such weapons or explosive devices directly, or indirectly and not in any way to assist, encourage, or induce any non-nuclear weapon State to manufacture or otherwise acquire nuclear weapons or other nuclear explosive devices, or control over such weapons or explosive devices.

Article 2 :

Each non-nuclear-weapon State Party to the Treaty undertakes not to receive the transfer from any transferor whatsoever of nuclear weapons or other nuclear explosive devices or of control over such weapons or explosive devices directly, or indirectly, not to manufacture or otherwise acquire nuclear weapons or other nuclear explosive devices and not to seek or receive any assistance in the manufacture of nuclear weapons or other nuclear explosive devices.

Article 3 :

1. Each non-nuclear weapon State Party to the Treaty undertakes to accept safeguards, as set forth in an agreement to be negotiated and concluded with the International Atomic Energy Agency, and the Agency's safeguards system, for the exclusive purpose of verification of the fulfilment of its obligations assumed under this Treaty with a view to preventing diversion of nuclear energy from peaceful uses to nuclear weapons or other nuclear explosive devices. Procedures for the safeguards required by this article shall be followed with respect to source or special fissionable material whether it is being produced, processed or used in any principal nuclear facility or is outside any such facility. The safeguards required by this article shall be applied on all source or special fissionable material in all peaceful nuclear activities within the territory of such State, under its jurisdiction, or carried out under its control anywhere.

2. Each State Party to the Treaty undertakes not to provide:

   a) Source or special fissionable material, or

   b) Equipment or material especially designed or prepared for the processing, use or production of special fissionable material, to any non nuclear weapon State for peaceful purposes, unless the source or special fissionable material be subject to the safeguards required by this article.

3. The safeguards required by this article shall be implemented in a manner designed to comply with Article IV of this Treaty, and to avoid hampering the economic or technological development of the parties or international cooperation in the field of peaceful nuclear activities, including the international exchange of nuclear

material and equipment for the processing, use or production of nuclear material for peaceful purpose in accordance with the provisions of this article and the principle of safeguarding set forth in the preamble.

4. Non nuclear weapon States Party to the treaty shall conclude agreements with the International Atomic Energy Agency to meet the requirements of this article either individually or together with other States in accordance with the Statute of the International Atomic Energy Agency. Negotiations of such agreements shall commence within 180 days from the original entry into force of this Treaty. For States depositing their instruments of ratification or accession after the 180 days period, negotiations of such agreements shall commence not later than the date of such deposit. Such agreements shall enter into force not later than eighteen months after the date of initiation of negotiations.

Article 4 :

1. Nothing in this Treaty shall be interpreted as affecting the inalienable right of all the Parties to the Treaty to develop research, production and use of nuclear energy for peaceful purposes without discrimination and in conformity with Articles 1 and 2 of this Treaty.

2. All the Parties to the Treaty undertake to facilitate, and have the right to participate in, the fullest possible exchange of equipment, materials and scientific and technological information for the peaceful uses of nuclear energy. Parties to the Treaty in a position to do so shall also cooperate in organizations to the further development of the applications of nuclear energy for peaceful purposes, especially in the Territories of non-nuclear weapon States Party to the Treaty, with due consideration for the needs of the developing areas of the world.

Article 5 :

Each Party to this Treaty undertakes to take appropriate measures to ensure that, in accordance with this Treaty, under appropriate international observation and through appropriate international procedures, potential benefits from any peaceful application of nuclear explosions will be made available to non nuclear weapon States Party to this Treaty on a non discriminatory basis and that the charge to such Parties for the explosive devices used will be as low as possible and exclude any charge for research and development. Non-Nuclear Weapon States party to the Treaty shall be able to obtain such benefits, through an appropriate international body with adequate representation of non-nuclear-weapon States. Negotiations on this subject shall commence as soon as possible after the Treaty enters into force. Non-nuclear weapons States Party to the Treaty so desiring may also obtain such benefits pursuant to bilateral agreements.

Article 6 :

Each of the Parties to the Treaty undertakes to pursue negotiations in good faith on effective measures relating to cessation of the nuclear arms race at any early date and to nuclear disarmament, and on a Treaty on general and complete disarmament under strict and effective international control.

Article 7 :

Nothing in this Treaty affects the right of any group of States to conclude regional treaties in order to assure the total absence of nuclear weapons in their respective territories.

Article 8 :

1. Any Party to the Treaty may propose amendments to this Treaty. The text of any proposed amendment shall be submitted to the Depository Governments which shall circulate it to all Parties to the Treaty. Therefore if requested to do so by one third or more of the Parties to the Treaty, the Depository Governments shall

convene, a conference, to which they shall invite all the Parties to the Treaty, to consider such an amendment.

2. Any amendment to this Treaty must be approved by a majority of the votes of all the Parties to the Treaty including the votes of all nuclear weapon States Party to the Treaty and all other parties which on the date the amendment is circulated, are members of the Boards of Governors of the International Atomic Energy Agency. The amendment shall enter into force for each Party that deposits its instrument of ratification of the amendment upon the deposit of such instrument of ratification by a majority of all the Parties, including the instruments of ratification of all nuclear-weapon-States party to the Treaty and all other parties which, on the date the amendment is circulated, are members of the Board of Governors of the International Atomic Energy Agency. Thereafter, it shall enter into force for any other Party upon the deposit of its instrument of ratification of the amendment.

3. Five years after the entry into force of this Treaty, a conference of Parties to the Treaty shall be held in Geneva, Switzerland, in order to review the operation of this Treaty with a view to assuring that the purposes of the preamble and the provisions of the Treaty are being realized. At intervals of five years thereafter, a majority of the Parties to the Treaty may obtain, by submitting a proposal to this effect to the Depository objectives of reviewing the operation of the Treaty.

Article 9 :

1. This Treaty shall be open to all States for signature. Any State which does not sign the Treaty before its entry into force in accordance with paragraph 3 of this article may accede to it at any time.

2. This Treaty shall be subject to ratification by signatory States. Instruments of ratification and instruments of accession shall be deposited with the Governments of the United Kingdom of Great

Britain and Northern Ireland and the United States of America, which are hereby designated the Depository Governments.

3. This Treaty shall enter into force after its ratification by the States, the Governments of which are designated Depositories of the Treaty, and forty other States signatory to this Treaty and the deposit of their instruments of ratification for the purpose of this Treaty, a nuclear weapons State is one which has manufactured and exploded a nuclear weapon or other nuclear explosive device prior to 1 January 1967.

4. For States whose instruments of ratification or accession are deposited subsequent to the entry into force of this Treaty, it shall enter into force on the date of the deposit of their instruments of ratification or accession.

5. The Depository Governments shall promptly inform all signatory and acceding States of the date of deposit of each instrument of ratification or of accession, the date of the entry into force of this Treaty, and the date of receipt of any requests for convening a conference or other notices.

6. This Treaty shall be registered by the Depository Governments pursuant to Article 102 of the Charter of the United Nations.

Article 10 :

1. Each Party shall, in exercising its national sovereignty, have the right to withdraw from the Treaty if it decided that extraordinary events, related to the subject matter of this Treaty, have jeopardized the supreme interest of its country. It shall give notice of such withdrawal to all other Parties to the Treaty and to the United Nations Security Council three months in advance. Such notice shall include a statement of the extraordinary events it regards as having jeopardized its supreme interests.

2. Twenty five years after the entry into force of the Treaty, a conference shall be convened to decide whether the Treaty shall continue in force indefinitely, or shall be extended for an

additional fixed period or periods. This decision shall be taken by a majority of the Parties to the Treaty.

Article 11 :

This Treaty, the English, Russian, French, Spanish and Chinese texts of which are equally authentic, shall be deposited in the archives of the Depository Governments. Duly certified copies of the Treaty shall be transmitted by the Depository Governments to the Governments of the signatory and acceding States".

134 Countries have signed this treaty, the notable nuclear weapon possessing absentees being France, China, and India. Israel, South Africa, and Argentina are considered as threshold countries and have not signed the treaty either. Because of Indian action and her efforts to produce nuclear weapons, Pakistan has not signed this treaty but has made commitment to sign it simultaneously with India and to open all facilities to international inspection if India agreed to the same. As stated earlier, the NPT was signed in March 1970. It was agreed that every five years the parties would get together to review the progress and to see how well the treaty is achieving its purpose. They are now meeting in Geneva for the third time.

FAILURE OF THE NPT

In spite of all the vocal holier that thou attitudes and rhetoric to the contrary the nuclear weapon states are expressing their blind faith in the value and usefulness of nuclear weapons in the most unambiguous way by investing billions of dollars to perfect and to enhance the more than 50,000 warheads already available. This way they have shown the hypocrisy of their own commitments to the NPT and are bound to get some very sharp criticism for their failure to do something towards nuclear disarmament. Unfortunately, the actions of the super powers have made nuclear weapons more attractive and less expensive compared to conventional weapons, to many nations which face potential threats to their existence and sovereignty.

The vertical proliferation by the nuclear weapon states has continued unabated and has unfortunately been a great source of encouragement and incentive to near nuclear states to press for acquisition of these awesome, monstrous and immoral tools of destruction.

There is then a great possibility, to the extent of certainty, that if the super powers do not make definite and concrete commitments to limit their own nuclear arms race, agree to a comprehensive test ban treaty, and do more than mere talking, major non nuclear threshold countries may go nuclear and quit the NPT. After all, one can give a notice of only 3 months to withdraw from the Treaty.

That would definitely mean the death of the NPT. If there is continued nuclear stock piling by the super powers, and observance of the treaty by the non nuclear countries, the non nuclear nations see the strong getting stronger and the weak getting weaker. This is the main reason why the non nuclear weapon States insisted upon a Review Conference every 5 years to keep pressure on the super powers to achieve agreements on the Comprehensive Test Ban Treaty and on Nuclear Disarmament. The Third Review Conference being underway now is just for this purpose and the Group of 77, which now consists of more than 100 states, will do all that is humanly possible to bring the super powers to their senses and to meet their obligations to humanity.

The Third Review Conference will continue from where the first two Review Conferences stopped. The First Review Conference of the NPT in 1975 featured an unusual alignment. The USA, the USSR and the UK joined forces to resist the demands of the non nuclear states, particularly the neutral and non aligned countries of the Third World. This conference made it evident to non weapon states that the super powers had not taken substantial and serious measures to halt vertical proliferation, nor were they prepared to make any definite commitments to specific measures to that effect, such as the Comprehensive Test Ban Treaty prepared by the non aligned states. The non aligned states had asserted that they had fully lived upto their commitments under the NPT whereas the nuclear states had not made good their promises. The non nuclear states emphasized the failure of the super powers to implement the treaty's provisions for stopping the nuclear arms race and cooperating in the peaceful areas of nuclear power. "During the First Review Conference, the non weapon states made several demands, amongst others an end to under ground testing, a substantial reduction in nuclear stockpiles, a solemn pledge not to use or threaten to use nuclear weapons against non nuclear states signatories to the Treaty and substantial assistance in developing the non weapon states in the peaceful uses of nuclar energy." The 1975 Review Conference achieved a fragile consensus, expressed in a communique in which the nuclear weapon states in effect promised to try harder to meet the demands of the non weapon states.

The failure of the NPT was again manifested by the Second Review Conference held in September 1980 which demonstrated the failure of the nuclear weapon states to fulfill their obligations to good faith negotiations and discussion towards stopping the nuclear arms race as soon as possible. No measurable or visible progress was made between the first and the second conferences: no Comprehensive Test Ban Treaty had been agreed upon and the Salt II agreement had not been ratified. On the other hand vertical proliferation of nuclear weapons by the super powers continued unabated and sophisticated and devastating nuclear and thermo-nuclear weapons were produced. It was in this atmosphere that the Second Review Conference was held. The conference failed to reach agreements or consensus on any aspect of stopping the nuclear arms race. Unfortunately the USA, which claims to be the champion of good causes, led the nuclear powers in refusing to make concessions on measures for the control of the mad nuclear race. Thus the conference ended without a final declaration or even any final reaffirmation of support for the NPT.

It is most unfortunate and a real source of anxiety that the outlook for the Third Review Conference is as bleak or even bleaker than the first two Review Conferences. The frustration and disappointment of the non weapon states is turning into resentment and anger because they are convinced that the super powers have cheated them. This Group will definitely renew its long standing demands for a Comprehensive Test Ban Treaty, nuclear disarmament and assurances that nuclear weapons will not be used or held out as threats against non weapon states. They will demand greater assistance in the peaceful uses of nuclear energy.

There is every reason to suppose and believe that the non weapon states will press harder than they did in 1980 that the nuclear powers must immediately stop vertical proliferation. Indeed all sane people believe that an end to vertical proliferation is the only way to stop horizontal proliferation and that both must be stopped simultaneously or neither will be. The refusal by the USA to agree to Comprehensive Test Ban Treaty and to refuse a moratorium on nuclear weapons testing even for a short time are not positive steps towards nuclear disarmament or non proliferation. Every step in the right direction, no matter how small, is a positive development. If the USA and other nuclear weapon states, submitting to this world opinion agree to stop all nuclear tests, it would be the most important step since the signing of the NPT and a major contribution to the nuclear non proliferation regime.

WHY IS THE NPT FAILING

The present Non Proliferation Treaty is based on set of rules, regulations, norms, agreements, procedures and institutions that try to control and regulate the international spread of nuclear technology and to constrain the ability of countries to acquire nuclear weapons capability. The NPT has been founded upon a semi imposed order and enshrines discriminatory principles and practices. This has made it both more politically fragile and less successfully adaptable to a changing situation than a treaty or a system established upon the basis of an openly negotiated treaty and non discriminatory principles and rules. Thus a treaty that was aimed at establishing an effective universal non proliferation regime, one which should have encompassed all peaceful nuclear activities and to which all countries were expected to submit, failed bitterly to reach a universal international consensus and its scope is seriously limited. Main reasons for the failure of the NPT are:

a) The Treaty is fundamentally discriminatory - it discriminates in its privileges and obligations between nuclear-weapon states and non nuclear weapon states. It fails to prohibit the possession of nuclear weapons by the nuclear weapon states.

b) The NPT has bitterly failed to stop vertical proliferation and has thus lost most of its credibility.

c) The NPT is also discriminatory with regard to the application of safeguards. These are not applicable to the peaceful nuclear activities of the nuclear weapon states party to the Treaty.

d) The NPT severely discriminates in its application of safeguards by making a distinction between two types of non nuclear weapons states-those which are parties to the Treaty and those which are not. Whereas the former are obliged to have all their peaceful nuclear installations and materials under IAEA safeguards, the latter are required to submit to IAEA safeguards only the nuclear materials and installations which are supplied by countries that are party to the Treaty.

Despite its explicit discrimination between nuclear and non nuclear weapon states and the highly unequal distribution of obligations and privileges between the two groups 134 countries have put faith in it and have signed it in the hope that it might save humanity from annihilation. The above mentioned discrimination has been tolerated in the short run considering the long term benefits at stake but in the long run it is reinforcing the idea that possession of nuclear weapons carries with it tremendous power, prestige and freedom of action. Therefore in the long period that the NPT has remained in effect without nuclear disarmament by the super powers and other nuclear weapon states, powerful and great forces have been there to tear the NPT apart. Such a scenario has already been witnessed in the last two Review Conferences.

The biggest single cause for the failure of the NPT is the attitude of the super powers. In blatant disregard to world opinion they have indulged in shameless proliferation of nuclear weapons. They have spent billions of dollars on increasing the number and killing power of these awesome and abhorrent tools of destruction. Art. VI of the NPT has been played with at will and has been torn apart to one's convenience. The Third World has completely lost faith in the words and deeds of the super powers. The only nuclear weapon state which has all along shown willingness and has insisted upon complete disarmament is China. Unfortunately, the USA and the USSR are engaged in a mad race of nuclear armament. The good faith reposed in the Treaty by the non nuclear states had been shattered to pieces. The feelings of the non nuclear weapon states have been aptly expressed by Mrs. Alva Myrdal of Sweden who has been a champion of nuclear non proliferation and one of the most important founding members of the NPT. According to her the last few years constitute a history of wilfully wasted opportunities to carry out disarmament. The major powers accepted not one iota of sacrifice of present or future nuclear weapon capabilities. She questions the value of the Non Proliferation Treaty as an instrument to bring about nuclear disarmament and feels that a number of so called international disarmament treaties, such as the Outer Space Treaty and the Treaty to keep the sea bed free from nuclear weapons, are just a means to avoid the criticism of super powers at the world platform. She has pointed out that in the last few years the arms competition has resulted in an unimaginable widening of the gap between the super powers and the non nuclear weapon states.

FUTURE THE NPT

If we try to judge the future of the NPT on the basis of the past behavior of the nuclear weapon states, the NPT should have died long ago or should die in the near future. Genuine hostility to the NPT has been shown in a number of conferences, meetings and forums. The UN Conference on International Cooperation in the Peaceful Uses of Nuclear Energy in 1983 had provided a forum for a critical scrutiny of the non proliferation system. This was initiated by Pakistan and Yugoslavia in 1977, partly as a reaction to President Carter's policies which were clearly aimed at attempting to restrain the transfer of peaceful nuclear technology to the developing countries. I believe this issue will play a dominant role in the Third Review Conference underway at present in Geneva.

There is, of course a danger to the NPT if there is a rift between the super powers despite their hostile behavior to each other in many fields, their close cooperation on non proliferation questions and in the IAEA has made a major contribution to sustaining NPT. Unfortunately the prospects are bleak even though the possibilities are numerous. A great setback to the NPT is the refusal of 10-12 significant non NPT countries to join the NPT and reverse their current policies. The proposals of international fuel cycle and enrichment centers, bank of nuclear materials and international plutonium system have all fallen on barren ground.

As I discussed in an earlier article some time back, perhaps the better prospects lie in regional initiations. The examples of the Treaty of Tlatelolco in South America and the recent creation of the South Pacific as a nuclear weapon free zone are highly commendable. Pakistan has been a staunch supporter of such a zone in South Asia and her proposal for it has been repeatedly approved by the UN. Unfortunately contrary to all the rhetoric and holier than thou statements by the Indians, they have not responded positively to this highly practical and useful proposal. It would save both the countries from an unnecessary and suicidal arms race.

Furthermore the creation of nuclear free zone in the Middle East is also imperative. For all practical purposes Israel has become a nuclear power, thanks to the connivance of, and actual help from, some of the Western countries. It may take a few years before the Arabs could manufacture nuclear weapons. As nuclear technology is expanding it is no secret and literature on how to make nuclear weapons is in abundance. The same holds good for South Africa. Unless and until both Israel and South Africa are forced to put all their nuclear facilities under IAEA safeguards the future of the NPT is doomed.

It is believed that a positive contribution to the NPT would be further expansion of the IAEA aid to the developing countries in the form of promoting the use of nuclear science techniques in power production, in agriculture, in medicine and in hydrology. This could bridge the wide gap referred to by Mrs. Alva Myrdal, as far as the peaceful uses of nuclear technology are concerned.

The only consolation we can have is the record of the NPT in the past 15 years. Except the blatant violation of the world trust by India, which cheated both the USA and Canada, and exploded her first nuclear device in 1974, international efforts to slow or halt nuclear proliferation have had reasonable success. It is eleven years since India detonated her nuclear bomb. Despite frequent cries of alarm in recent years, especially aimed at Pakistan, Libya, Iraq and Argentina, there was in fact no overt proliferation and if the threat to our beautiful world looks credible it is only due to the arms race unleashed by the nuclear weapon states themselves.

In the light of the preceding arguments, it would be an important positive step on the part of the nuclear weapons states to stop the nuclear arms race (the foremost obligation under Article VI of the NPT) to put a halt to the manufacturing, testing and development of these weapons. Hence a Comprehensive Test Ban Treaty will be a most important first step towards ending the nuclear arms race. This step is both feasible and the most easily attainable measure to halt both the horizontal and vertical proliferation of nuclear weapons. The Third World would consider a Comprehensive Test Ban Treaty as a definite proof of intention of the super powers and their willingness to comply with their obligation under Art. VI of the NPT. In the view of the Secretary General of the UN, "It is of direct importance to the future of humanity to end all nuclear explosions. No other means would be as effective in halting the further development of nuclear weapons." Let us hope the Third Review Conference is able to bring home these points and takes positive and concrete steps towards global disarmament.

About the future of the NPT, Rodney Jones of the USA says that the number of countries comprising the official nuclear club could change drastically at any time. The problem countries, according to him, are creeping to the edge. There are only five now (he is omitting India, though India is a nuclear weapon state) and if there are suddenly two more, that is a very rapid break out. If more countries go nuclear and get away with it and there is a new respect for them, or their influence rises, there is a real danger of it becoming like a dam that breaks and you have a flood he says.

Bernard Feld, the US physicist who helped produce `Little Boy' and `Fat Man' in a report to the Congress to mark the 40th anniversary of the nuclear bombing of the Japanese cities, says, "Indeed, the indications are that the dangers of nuclear weapons use are increasing year by year that it is quite likely that a nuclear weapon will again be used in a conflict situation before the end of the century." Let us pray and hope he is wrong but we must remember that the politicians and those in power at that time had ignored the sane advice given by the genius Neils Bohr that "temporary advantage" (from using nuclear weapons against Japan) would result in perpetual menace to human security." The advice given subsequently by Szilard, Franck, Einstein, etc., was also ignored. Scientists and engineers think rationally and their advice can play a positive role, but unfortunately, because of their dedication to work and isolation, they have not been able to influence the course of the politicians with the result that we are now at the brink of doomsday.

CONSEQUENCES OF A NUCLEAR WAR

The direct consequence of the failure of the non proliferation regime will be an unabated spread of nuclear weapons and, as Bernard Feld fears, the use of a nuclear weapon before the end of the century is a real possibility. Those participating in the Third Review Conference carry a grave responsibility on their shoulders as their failure to reach a consensus towards non proliferation and total disarmament would directly contribute to a nuclear Armageddon. The nuclear weapons of today make the bombs dropped on Hiroshima and Nagasaki look like children's framework. A single present day hydrogen bomb is more than 1000 times more powerful. Recent estimates by the World Health Organization WHO have concluded that about 1 billion (1000 million) people would be annihilated outright and a billion severely injured if only 1/3 of the estimated present stock of nuclear weapons is utilized. There are about 50,000 warheads stored in the nuclear weapon states and that is enough to kill each and every individual on this earth and to blast this beautiful world of ours many times over. It has now been realized that those who will survive the nuclear war will perish in a nuclear winter brought on by huge amounts of dust and soot which will stop the sun rays from reaching the earth. Let us hope that both the nuclear weapon states and the threshold countries realize that there is no secret about the atom bomb any more and there is no defence against it. If they allow this opportunity, the Third Review Conference, to squander away they will be responsible for the inevitable nuclear holocaust, and, as Bernard Feld has predicted, that day is much nearer than the nuclear weapon states are realizing. The looming danger of a nuclear holocaust is being ignored in the same way as people have been ignoring traffic accidents, starvation, etc. The person sitting at the steering wheel never accepts or believes that there is a great probability of his getting killed in an accident. And hundreds of people do get killed every day, either due to their own fault or due to the faults of others. Seeing thousands of starving people never makes you realize that you could meet the same fate some day. And these things have happened and we have all seen them happening. The second world war brought unimaginable miseries to millions of people. It was only a conventional war. A nuclear war will leave no help, no hope and no civilization. Let us hope that the nuclear weapon states realize this and play their part of the bargain of Art VI of the NPT to reduce, and eventually to destroy, these monstrous tools of destruction. Never before has the need of such an action been felt so much as now. It is getting too late. If there is no agreement this time, the NPT is doomed and a vicious new second cycle of proliferation will start which will make the predicted nuclear holocaust a reality.

PAKISTAN AND THE NPT

Since the creation of the NPT in 1968, Pakistan has been one of its staunchest supporters. Pakistan voted for the NPT in the UN in 1968. However, because of its grossly discriminating nature, Pakistan has not officially signed it. While India refrained from signing it as a long range strategy to explode a nuclear bomb in 1974, Pakistan has all along supported it and has not indulged in any attempts to sabotage it. As a very useful and concrete step, Pakistan launched a proposal many years ago to declare South Asia a nuclear weapon free zone and the declaration by the regional states to officially renounce the manufacture and use of these monstrous tools of destruction.

Notwithstanding the general discriminating charter of the NPT, Government of Pakistan offered to India many concrete suggestions to save the sub-continent from a mad nuclear race. These proposals have been put forward to India by no less a person than the President himself. Summarizing all these proposals in a recent interview to Mr. Tom Brokaw of the NBC, the President offered to India;

a) To declare South Asia a nuclear weapon free zone.

b) *To* sign the NPT simultaneously with India.

c) To sign a bilateral nuclear non proliferation treaty.

d) To agree to an international inspection team to visit and inspect each and every nuclear facility in each of the two countries and

e) To renounce the use of nuclear weapons.

Unfortunately, and understandably, the Indians do not accept any one of these sincere and straight forward proposals. The Indian scientists and politicians are engaged in misleading the whole world and are trying to insult the intelligentsia of the world by creating a hoax of the so-called peaceful nuclear explosion. Every body knows that the so-called peaceful nuclear device incorporates the same basic technology as a nuclear bomb. It is most unfortunate that following the tradition laid down by Gandhi, Nehru, and Indira Gandhi, the Indian Prime Minister is also engaged in misleading the whole world. A country that exploded a nuclear bomb 11 years ago and is engaged in clandestine production and stockpiling of huge quantities of plutonium in unsafeguarded facilities is trying to mislead the world in the role of a peace lover. Notwithstanding his recent entry into public life and lack of understanding of world affairs, Mr. Rajiv Gandhi must realize that those who indulge in misleading the world and act stupidly are taken for fools. He must not allow himself to be projected as an ignorant person by following the advice of crooks. It would be more appropriate for Mr. Rajiv Gandhi to act and behave as a Prime Minister of 800 million people and he should not indulge in mud slinging on Pakistan's peaceful nuclear programme. If he has any doubts about our peaceful programme and is sure of his own position, he should accept the challenge thrown by our President and sign the NPT simultaneously or open all the nuclear facilities to an international inspection team. Naturally, Pakistan cannot take a unilateral action, as it will mean a sure end to our existence as an independent and sovereign state. India, in keeping with its aggressive policy (East Pakistan, Kashmir, Junagarh, Manavadar, Hyderabad, Goa, Sikkim), will definitely indulge in nuclear blackmail against us and will not hesitate to deliver a mortal blow to our beloved country. No government can write the death warrant of her own country. At least we would not.

Coming back to Pakistan and the NPT, Pakistan is attending the Third Review Conference as an Observer. Pakistan refrained from attending the First and the Second Review Conferences due to the hypocritical attitude of the Super Powers. Pakistan's decision to attend the Third Review Conference for the first time demonstrates its consistent support for the NPT's central obligation not to manufacture or acquire nuclear explosives — peaceful or otherwise. It also shows its desire to evoke at the global and regional levels effective and non discriminatory arrangements to prevent proliferation of nuclear weapons.

Let us pray and hope for the sake of humanity and for this beautiful world of ours, that the Third Review Conference evolves a general consensus and agrees upon concrete and substantial measures to reduce, and then to ban, these monstrous tools of destruction.

CHAPTER - 3

INDIAN NUCLEAR DUPLICITY*

The success of the Indian campaign to cheat the world under the guise of non-violence is vividly manifested by the writing of many Western journalists and even some politicians. What is most astonishing is that a person of Dr. Hans Blix's position (Director General of IAEA) and knowledge seems to have been fooled (or is it a convenient way of accepting India as the sixth nuclear weapon state?) by the continuous propaganda sustained by the Indians at the international level.

In a recent article (Nuclear Power Without Nuclear Weapons) in The New Scientist of London dated 22.8.1985, Dr. Blix made a statement "No new nuclear weapon state has emerged since 1964 (when China exploded its first atomic bomb), in spite of the fact that nuclear technology became accessible to or was acquired by more than a dozen states". It is tantamount to giving a clean and blank approval to India's nuclear explosion of 1974. Dr. Blix is trying to deceive himself and ignores hard facts.

BASIC TECHNOLOGY

Starting from top nuclear scientists to high school students, everybody knows that there is no technical difference between the so called peaceful nuclear device which incorporates the same basic technology as the horrible, abhorrent tool of destruction, the nuclear bomb. Every scientist and engineer

---

* This article appeared in daily 'The Muslim', Islamabad, Pakistan on November 13, 1985.

knows that peaceful nuclear device incorporates the same basic technology as a devastating nuclear bomb. Otherwise, Mr. Rajiv Gandhi would not have boasted to a French newspaper publicly in June 1985 that India could produce nuclear weapons in weeks. Even a loud boasting claim was made by the former Indian State Minister of Foreign Affairs, Mr. Khurshid Alam Khan, who said people would be awestruck if India disclosed its capabilities in this field, as it did in 1974 (when India exploded an atomic bomb.)

You can not produce nuclear weapons in weeks if you have not been working on this for years and have all the components ready. By intentionally ignoring this fact, and excluding India from the nuclear weapon club, Dr. Blix has not done justice to the charter of IAEA. Why is he afraid of calling a spade a spade? As Leonard Spector puts it, "India has already prepared the high precision components for atomic weapons, leaving it only `a screw driver away' from a nuclear arsenal." And then he says, "if the Pakistani programme can be arrested, India seems unlikely to take major steps in this direction" What a naive analysis ! Such self proclaimed experts on nuclear affairs as Leonard Spector of the USA have intentionally and conveniently swallowed all the misleading statements put forward by India. While he questions and doubts all our efforts and solemn pledges, he gulps down the Indian lies without the least hesitation. I guess he is probably highly impressed, and bewitched, by the Indian government paid advertising film, Gandhi.

SIMPLE CHICANERY

According to the well known Indian writer, Ashis Nandy, India's nuclear establishment is an example of sycophancy, dishonesty and plain, simple chicanery. The Indian duplicity has been further exposed by another noted Indian journalist Dhirendra Sharma. He points out how D.S.Kothari, who for many years served as chief Scientific Advisor to the Indian

Defence Ministry (making destructive weapons), has become an outspoken spokesman for spiritualism through modern science. Similarly Ashok Paarthasarathy, an ultrahawk, has been cheating the great pacifist of the Indian branch of the Pugwash, the so called movement of scientists against nuclear weapons and nuclear armament.

Then, of course, we have the self proclaimed nuclear hawk, K. Subrahmanyam, who according to his own confession, has been advising India to produce nuclear weapons for the past 17 years. You will find this gentleman at every disarmament conference, whether be it at Stockholm or at Geneva, telling others not to make nuclear weapons but advising India to make these horrible weapons of destruction.

As Shenihymay has put it:

> "It is ironical that in spite of Indian decision to go nuclear right from 1947, its preparation and then detonation of the device (atom bomb) went unnoticed, intentionally or unintentionally, by the West. In fact the US, Canada, France and the UK whole heartedly gave all assistance without any hesitation. The question is whether these champions of non proliferation were befooled by India or they kept their eyes shut; the answer seems to be `yes' for the latter part and `no' to the former. Right from the very beginning it has been the cornerstone of Indian policy, specially in foreign affairs, to remain elusive. The world has been accepting bare facts and forgetting what was uttered, claimed and promised earlier. This only means that it has been living with a scenario of double standards. India has taken full advantage of this weakness and has turned it into its advantage."

Pakistan is being singled out by the mischievous Indian press, and biased Western news media, to be indulging in all out efforts to produce nuclear weapons. Ours is a modest research and development programme solely aimed at peaceful utilization of nuclear power and in this connection I want to reproduce the repeated sincere and straight forward proposals presented to India by no less a person than the President of Pakistan, both in bilateral communications to the Indian Prime

Ministers, as well as at international level, the latest being at the floor of the United Nations in the presence of world leaders from more than 150 countries. These proposals include;

a) To declare South Asia a nuclear weapon free zone.

b) To sign the NPT simultaneously.

c) To sign a bilateral nuclear non proliferation treaty.

d) To agree to an international inspection team to visit and inspect each and every nuclear facility in each of the two countries.

India's response is negative as the Indians are not only dreaming of competing with China in nuclear weaponry, but also of subjecting Pakistan to perpetual nuclear blackmail.

INDIAN QUEST

A country that exploded a nuclear bomb 11 years ago has been stockpiling huge quantities of unsafeguarded plutonium, and is engaged in deceiving the whole world under the garb of non violence and fakir style Gandhi-ism, has the cheek to indulge in mud slinging on Pakistan's peaceful nuclear programme. What more does the world want from us?

The Indian response, as is understandable from their past hypocritical and aggressive attitude towards Pakistan, is negative. The Indians are under the illusion of matching Chinese capability and potential. Those who have lived in India, or know the Indian mentality, would tell you that this will never happen. You just have to read the history of Gandhi, Nehru and others written by some of the Indians themselves. A country which has millions of starving people, hundreds of thousands sleeping and dying on the footpaths, does not hesitate to squander billions of dollars on prestige seeking space and nuclear projects and hegemonic activities, is dreaming of becoming a superpower. That Mr.K Subrahmanyam considers our proposals a trap to disarm India against China confirms that India is dreaming of becoming a match for China in nuclear weaponry.

The Indian quest for weapons is very old indeed. It was Bhabha who put in Nehru's head that an atom bomb would put India in the group of superpowers. Ashok Kumar, the noted Indian writer and analyst has exposed it in many of his writings. Now Mr. K. Subrahmanyam has been openly encouraging and advising India to go nuclear, to produce horrible nuclear weapons. Where is all that preaching of non violence? Where is that Gandhi's or Nehru's big talk of India to be the champion of non violence and torch bearer of peace. The fact is that the Indians have never practised what they have preached. If you just pick up all the solemn commitments and declarations made by the Indians, including Gandhi and Nehru, and then see their later statements you will know conveniently they were back on their words and cheated the other party.

Some in Pakistan were under the false impression that when Mr.Rajiv Gandhi settled down he would be more realistic and would try to establish friendly relations with Pakistan. Those who have lived with Indians and are familiar with their character had no illusion that this would happen and they knew that the old hatred against Pakistan would be increased. The brutal killings in Assam, the merciless butchery of the Sikhs in Punjab and desecration of their holiest Golden Temple were carried out with great impunity and comfort by those who professed non violence.

The vehement, persistent and mischievous propaganda against Pakistan's peaceful nuclear programme has a sinister character. It has been built over many years. First there was talk of Pakistan making enriched uranium, then of making weapons grade uranium, then false and malicious accusations that China gave us the technology for making a bomb. As if that was not enough, those liars indulged in notorious suggestions that Pakistan would test its atomic bomb in Sinkiang.

FALSE ACCUSATIONS

As ours is an exclusively peaceful nuclear programme, there

is no question of either China giving us help in this matter or our testing a device in China. If ever the government of Pakistan were to use the nuclear option and asked the scientists and engineers to manufacture a nuclear bomb, I believe it will not go to a foreign country to test it. If the aim is to establish credibility it would be established on our own soil. But I don't look forward to that day.

A latest wave of false and unfounded accusations against us has recently been started by Mr Rajiv Gandhi. First he was frightening the world with an impending Pakistani nuclear bomb and when it did not materialize he was fed by those around him, to indulge in a bigger mischief to frighten the world that Pakistan was not only indulging in the production of chemical weapons but that the Arab countries were providing substantial financial resources for the manufacture of nuclear weapons and that Pakistan would thus be obliged to give them these weapons, thus creating an imaginary threat to world stability and peace. This is a highly mischievous and well thought out accusation to create problems for Pakistan at the international level.

Let us now have a look at India's own deeds. The Indians exploded an atomic bomb in 1974. Yes it was an atomic bomb as there is no difference between a device or a bomb. The noted Indian author, Arvind-Vedhyadharan has no hesitation in calling it an atomic bomb. Any average engineer could turn a device into a deliverable bomb in few months. The Indians are not such geniuses or intellectuals as they try to profess and proclaim. They were helped in their efforts by many other countries.

GOOD FAITH?

Immediately after the Chinese nuclear explosion the Indian nuclear scientists and engineers started paying regular visits to foreign countries and were given sensitive data on nuclear matters. We all know that the Indians openly and blatantly cheated Canada and the United States by using the facilities of reactor and heavy water provided by these countries in good faith to a self proclaiming `Guru'. Nobody is asking India (or coming with an explanation or exposure) where it got the Klystrons or like wise triggers from, who supplied the fast storage oscilloscopes and diagnostic coaxial cables for her atomic explosion in 1974. These are questions no body is asking the Indians. The Indians managed to cheat the world and got away with it.

After having exploded her first atomic bomb Mrs. Indira Gandhi and the Indians were flying high really very high. I was in Europe and I still remember the Indians wagging tail and boasting about their competence in science and technology even though one can still remember the cartoon in Newsweek (or was it Time Magazine?) in which a turbanned Indian faqir was trying to join nuclear weapon states. The dismemberment of Pakistan, the feat of cheating the world and the possession of the atomic bomb gave the Indians the false hope of becoming a superpower in South Asia and treat Pakistan and other Middle Eastern countries just like Sri Lanka, Bhutan, Nepal and possibly Sikkim.

By mounting a vehement, sustained, baseless, and concocted propaganda against Pakistan's peaceful programme, the Indian leaders and politicians hope, rather naively, to persuade Pakistan and other countries to be committed to denuclearization while India could arm itself with nuclear weapons to the teeth. Indian assertions that the 1974 atomic explosion was nothing more than a peaceful nuclear test has fooled only very few ignorant people.

While the Indians have been indulging in this vehement anti Pakistan campaign to divert the attention of the world, they themselves are shamelessly busy in making not only atomic weapons but also the most horrible tool of destruction, the hydrogen bomb. In a recent article in Newsweek, USA the famous American columnist Jack Anderson has exposed the Indian mischief. Mr. Anderson says, "India exploded a nuclear bomb 11 years ago, can set off a second one within two months of decision to do so, and is already storing enough unsafeguarded material to build an entire nuclear arsenal. In addition, the Indians appear to be mastering the more sophisticated technique of building a hydrogen bomb". According to CIA sources, India is simultaneously going ahead with work on a hydrogen bomb. Unlike the crude atomic bomb it detonated in 1974 a hydrogen bomb is far more complex to develop. The hydrogen bomb is being built at the Bhabha Research Centre BARC near Bombay. About 3 dozen scientists are trying to refine a process called inertial confinement fusion. India, since 1983, has been stockpiling separated plutonium that is ideal for weapons. At full capacity the plant can process 100 tons of spent fuel a year separating as much as 150 kg of weapons grade plutonium. Six to eight kilos are enough for a nuclear bomb. This is what India herself is indulging in and has the mischief to sustain a world wide misleading propaganda against Pakistan's peaceful nuclear programme.

VICIOUS CAMPAIGN

Mrs. Indira Gandhi was satisfied with the creation of Bangladesh but did not like to make it a part of a bigger India as more than 100 million poor Bengalis did not offer a bright prospect for India. However, the Indians have always been eyeing Pakistan which is much more prosperous and has abundance of food, fruits and mineral! Any legitimate attempt by Pakistan to boost its security, or status, immediately brings a mischievous and violent reaction from the Indians. Whether we buy a few fighter aircraft or a few tanks, or put up a modest nuclear research and development programme, it hurts the Indians very badly and they immediately start a vicious campaign. Look at their hue and cry at our few F-16 planes. They have armed themselves to the teeth and are engaged in fanatic armaments purchasing at the cost of welfare of the common man.

Before the death of Sanjay Gandhi Mr. Rajiv Gandhi was an airline pilot. Thanks to the position of his grandfather and his mother and the unexpected turn of events he became the Prime Minister. Now a large number of selfish people have surrounded him and are feeding him with poisonous and malicious ideas against Pakistan. We appreciate the limitations of Mr.Rajiv Gandhi due to his background but now that he is the Prime Minister of such a large country he should behave like one. Hitler, Mussolini and Tojo were also surrounded by such extremist and selfish people. Even though the three nations consisted of some of the most capable and intelligent human beings on earth but see what happened to them. The Indians are behaving like that vulgar damsel who is standing naked in the market place and shouting her throat hoarse that her neigbour is thinking of taking his clothes off and is coming out of his house, forgetting her own vulgarity.

The simple and straight forward fact which Mr Rajiv Gandhi and his colleagues must realize is that neither is Pakistan interested in any mischief or adventure against India nor should India try to bully or put Pakistan to perpetual submission and nuclear blackmail. We can live as equal, independent and sovereign neighbours, and on this basis it could be in the mutual interest to cultivate a friendly relationship, increase trade, remove visas and sort out the outstanding disputes in an amicable manner either bilaterally or through the good offices of the International Court of Justice or the UN. The two countries could even use the good office of a group of such neutral countries as the Netherlands, Sweden, New Zealand and Switzerland to stop nuclear proliferation once for all.

The Simla Agreement is there to function as good and solid foundation. The five extremely fair and balanced proposals regarding nuclear non proliferation proposed by President Zia-ul-Haq can save the sub-continent from a destructive nuclear arms race. An eventual nuclear war will completely destroy decades of progress and hundreds of years of civilization with innumerable casualties. I hope sanity will prevail on the Indian leader and they will appreciate that baseless and concocted propaganda against Pakistan will not bring them any benefits.

Both India and Pakistan must learn from the history of Germany and France. The two countries were worst enemies for centuries, fought many battles resulting in the annihilation of millions of French and Germans and then realized that enough was enough. They are now very good friends and have committed to stand by each other against outside aggression. The two peoples have totally different tempers and cultures. On the contrary, the Indians and Pakistanis have many things in common, have lived together for centuries and can easily surmount the present difficulties if the Indians show reasonableness and accept very sensible and fair proposals of President Zia-ul-Haq. The two countries should live like France and Germany and concentrate on the prosperity and welfare of their nationals.

CHAPTER - 4

URANIUM ENRICHMENT : YES, IT IS SO UNIQUE!*

We are one of the 8 or 9 nations in the world which are capable of enriching uranium to 3 percent concentration for any practical use. We have done this in record time and for a record low cost. This achievement is no less than a miracle, especially in a country where one cannot make a sewing needle, a good ball bearing or a rust free stainless steel cooking pot, not to talk of broken, pitted wavy metalled roads. The enormity of the achievement becomes more outstanding and invaluable, and to be proud of as a nation, when one realizes that enrichment of uranium is the most difficult and most valuable and the hardest nut to crack in the whole nuclear fuel cycle. Yes, the hardest and the most difficult, otherwise many nations, and not only 8 or 9, would have been able to put enrichment plants, as is the case with aircraft, locomotive, automobile, nuclear reactors, etc., within their territories. Pick up any standard book on nuclear engineering or go through the articles by top notch experts in the field of nuclear sciences, nuclear armament and nuclear non proliferation and you will immediately realize the importance of uranium enrichment and its potential application. Pakistan is rightly proud of mastering this technology.

"NUCLEAR EXPERTS"

Now some "nuclear experts" are proclaiming that there is nothing special about uranium enrichment and that the

---

* This article was published on daily `The Nation', Lahore, Pakistan, on November 5, 1986.

centrifuge technology is neither a secret nor such an art of technology that it should be considered beyond the reach of most countries. Instead of belittling and ridiculing our tremendous and highly commendable efforts in the enrichment field and comparing our achievements with those of the United States, they should have the moral courage to compare their own achievements with such backward countries as India, Philippines, Yugoslavia, Spain, Argentina, etc. While in West Germany and working in a top notch Nuclear Research Centre at Karlsruhe, I came to know of our success in this most important field. It was, at the first instance, difficult to believe that we had obtained mastery in this most elusive and valuable technology in such a short time. My German collegues were full of praise for our success and accomplishment. The break through by our scientists and engineers at Kahuta came as a real heart warmer to all the Pakistani scholars working abroad and it was for the first time that we could walk tall and straight. We were proud to be Pakistanis.

URANIUM ENRICHMENT

A number of articles in the local papers have dealt with this subject in the past. Some of the articles were authentic, having been written by experts in the field with first hand knowledge and experience. Others were by ignorant, ill informed, self proclaimed experts with no knowledge or experience in the field. In an article in the Karachi English Daily of 5.9.1986, the noted scientific writer, Mr. Azim Kidwai, has admirably explained the whole process for a layman. It is reproduced below:

> "When you dig out uranium from the crust of the earth, it is not one brand of uranium, it is a mix of several types of uranium. The particular elements have identical chemical properties but physically they are different, for their atomic weights are different. In other words, the mass of their atoms differs and so do some of their physical properties".

"The two isotopes in natural uranium dug out from the earth and which the world is deeply concerned with for the last 40 years or so, are Uranium-235 (U-235) and Uranium-238 (U-238). Out of the two, the real meat is U-235 that fissions and creates energy. It acts as the fuel in atomic reactors; it makes the atomic bomb (the so called uranium bomb). The bomb thrown on Hiroshima was a uranium bomb. The atoms of the other isotope, U238, do not fission, do not split, and so, it cannot be used directly for production of atomic energy."

"Nature has condescended to play a joke. The proportion of U-235, the meat in the natural uranium dug out from the earth, is very low. It is only 0.7 percent, that is, less than one per cent (one in 140 parts). For production of energy, therefore, the uranium has to be "enriched", invariably. In other words, the percentage of U-235 has to be increased from less than one per cent to higher proportions. That is known as `enrichment. The enriched uranium used in atomic reactors has the U-235 content of 3 to 4 per cent. For making a bomb, the bomb grade uranium has to have U-235 to the extent of 90 per cent or above. A crude device can also perhaps be made out of uranium with an enrichment of 70 per cent."

It may, however, be mentioned that an atomic reactor can also be run with natural uranium that has less than 1 per cent of U-235. KANUPP at Karachi is one such reactor — its fuel consists of natural uranium. But over 90 per cent of nuclear reactors producing nuclear power in the world are run on enriched uranium, containing 3 to 4 percent U-235 because of certain advantages in having enriched uranium as the fuel. As power producers, the reactors run on enriched uranium are graded as superior. The reactor envisaged for the proposed Chashma power plants is to have enriched uranium as its fuel.

Uranium can be enriched (that is, the percentage of U-235 increased) only by very cumbersome physical methods. The isotopes of uranium being chemically the same, no chemical method can work. The physical method invariably has to exploit the meagre difference in the atomic weights of U-235 and U-238, a difference of 3 in 238. U-235 is just a shade lighter than U-238. That is why uranium enrichment is so difficult, so cumbersome, and so far has remained almost beyond the resources and expertise of developing countries (Pakistan being an exception).

The methodology used at Kahuta is the latest, least power intensive and very sophisticated. It is known as ultra-centrifuge technique and is only one tenth power intensive as compared to the old traditional method, called diffusion process (that yielded the enriched uranium for the bomb dropped on Hiroshima). The ultra centrifuge rotates at terrific speeds of 70,000 to 100,000 revolutions per minute. Any mix of lower and higher density put in it tends to separate towards the centre and the rim. Natural uranium, a mix of U-235 and U-238, thus yields richer mixture of U -235. Scores of ultra-centrifuges in cascade can give very high enrichment of U-235.

The fuel of any reactor contains both U-235 and U-238. As the reactor is run, the U-235 atoms fission and produce energy. But then in the proximity are also present the atoms of U-238 which undergo metamorphosis due to the nuclear reactions going on there. The U-238 atoms are transformed into plutonium atoms as a result of the nuclear reactions generated there. A new element is born in the atomic reactor, called plutonium, which can be used as fuel of reactors or for making a bomb.

In simpler words, one gets plutonium as a byproduct in an atomic reactor without asking. Plutonium being a different metal from uranium, chemical methods that are not cumbersome can be employed to separate it from uranium if you have the burnt fuel from an atomic reactor. The apparatus that does the separation is called reprocessing plant. Incidentally, in such a plant, the unburnt uranium is also recovered to be used again in the reactor. That is an additional bonus. The uranium enrichment plant at Kahuta is a full size commercial plant.

ENRICHMENT TECHNOLOGIES

Yes, theoretically there are a number of processes to enrich uranium but for technical or commercial, or for both reasons, the only ones being used commercially are the diffusion and centrifuge technologies. The diffusion process was invented in the USA in early forties during the Second World War and delivered the enriched uranium for the bomb dropped on Hiroshima. The process is expensive as it uses a lot of energy but only a stupid and an ignorant person would call it out dated, backward or simple. It is relatively more expensive and only when you have a more economical alternative you adopt it. Once the feasibility and cheaper operation for centrifuge process was established in 1972 by the first pilot plant it was adopted for industrial plants and 2 big industrial plants, 1000 ton each, are full operational at Almelo, Holland, and Capenhurst, England. Germany has put up a 1000 ton centrifuge enrichment plant at Gronau. It will reach full capacity by 1989. Japan considers the gas centrifuge process as the most promising and preferred enrichment technology.

Huge diffusion plants are operational in the USA, UK, France, Russia and China. A small pilot plant has recently been made operational in Argentina. The success of the centrifuge technology can be judged from the fact that Urenco Consortium of England, Germany and Holland) has succeeded in obtaining contracts worth 2.5 billion (2500 million). Another enrichment process, the Nozzle Process, which was invented by Prof Becker of Karlsruhe Nuclear Centre, did not get off the ground because of technical and commercial considerations. While I was at Karlsruhe I did some work on it in Prof Becker's department. In spite of widespread publicity and promise of assistance in setting up plants based on this technology, it could not win any country to adopt it.

A combination of the Nozzle Process and the Centrifuge Process, known as the Kelikon Process, has been adopted by South Africa and the test facility is expected to be operational in 1987. Any extension will depend on the success of the current process under way, according to a recent statement of the senior General Manager of the South African Atomic Energy Commission. Thus, it has not yet been fully proven or established.

Most recently the Americans have come up with a process known as the Laser Separation Process or more appropriately the Atomic Vapor Laser Separation Process. The claimed advantages of the Laser Separation Process as the future enrichment technology have been widely published by the Americans. Its choice as the replacement for the energy intensive diffusion process looks attractive because of its potentially lower energy cost and separation factors. However, the commercial reality or the laser process is still many years ahead and the practical benefits have yet to be demonstrated. When I was in Europe an international conference was held in London in 1974 on uranium enrichment. It was claimed that within 10 years there will be many industrial plants all over the world. Now 12 years later there is not a single one. I tell you why. The process is not so easy, as tuning of lasers to emit colours that will be absorbed only by a U-235 atom is a highly complicated and most difficult task.

AMERICAN POLICY

One more rather intriguing and interesting point is the policy of the Americans. With the European's successful pilot plant at Almelo in 1972 they started a widely published campaign that they had made huge centrifuges many meters high and about a meter in diameter and with 15 to 20 times the capacity of the European centrifuges. It was a a subtle and rather unethical attempt to frighten the Europeans that they would never be able to compete with the Americans in the cost of enriching uranium and it was useless fcr them to indulge in the luxury of investing huge amounts in this field. They went so far as to announce the construction of a centrifuge plant at Portsmouth at a cost of US$ 10 billion. The Europeans saw through the game and my German friends scornfully observed that the Americans should not insult their intelligence. They went ahead with the expansion of the plants at Almelo and Capenhurst and with a new plant at Gronau. It was clear that the Americans were not interested in investing such huge amounts in enrichment industry. During and after the Second World War they had put up huge diffusion plants which could meet all their civilian and military requirements and they still had more than enough capacity to sell to the world, of course, with political strings and conditions.

Failing in their game to trick the Europeans into giving up their enrichment programme the Americans came again with widespread publicity, and tall claims, of having mastered the laser technique to enrich uranium. Again it was claimed that it was even cheaper than the centrifuge technology and that the proposed US$ 10 billion centrifuge plant at Portsmouth was being dropped in favour of the newly mastered laser technology. The Japanese were the first to react by announcing that they would stick to the well proven and well established centrifuge enrichment technology. The Europeans (England, Germany and Holland) have totally ignored the American subtle game and are going all out with the expansion of their centrifuge plants. However, since there is so much publicity and talk about potential benefits the Europeans and the Japanese have initiated very small research programmes to see if there is any truth in the tall claims being made by the Americans. This is not strange as these advanced nations maintain a lot of research and development programmes on a number of exotic topics to keep their scientists and engineers busy. Notable examples are the work on fusion reactors, Tokamaks, Magneto-hydrodynamic power generators and solar energy plants. The biggest joke is that while such tall claims are being made about laser enrichment process by the Americans they have not yet been able to offer solar energy at acceptable reasonable price.

The French, the Russians and the Chinese are still fully committed to their diffusion plants and are in a position not only to meet their own military and civil enrichment requirements but can also sell huge quantities of separation wook units (swu) to other countries. The EURODIF plant at Tricastin in France alone has capacity of about 11 million swu/year. A 1000 MW reactor requires enrichment amounting to around 100,000 swu/year. It is thus enough to feed more than hundred 1000 MW reactors.

The so called nuclear experts have conveniently ignored all the above mentioned facts and figures and are trying to project laser enrichment technology as if it were no more than mastering the technique of grinding flour pouring the wheat grains in between the grinding wheels and collecting, flour media from different outlets. They have suggested that all you have to do is to convert uranium hexaflouride gas into plasma, hit it with a laser beam and collect U-235 and U-238 in different bags or rather containers. It looks rather simple but if it were so simple then why those who have widely publicized laser groups at their disposal in the country have so miserably failed till today to deliver even 5 gms of uranium enriched to 3 percent U-235, and if this is not a new and advanced technology then come with a good operational centrifuge not a copy of the Kahuta machine capable of enriching uranium and accept my neck.

SOPHISTICATED AND MODERN TECHNOLOGY

Let us come back to the centrifuge technology. The Capenhurst plant in England has a capacity of 65000 swu/year, the Almelo Plant in Holland a capacity of 1 million swu/year. This is a huge capacity and proof enough of the success of the centrifuge technology. Contrary to this not a single, I repeat not a single, plant based on the widely publicized laser technology is in operation. All is based on guesses and future hopes of good luck.

A major advantage of the centrifuge enrichment lies in its suitability to re-enrich the reprocessed or recovered unranium due to modular nature of the plant. Reprocessed material can be segregated into a particular operational unit which prevents cross contamination with other natural uranium.

There is not the least doubt that the success of the gas centrifuge process and its further potential are such that it will maintain its superiority on other processes, be it diffusion or laser, for many decades to come. Pakistan does not need better than that. Now let us also discuss the rather stupid and ignorant assertions by anti Pakistan element that the Kahuta plant is a rather insignificant facility not capable of meeting the requirement of fuel for our "dream reactor".

The statement by the ignorant self proclaimed experts that 1000 MW nuclear reactor requires a large inventory of enriched fuel which will need 100,000 centrifuge for annual reloading of fuel is not only baseless but a blatant lie to mislead the nation. A 1000 MW reactor requires only about 100,000-120,000 swu/year and thus simple mathematics tell us that one does not need more than 12000-15000 machines to meet the requirement. From all reliable and published data available Kahuta should be able to more than meet the demand. But what about the reactor? Whereas a full fledged enrichment plant has been operational for a number of years there is no trace of a nuclear reactor in the country. There has been gross inefficiency and lack of foresight in this respect. Even if today a foreign country agrees (which is totally impossible) to sell us a reactor it will take at least 10 years to erect and commission it. But nobody is offering one and those who are selling it to the nation will most probably be answering the questions of Munkar Nakir in their graves before this nation will ever see an indigenous reactor. You mark my words and keep this article to go over it after 10 years to see if it was not true.

SIGN OF PRIDE AND SOURCE OF STRENGTH

As is now well known to the whole nation, the Kahuta enrichment plant at Dr. A. Q Khan Research Laboratories Kahuta is a pure Pakistani effort and success. No foreign country or experts were involved in its planning, design, construction, erection, commissioning and operations. The Pakistani scientists and engineers did a marvellous job and put Pakistan on the world nuclear map. They gave Pakistan the latest and most economical enrichment technology and put a solid foundation to make Pakistan self sufficient in all its future requirements of the job and delivered the goods on time.

Let us now see what Kahuta or the centrifuge uranium enrichment process has given to Pakistan.

1. It has given tremendous amount of self confidence and pride to the concerned engineers and scientists that they have done a marvellous job for the country by mastering the most difficult of all the processes of the nuclear fuel cycle.

2. It has put Pakistan on the world nuclear map. Pakistan cannot be ignored now when the world talks about uranium enrichment and nuclear capability.

3. It has made Pakistan self-sufficient in enriched fuel for all our future nuclear power reactors. By the time (10-15 years) we have any reactor Kahuta would have procured enough enriched uranium for its initial loading and sufficient stock for its annual reloading.

4. The possible military aspect of the achieved technology has sent chills into the spines of our enemies and has forced others to treat us with respect and consideration. We are no longer being taken for granted by friends or foes. This could be explained to you much better by those in the Government who matter and who have to deal with other countries and their leaders/officials.

Ours is solely a peaceful programme. The President, the Prime Minister, the Foreign Minister and other senior government officials have time and again reiterated our commitment to peaceful uses of our enriched uranium. We are the sponsors of a nuclear weapons free zone in South Asia but we have made it very clear that we will not take any action unilaterally to jeopardize the safety and integrity of our country.

However, in spite of our peaceful policy and our commitment to use our newly acquired invaluable technology for the betterment of our people the world has not overlooked the potentials this technology has given to Pakistan. A recent article "Pakistan Slips into the Nuclear Fold" in a prestigious London weekly, the New Scientist, says:

"Many observers believe the US change of heart is a tacit recognition that Pakistan now has the capability to build the bomb, and that continued trade restrictions are pointless. Pakistan's importance strategically in the face of the perceived Soviet threat in neighbouring Afghanistan is now the US's overriding concern. Washington has poured $3.2 billion in military and economic aid into Pakistan since 1981 with promises of more to come".

"Nuclear parity with India has been a cornerstone of policy for successive Pakistani governments since India exploded a nuclear device in 1974. Even the suspension of American aid by President Carter during the 1970s did nothing to deflect them. Now there is strong evidence that Pakistan has achieved its goal by mastering uranium enrichment."

"Ironically, Pakistan's achievement of its goal may turn out to be the key to peace in the sub-continent. For India now seems ready to listen to Pakistan's suggestions for a nuclear free zone in South Asia. Last December, India and Pakistan signed an agreement undertaking not to attack each others nuclear facilities.... The Kahuta facility has been built to provide fuel for the eight light water reactors for civil nuclear power, which Pakistan plans to install by the end of the century. Such reactors run on uranium enriched to contain 3 percent of the isotope U-235. A successful bomb requires uranium enriched to 90 percent. The technique of centrifuge enrichment can accomplish both tasks."

This is the true picture of the potentials of what we have at Kahuta. If at any time any Pakistani government decides to use this technology in the best interests of national security it will have a full Pakistani option. It will not have to look for some help or assistance from abroad to protect its integrity and sovereignty. This solid foundation is based on the well established American research work carried out at Los Alamos and reported by J.T. Markin *et al* at an international conference held on 22-29 April, 1982 at Petten, Holland, whereby centrifuge technology was actually used to produce 16 percent, 52 per cent and 90 per cent enriched uranium samples for perfecting a technology to monitor concentration of enriched uranium in a centrifuge enrichment plant.

What was true 15 years ago is still true today. Without Kahuta they are still zero. In short, without Kahuta zero plus will give you zero.

CHAPTER - 5

THE CONCEPT AND DOCTRINE OF NUCLEAR WARFARE*

History has shown us that most of the technologies have worked as a double edged sword, double edged because advances that promised to better the lot of some of the human beings often not only threatened but actually harmed others in this process. And when the threat got rather serious, drastic actions on the part of the threatened were the result. Following the classical Murphy's law that a thing will happen if it can happen, the proliferation of nuclear weapons has taken place and will go on taking place even more rapidly to gain edge on the neighbouring states.

Humanity has always concentrated its efforts on developing new technologies and special applications of them. Even though these technologies were developed initially for peaceful purposes, they all ended up being used for killing fellow human beings. The work on fission by Hahn and Strassman and related work by Fermi, Bohr, etc. was of purely academic nature, but the sudden terror of war and butchery unleashed by the Nazis forced the scientists (viz Oppenheimer, Szilard, Teller, Frisch, Peierls etc.) to use this technology, which offered so much to humanity for the destruction of that same humanity. Never in history were such talented manpower and so many resources used for such a terrible weapon of destruction as the atom bomb. Victory in World War II was by an alliance of the USA, the USSR and the UK, and its

---

* This lecture was delivered at a conference of Scientists and Engineers at Islamabad on February 7, 1989.

contribution to the defeat of Fascism was crucial and essential. I will now give you a brief summary of nuclear reactions and atomic, hydrogen and neutron bombs.

NUCLEAR REACTIONS

All atomic nuclei carry positive charges. Under ordinary conditions the electric repulsion between like charges prevents nuclei from approaching each other more closely than by the diameter of an atom. This distance is few times one billionth of an inch. The size of a nucleus is approximately one ten thousandth of this distance. Unless two nuclei touch, no re arrangement of nuclear constituents is likely to occur, and no nuclear reaction can be expected. Thus the great energy content of the nucleus cannot be put to use under ordinary conditions.

There are four conditions under which a nuclear reaction occurs. The first is the reaction between a nucleus and a neutron, a nuclear constituent that is not found in nature in a stable state. Since a neutron does not carry an electric charge, it can freely approach a nucleus and react with it. This reaction may produce more neutrons, which in turn give rise to more reactions. Thus a chain reaction can be obtained. This is what happens in controlled or explosive fission processes.

The second condition occurs when a small number of nuclei are accelerated to a high speed in the laboratory. Some of these fast nuclei collide with other nuclei and reactions can be observed. This is how nuclear physics began, and it made the use of nuclear energy possible.

The third condition occurs in the sun and the stars. The central regions of these bodies have temperatures of many millions of degrees. At these temperatures, the nuclei may have a high enough energy to approach each other and react. This holds particularly for light nuclei, which carry few charges and do not repel each other so strongly. Hydrogen nuclei carry only one proton and can participate most vigorously. Since an extremely high temperature is the condition for these reactions, they are called thermonuclear reactions. Almost all energy available to us on the earth can ultimately be traced to thermonuclear reactions deep within the sun.

The fourth condition occurs in a man made thermonuclear reaction such as a hydrogen bomb (more properly called a thermonuclear bomb). The reaction in such a bomb differs from the reaction inside a star in that it proceeds very much faster. One reason for the greater speed is that the temperature in man made thermonuclear explosions is higher than in the interior of the sun. A more important reason is that the thermonuclear explosives are carefully selected.

REACTION IN THERMONUCLEAR EXPLOSIONS

The most common of the selected explosives is deuterium (heavy hydrogen). In nature it occurs in hydrogen as one part in 5,000 and can be separated from normal hydrogen with moderate effort. The deuterium nucleus, called a deuteron consists of a proton P the nucleus of common hydrogen, and a neutron.

$$D = p + n$$

In principle two deuterons can form a common helium nucleus He^4 which consists of two protons and two neutrons:

$$He^4 = 2p + 2n$$

He^4 is a particularly stable nucleus. Actually, two other reaction occur with high probability. One is:

$$D + D \longrightarrow T + p$$

where T is tritium the heaviest hydrogen isotope. It contains a proton and two neutrons. The reaction can also be written as:

$$(p,n) + (p,n) \longrightarrow (p,2n) + p$$

The other competing reaction is

$$D + D \longrightarrow He^3 + n$$

where He^3 is a light helium nucleus containing two protons and one neutron. For this reaction we can write:

$$(p,n) + (p,n) \longrightarrow (2p,n) + n$$

Another reaction that plays a role in thermonuclear explosion is

$$D + T \longrightarrow He^4 + n$$

This is very effective whenever tritium is present.

$$(p,n) + (p,2n) \longrightarrow (2p,2n) + n$$

In all these reactions, heavier nuclei are built by the process of fusion the union of parts into a bigger whole. For this reason the hydrogen bomb is also called the fusion bomb.

Finally one may mention a reaction between lithium 6 and a neutron. The light lithium nucleus has the structure:

$$Li^6 = 3p + 3n$$

The reaction is

$$Li^6 + n \longrightarrow He^4 + T$$

or

$$(3p,3n) + n \longrightarrow (2n,2n) + (p,2n)$$

It is not proper to say that this is a thermonuclear reaction since the neutron is not repelled by the lithium nucleus and high temperature is not needed for the reaction to proceed. However the reaction produces tritium which can enter into the thermonuclear process.

WHAT IS AN ATOM BOMB?

An atom bomb is a basic nuclear weapon which derives its energy or destructive power from the splitting or fission of the nuclides (nuclide is a species of an atom characterized by the number of protons and the number of neutrons in its nucleus) of very heavy atoms such as uranium or plutonium by the impact or bombardment of a neutron. U-235 and Pu-239 have been used so far in nuclear weapons. The main steps in a fission process are:

a) large amount of energy released at each fission,

b) the radio activity of nuclides resulting from the fission of the original nuclides,

c) release of several neutrons.

It is the release of neutrons at fission that makes a chain reaction possible. There exists a critical mass at which self sustained chain reaction can take place. If an amount of fissionable material larger than the critical mass is put together an explosion takes place, because only one neutron is needed to start the chain reaction and the cosmic radiation can always provide this very easily. For this reason the bomb consists of two species of fissionable material, each smaller than the critical mass, and these are brought together extremely fast. Two methods of rapid assembly are known to be used, viz:

a) The Gun Method in which this fissile material is in two parts placed at the extreme ends of the barrel of the gun. The pieces are brought together by shooting one piece into the other using ordinary explosives, and

b) The Implosion Method, in which a sphere of the fissile material smaller than a critical mass is surrounded by segments of suitably shaped plastic chemical explosives. At the required moment all these charges are simultaneously exploded, pushing the fissile material inwards and compressing it to a higher density and making it supercritical. The shaped plastic explodes, and pushing the fissile material inwards and compressing it to a high density and making it supercritical. The shaped plastic explosives are known as lenses and serve to focus the shock wave at the centre of the sphere where a neutron source is put to ensure availability of neutron at the right moment. The principle is roughly similar to focusing of light rays at a point by an optical lens.

According to available literature about 15-20 kg of U-235 or 5-7 kg of Pu-239 is needed for making an atomic bomb. The bomb dropped on Nagasaki was the implosion type with Pu-239 and was known as the `Fat Man' whereas that dropped on Hiroshima was the gun type using U-235 and was known as the `Little Boy'.

The explosive yield of the bomb depends on the amount of fissile material that undergoes fission before the whole assembly is blown apart by the force of explosion. The neutron reflector, usually U-235, plays an important role in this respect by acting as a tamper to hold the material just a little longer for the last important fissions to take place. For this reason the high density of U-238 is used which also acts as reflector for neutrons emitted from the fissile core. The schematic diagrams show the configuration of components of an atomic bomb both for the implosion and the gun type. Table 1 shows the critical masses for fissile materials. Both the Nagasaki and Hiroshima bombs were of about 1kg of the fissile material. The size of an atomic bomb varies from 1 foot to 3 feet in diameter.

Table 1

Enrichment % of U-235 or Pu-239	Critical mass (kg) in metal fom					
	U-235 Without reflector	Be as reflector	Pu-239 Without reflector	Be as reflector	U-233 Without reflector	Be as reflector
0	-	-	-	-	-	-
10	-	1300	-	-	-	-
20	-	250	-	-	-	-
30	-	-	-	-	-	-
40	-	75	-	-	-	-
50	145	50	-	9.6	-	-
60	105	37	-	7.8	-	-
70	82	-	23	6.7	-	-
80	66	21	-	5.6	-	-
90	54	-	-	5.0	-	-
100	50	15	15	4.4	17	4 to 5

HYDROGEN BOMB

Hydrogen bomb is an explosive device that derives its energy from the formation of helium nuclei. The energy that can be released by a given weight of explosive is approximately four times as great as for a fission of atomic bomb in which heavy nuclei like uranium or plutonium split into two fragments called the" fission products. In both cases the energy released by a pound of explosive is many million times as great as for a chemical high explosive or any chemical reaction.

There are two important differences between a hydrogen bomb and a fission bomb. One is that the explosive in the hydrogen bomb is less expensive. Once the explosion (for which a fission bomb is required) is started, the production of additional explosive energy is relatively inexpensive.

The second important difference is that the radioactivity generated by a hydrogen bomb is much more amenable to modification than the radioactivity produced by a fission bomb. This leads to the possibility of constructing a clean bomb in which the quantities of dangerous radioactive products are greatly reduced relative to the total yield. This is important in some applications for defence, even more so in the peaceful uses of hydrogen explosives.

Most of the details of the construction of the hydrogen bomb are secret. Only the most general principles have been published. As has been mentioned previously a thermonuclear explosion requires exceedingly high temperatures. These can be produced by utilizing the high energy concentrations produced by a fission bomb. Therefore, the fission bomb is used as the watch to ignite the thermonuclear explosion.

NEUTRON BOMB

Neutron bomb is a very small hydrogen bomb that releases massive amounts of high speed neutrons, which kill anyone within a limited range. The bomb is designed to increase the effects of short lived neutron radiation in the immediate area of a bomb blast while confining damage by blast and heat effects to a radius of only 200 to 300 yards (185-275 meters). The radiation kills people slowly and painfully, with some victims surviving for about a week.

The neutron bomb would be used as a low yield, very accurate weapon, as in killing troops of invading forces while sparing nearby civilian population and structures. Thus the bomb is a tactical weapon for use on the battle field.

The neutron bomb was developed at the University of California's Lawrence Livemore Laboratory. Its technology has been under development since the 1950's with some intensive work having been done in the 1970s when it was tested underground. President Carter approved production of the bomb in 1977.

DELIVERY METHODS

In general, the delivery methods for a nuclear bomb are the same as for any other conventional bombs. Great emphasis has been placed on rocket delivery. This is partly due to the circumstances that in this way one can retain maximum control and yet make the bomb available in a short time at a distant location. Furthermore the big yield of some hydrogen bombs, which ranges from 10 to 1,000 times the yield of a fission bomb, makes it less necessary to deliver these weapons with very high accuracy.

DESTRUCTION OF NUCLEAR WEAPONS

This is an undisputed fact that nuclear weapons are the most destructive technology ever devised by man. As mentioned earlier, the first and the last use of atom bombs was by USA against Japan in August 1945 during World War II which led to the destruction of Hiroshima and Nagasaki and killing of 70,000 and 40,000 people respectively. Another, 1000,000 people had died till the end of 1945.

The number of casualties are to some extent estimates but they give a true picture of what a small nuclear bomb can do. The fact that Nagasaki did not suffer as many casualties as Hiroshima was due to its different layout. Nagasaki is built in a series of valleys whereas Hiroshima is spread over a plain.

In a nuclear bomb explosion, **blast and fire** are the two main factors which do most of the immediate damages. The blast i.e. shock wave of a nuclear warhead, has the same general characteristics as that produced by the explosion of TNT. However, the far greater energy released by a nuclear explosion causes destruction in a vastly greater area. The "matter" or "nuclear explosive" embodied as a solid in a small mass is instantaneously converted into a balloon of, let us call it, gas (figure 2). The balloon expands at supersonic speed. Its speed falling off at its front, which is the shock wave, moves from the point of explosion. So does the pressure at about four miles from the centre of explosion. At that distance the wind behind the front is moving at a speed nearly 200 miles an hour which is greater than the speed of the worst hurricanes ever recorded. Moreover, flesh burns, fires, radiation and radioactive fallout increase the amount and rate of destruction to the population and property of the affected area.

WHY ATOM BOMB IS REQUIRED?

It would not be out of place to say that the use of the atom bomb in World War II has fundamentally changed the nature of the military conflict and the balance of power. It gave the USA the unrivalled position of a prime arbiter of international affairs. The USSR having suffered so much initially at the hands of the Nazis got down to safeguarding her interests and to breaking this monopoly, and developed its own nuclear weapons. Furthermore, United Kingdom and France did not want to accept the role of second rate powers and to be ignored in international politics. The same argument forced the People's Republic of China to go all out for nuclear weapons.

Chairman Mao had earlier described the philosophy of politics that, political power grows out of the barrel of a gun and Marshall Chen Yi, feeling rather ineffective as a Foreign Minister, felt he could not straighten his back. The Marshall insisted that "even if we have to pawn our pants, China should develop a nuclear arsenal so it could start on equal terms with other nuclear powers." A country of 700 million people now over 1 billion) had to exert herself and not be treated as a second rate power.

Moreover the industrial fall out of the nuclear weapons programme was so attractive that even President De Gaulle was obliged to say, "A weapons programme gives a technical rub off that makes you compete on the world market in a thousand other ways."

As mentioned earlier, the first nuclear bombs produced by the United States were manufactured as a noble cause. All those involved in it did it with a sense of duty and as means for safeguarding humanity from Fascism. The development of these awful weapons by the Soviet Union was to protect its security after the bitter experience of the Nazi invention, and butchery of millions of her citizens. The production of nuclear weapons by England and France was not based on reasons of danger to their security but more as to gain status and weight in international affairs. The same reasons can be attributed to the development of the Chinese and Indian nuclear devices.

In the past 40 years since the first nuclear bomb was dropped on Japan by the United States, 5 additional states, mentioned above, have detonated nuclear devices and all have developed and deployed (India has not deployed so far) very sophisticated and costly nuclear weapons delivery systems. Lack of technological and financial resources has stopped many nations from acquiring this capability and many nations have chosen to refrain from doing so despite having all the necessary facilities at their disposal. Even though the arsenal of nuclear weapons has become awesome (vertical proliferation) the records shows that at least for those countries which were in a position to develop or acquire nuclear weapons, either the motivations to do so were not very strong or the disincentives have been stronger.

I would like to present here examples of South Africa, Israel and India. Only India has already tested an atom bomb and other two nations are strongly believed to possess the weapon. This has created an unbalance in the respective regional political and military situation. The neighbouring states are facing great problems of protection of their geographic territories and political freedom. Thus they are left with no other choice except to develop nuclear weapons to regain and protect their political importance and regional respect and sovereignty.

CHAPTER - 6

WHAT IS KAHUTA?*

An Interview

Brig. Sid: Kahuta remains surrounded by deep mystery. It does not have much to show for all the years it has been there. Would you like to comment?

Dr. A. Q: All sensitive or high technology projects all over the world are kept away from the approach of every Tom, Dick and Harry. Kahuta is no exception. You can not go to Harwell, Karlsruhe, Los Alamos or Bhabha Atomic Centre. Our government has so often spoken about the work being done at Kahuta. In addition to the difficult task accomplished in the field of uranium enrichment, we are now producing some sophisticated weapon systems for our Armed Forces. I believe we have shown more than enough to the nation to worry about our image or credibility.

Brig. Sid: How much of the Pakistani bomb is fiction and how much of it is reality? Do not you think, as time passes, it is becoming something of a dream than a matter of substance?

Dr. A. Q: It is all fiction and a creation of the minds of the anti-Pakistan lobby. Our governments all along have been solemnly declaring that our nuclear

---

* What Kahuta actually is and has this mystical-mythical giant stood a deterrent against Indian aggression? This is brought out in an interview with Dr.A.Q.Khan by Brigadier Abdur Rahman Siddiqui, Editor-in-Chief of the monthly "Defence Journal" and carried in its issue of May-June, 1989.

programme is peaceful. I have not been asked to do otherwise. We are a poor country, and very short of electric power. All our efforts in this field are aimed at producing nuclear power in the country.

Brig. Sid: Besides bomb making what are the uses of the kind of enriched uranium you are making at Kahuta particularly when we do not have any Light Water Reactors?

Dr. A. Q : The 3-3.5% enriched uranium we are making at Kahuta is mainly meant for making fuel for Light Water Reactors. When we started Kahuta we were hopeful that by the time we start producing enriched uranium we will be having our own LWR. This unfortunately has remained a dream. If we had LWR we would be saved from so much insinuation and doubts about our peaceful nuclear programme. We have been let down in this case.

Brig. Sid: Can you build LWRs? If you can, why don't you go ahead with that?

Dr. A. Q: Technically speaking, yes. As an engineer I do not see any problem in it. Why we do not go ahead, well we can do only those things which the government asks us to do. We can't initiate any projects on our own.

Brig. Sid: What are the chances of collaboration between PAEC and KRL? Why cannot the manufacture of LWRs be undertaken as a joint PAEC - KRL project?

Dr. A. Q: Under the present circumstances this is not possible. We have different norms and approaches to work. If I accept a job or if I am asked to do a certain project I make sure it will be successfully completed within a definite time and for this you should be free to handle the job on your own. In this country working with others means delays, obstructions, failures, etc. We are not yet mature enough to work honestly and as colleagues.

Brig. Sid: The existence of a certain amount of bitterness between PAEC and KRL is becoming increasingly clear. Would you like to say something on that?

Dr. A. Q: If the politicians can have difference of opinion why not the scientists and the engineers? I am not bitter about anybody. I have been entrusted with a very important, difficult and sophisticated job and by the Grace of Allah my colleagues and I have done our job very well. The government is satisfied and happy and we are proud of our achievements.

Brig. Sid: Do you not think, any unseemly debate between two or more scientists is best avoided?

Dr. A. Q: I guess so , but you and other Pakistani friends know the reasons behind it. I do not want to go into details.

Brig. Sid: How long might it take you to present the finished product under development at Kahuta? In case you cannot in foreseeable future it might seriously compromise your credibility as a scientist engineer.

Dr. A. Q. I do not know what you mean by the finished product. As far as we are concerned we have been producing the finished product, viz 3-3.5% enriched uranium, for many years and the government and the whole nation knows about it. We have established our credibility on a very solid foundation and on truth, and we are not worried about the few mischievous or concocted articles or gossips by selfish journalists or PROs. You should judge our credibility from what the whole world, friends and foes alike, say about us. Pick up any foreign journal or magazine and see what respect Kahuta commands at international level.

Brig. Sid: Would you like to comment on the reported downgrading of Kahuta and its potential for weapon grade enriched uranium?

Dr. A. Q: This is a highly mischievous and false propaganda. Kahuta is meant for peaceful uses of nuclear energy. We are working exactly the same way and with the same tempo as before. The government is keen to get rid of load shedding and Kahuta will play the pivotal role in it.

Brig. Sid: Do you find the references made to you as James Bond, Dr. No, Dr. Strange love, etc. flattering or embarrassing?

Dr. A. Q: I would say it is amusing to see how unfertile brains can work and concoct things and stories. It does not bother me what the Western press says about me. They dislike our God, they dislike our prophet, they dislike our national leaders and no wonder they dislike anybody who tries to put his country on an independent and self reliant path. As long as I am sure I am doing a good job for my country I will ignore all such insinuations and concentrate on my work.

Brig. Sid: Would you like to say something about your achievements other than nuclear enrichment?

Dr. A. Q: Yes, in addition to the Herculean and seemingly impossible task of establishing a uranium enrichment plant, we have been helping our armed forces with some modern weapon systems. We have been supplying them with surface to air, anti-aircraft shoulder-fired missiles, hand-held laser range finders (the first and the only one approved by the Pakistan Army and in use with it), special anti-tank munition multi-barrel rocket launchers etc. We are also developing sophisticated anti-tank missiles and some other weapon systems. We are making all the sophisticated equipment and instruments for our facilities at Kahuta thus keeping it totally self reliant and safe from political pressures or blackmail.

Brig. Sid: Would you like to throw some light on the circumstance of your interview with Kuldip Nayyar? You would agree it caused much embarrassment to the government at a time when the US Administration was about to consider the question of military assistance to Pakistan.

Dr. A. Q: This is now an old story but I want to reiterate that it was never an interview. That was the biggest mischief perpetrated by a Hindu and was a shame on journalism. You know Mr. Mushahid Hussain was a dynamic editor of the daily Muslim. He wrote good editorials and commanded a lot of respect. Whenever we ran into each other it was a pleasant experience. One day he phoned me and said that a good friend of his, Mr.Nayyar or Kuldip Nayyar, I honestly do not remember, and it does not matter any way, from India was coming to attend his marriage and would be in Islamabad the next day. He was one of my admirers and would love to see me. I asked Mr. Mushahid Hussain to check with me the next day at about 5 p.m. as I had visitors and had arranged a dinner for them at 7 p.m. Mr. Mushahid phoned the next day and I agreed to receive him and his friend at about 6.30. They came the next day. It was almost dark. I guided the two gentleman into the house. My wife prepared some tea and brought some biscuits. We talked on general topics and Mr. Nayyar said that he was from Sialkot and was in India and I was from Bhopal and was in Pakistan. I told him that was history and we were happy that we had a land of our own. Then he said that Pakistan should not indulge in nuclear weapons programme as India could make hundreds of them and Pakistan could never match that capacity. I responded by saying that India could use only 3 or 4 bombs against us and we did not need more than 4 or 5 against them either and as such the numbers did not play any role. Moreover, we should concentrate on improving the conditions of our poor people. They left at about 7 and I went straight to the nearby Guest House to attend the dinner. Kuldip Nayyar went back and after more than a month published that piece of yellow journalism. If I had said we have an atomic bomb, Mr. Mushahid Hussain would not sit on it for one month and let Nayyar get away with the prize. No newspaper in the world wanted to buy this fictitious story but another Hindu Shyam Bhatia of the Sunday Observer came to Nayyar's help and managed to get the consent of Mr. Trelford, editor of the Observer, to publish it. You already know about the stories of illicit relations of London Observer editor with an Indian call girl, Pamela Bordes. All these things led to the publication of a concocted and false interview. The respectable and noted American nuclear expert Mr. Leonard Spector has recently exposed this yellow journalism in his new book and shown how Nayyar used my Dawn article and other publications to concoct and fabricate that article. It caused some inconvenience to our government but in the end the truth prevailed and the Indians failed to sabotage the US aid to us.

Brig. Sid: How would you substantiate your claim that Pakistan is ten years ahead of India in the nuclear enrichment technology?

Dr. A. Q: I meant what I said. You know all the nuclear experts of the world have described enrichment technology as the most difficult of the whole nuclear fuel cycle. Only 8 countries in the world can enrich uranium and out of them only 5 can enrich with the most modern ultra centrifuge method being used at Kahuta. I know for sure that the Indians have been trying very hard for the last 15 years to master this technology and have not yet succeeded. That's why I say that we are way ahead of India in this important and sensitive field,:

Brig. Sid: Thank you very much, Dr. Khan.

CHAPTER - 7

ADVANCED MATERIALS - I*

I consider it appropriate to open this keynote address by the words of Sir George Thompson, the Nobel Laureate, who said, "We have for some time labeled civilizations by the main materials they have used: The Stone Age, The Bronze Age, and the Iron Age. A civilization is both developed and limited by the materials at its disposal. Today, mankind lives on the boundary line of the Iron Age and a new Materials Age". In my opinion, we have now entered into the Advanced Materials Age. Rapid and multi dimensional growth of high tech industries has continued to expand the role of Advanced Materials. High strength and high temperature alloys, ceramics, composites and polymers were and are being developed to meet specific technical requirements. Recent technological advances such as space shuttle, optical fibres and personal computers would not have been possible without the availability of Advanced Materials. Materials developed for high tech use, with the passage of time, filter down to touch the every day lives of the citizens.

This International Symposium on Advanced Materials is the first of its kind in Pakistan. It is being held when the country is venturing into an era of expanded industrialization. The symposium will increase our awareness about the materials being developed, the modern analytical techniques involved to characterize them, their important physical and mechanical properties, oxidation and corrosion behaviour, application of

---

* Keynote address on the opening day of the First International Symposium on Advanced Materials held at Islamabad, Pakistan from September 18-20, 1989.

corrosion protective coatings and the processing of these materials by electron beam. The development of materials with superior properties cannot be perceived without advanced analytical techniques for materials characterization. The abilities of modern analytical techniques can help us to study even the minutest details of the micro structural features. Using an average scanning transmission microscope system for example, we can see individual atomic planes, identify the crystal structure of submicron size secondary particles and determine their chemistry. A multitude of analytical techniques involving X-ray neutron and electron diffraction spectroscopy are available to obtain qualitative and quantitative information about the crystal structure and crystal imperfections, dislocation, atomic sites in inter-metallic compounds, magnitude of strain, surface texture, magnetic ordering, micro-structural refinement and grain interaction studies in composites. These micro-structural features of materials are being related to the important mechanical and corrosion properties which can further be used to predict the life of components in a given environment. Non destructive techniques (N.D.T.) are also being used for materials characterization. In addition to the classical methods of N.D.T like X-ray diffraction, ultrasonic attenuation and radiography, some of the innovative N.D.T techniques being used are laser beam optical topography and electron acoustic imaging. The techniques of non-destructive materials evaluation have grown up to such a variety and their scope is increasing with such rapidly, that it becomes increasingly difficult for an average investigator to make the best choice of a technique for a particular requirement. Efforts should be devoted in Pakistani industry to develop and improve techniques to monitor and control the quality of materials being produced and stored.

It is very heartening to note that an exclusive session is devoted on fatigue, fracture and creep. On a global scale, metal fatigue and fracture and creep have been studied extensively. Relatively recent efforts have been directed towards an understanding of damage in composites and other non metallic material. In Pakistan, hardly an effort has been made to recognize the importance of a thorough understanding of fracture at macroscopic and microscopic levels. Spreading of that knowledge is crucial so that in the designed service life of equipment, premature failures do not occur. In our efforts to evolve economic designs of equipment and structure we have not yet progressed enough to predict the fatigue life of engineering components.

In order to enter into an era of high technology, we should advance ourselves in each and every field of science and technology. Other nations have established strong national programs in science and technology, whereas we are yet planning our Science and Technology priorities. We must realize that we would stand nowhere in the battle of international competitiveness if we do not become aware of the needs of the present time. We should put more emphasis on engineering science. There must be a proper balance between research in traditional engineering sciences and emerging engineering fields. We should use our engineers more effectively and become directly involved in educating our engineers throughout their life time. We should hold technical seminars and discussions at national and international levels.

Metallurgy in Pakistan has emerged from neglected isolation in the past into a hopeful future, integrated metallurgical plants and complexes like Pakistan Steel, Precision Engineering Complex of Pakistan International Airlines, People's Steel Mills Heavy Foundry and Forge, Karachi Shipyard and Engineering Works, Space and Upper Atmosphere Research Commission, Pakistan Atomic Energy Commission and Dr.A.Q.Khan Research Laboratories are some of the major metallurgical industrial and research centres. They are sensitive to the national demands and have responded to the country's requirements.

CHAPTER - 8

DR. A.Q. KHAN SPEAKS TO DEFENCE JOURNAL*

Defence Journal: Dr. A.Q. Khan, your are almost a legend for most Pakistanis because of your monumental work in the nuclear field, but somehow many of them don't know much about your early life. Could you kindly tell briefly about your younger days and how you reached Kahuta that has made you famous internationally.

Dr. A.Q. Khan: I was born in the State of Bhopal of British India in 1936. I migrated to Pakistan in 1952 and graduated from the University of Karachi. But soon I left for higher studies in Europe. While in Europe, firstly I studied at the famous Technische Universitat at Charlotenberg, West Berlin. Subsequently, I moved to the Technological University of Delft in Netherland and took my Master's Degree in a record time of 5 years[1]. And finally I went to the famous old University of Leuven in Belgium where I earned my Doctorate in Physical Metallurgy.

Defence Journal: When you started work at Kahuta, Did you really envisage what you accomplished

---

* Interview given to Defence Journal (12'90)

1. The normal time taken by students to complete this degree is six and a half to seven years (editors).

finally?

Dr. A.Q. Khan: Yes, I had never looked at anything else but at our goal. We had an objective and we never doubted that we will not achieve it. Thanks to the kindness and guidance of Almighty Allah, the unreserved support, encouragement and guidance of our President, Mr. Ghulam Ishaq Khan, and the untiring efforts and dedication of my colleagues, we achieved our goal in record time and without wasting any money.

Defence Journal: Why did you choose the rather new ultra centrifuge technique for uranium enrichment in preference to old well tried technology like gaseous diffusion that a less developed country like China had used?

Dr. A.Q. Khan: The gas ultra centrifuge method is the most modern and the most difficult enrichment method . Only 5 or 6 countries in the world can claim to have achieved mastery in this field. I chose it because I had good experience in it and because it was cheap. It was within our reach. A country like Pakistan could not undertake the diffusion route as it was very expensive and non economical.

Defence Journal: Do you think ultra centrifuge is a better technology than other latest ones like laser being tried now?

Dr. A.Q. Khan: Any method which has proved its viability is better than the one on the drawing board or more simply said, a bird in hand is better than 2 in the bush. As long as there is no other proven and established technology available, centrifuge technology is the best because it is cheaper, it uses 1/10 of energy compared with the diffusion method. One hears a lot about the laser technology but there is not a single plant, not even a pilot plant, in the world based on this technology. Producing a few grams of enriched uranium by this method does not make it a viable process though some so called nuclear experts in this country have tried to make the government believe so. Even the USA is using this technology in a joint venture with the URENCO the European Consortium consisting of England, Holland and Germany. I have my reservation about the laser technology and even if the USA, UK or France gain mastery in it, this does not make it cheaper or available to us.

Defence Journal: What are the main constraints in uranium enrichment that did not allow even a scientifically advanced developing country like India to graduate to enrichment?

Dr. A.Q. Khan: Uranium enrichment is the most difficult of all the processes in the whole nuclear fuel cycle. Because of similar chemical properties of the 2 isotopes of uranium, viz U-235 and U-238 and of every little difference in their physical properties, it is extremely difficult to separate the 2 isotopes. Because of this very few countries in the world have been able to achieve it. India will have to really work hard to have any success in this field.

Defence Journal: Do you think Kahuta can be upgraded to provide enough enriched uranium for the proposed 300 MW Chinese nuclear power reactor and the 900 MW French nuclear reactor to be completed in the 90s?

Dr. A.Q. Khan: You know that it will take at least 7 or 8 years from the date of signing the contract before a reactor can be commissioned. We are not yet that far and knowing the ability and the competence of those responsible for doing it, I do not see it being done in the near future either. We have an operational enrichment plant. It is 100% indigenous. We can expand its capacity and we already have reasonable quantity of enriched uranium suitable for nuclear reactors with us. Hence, I do not see any problem in meeting the fuel requirement as/when it arises.

Defence Journal: What is the difference in the enriched uranium you are producing at Kahuta for peaceful purposes and the one needed for a bomb, and can you make bomb grade uranium if asked to do so?

Dr. A.Q. Khan: The fuel you use in a reactor consists of about 3% enriched uranium whereas for making nuclear weapons you need more than 90% enriched uranium. Ours is a peaceful nuclear programme and we have all along concentrated our efforts to produce 3% enriched uranium. However, theoretically it is possible to enrich uranium to any concentration by centrifuge method. Since our government is not interested in using the enriched material for nuclear weapons, we have not tried to produce weapon grade material. But there is no doubt about it that we have the capacity and the potential to do so — some other countries like Holland, Germany and Japan have it also.

Defence Journal: Can your team, if asked to build an indigenous nuclear plant, accept the challenge. If so, what type of nuclear power plant you think could be feasible and of what power?

Dr. A.Q. Khan: I can say without any exaggeration and hesitation that I have the best brains in the country. I have the most capable and devoted scientists and engineers in the country and they are as good as the best in the world. We have proved it by putting Pakistan on the world nuclear map in a record time of 5 years. You will not find a single colleague of mine who will make lame excuses or will try to convince himself or others of country's inefficiency or inability to undertake this job. I believe that if the task is given to us we will not disappoint the nation. My colleagues and I never undertake a challenge without meaning to finish it, and I believe we can definitely do the job. We believe that light water reactors will be most suitable for Pakistan and we also believe that we should go initially for a few 300 MW reactors. The country is not yet ripe to put 900 MW reactor on the national grid. You can imagine the effect on the industry when the reactor is not working every now and then as is the case with all the nuclear reactors. It will be highly unwise at this stage to go for 900 MW reactors. We should build a number of 300MW reactors in collaboration with our tried and trust worthy Chinese friends.

Defence Journal: You have also built some weapons for the defence forces of Pakistan. What type of weapons? Could you kindly explain a little about their character complexion?

Dr. A.Q. Khan: Yes, we are helping our Army with some good and effective weapons systems. We are supplying them with shoulder fired surface to air missiles which are sophisticated and effective. We are also producing anti-tank missiles. We are also supplying to army mine sweeping equipment, highly sophisticated laser range finders, multiple barrel rocked launchers, special anti tank munition, etc. This is a substantial contribution and is saving the country large amounts in foreign exchange besides making it self reliant.

Defence Journal: You are also the Project Director of a very prestigious institute of higher learning the GIK Institute. How you find time to indulge in so many intellectual pursuits at the same time?

Dr. A.Q. Khan: It has always been my greatest desire to be associated with education. At Kahuta I have established a team of excellent scientists and engineers and we publish a number of original research papers in international journals. When the President showed his keen interest in the establishment of an Advanced Institute of Engineering Sciences and Technology and asked me to do all the planning ad implement it. It is sometimes very difficult to find time to do all the things I want to do but education is definitely one I will sacrifice all others for. We have a good team to do the job Mr. S.S Jafri, a very senior and competent former civil servant is the Chief Coordinator and Prof Dr. Jamal Khan, Former Vice Chancellor of the NWFP University of Engineering and Technology is Additional Project Director. I believe we can do a good job. We have the capability and the experience to do it. Inshallah the institute will start functioning in October 1993. It will be an exemplary institution

Defence Journal: You seem to be very fond of learning different languages. In fact, you appear to be almost a linguist. In how many languages you have attained proficiency and how? Any comments on this rather strange blend of an exceptionally brilliant scientist and a linguist?

DR. A.Q. Khan: I know a few languages. First of all Urdu is my mother tongue. Then after partition I had to learn Hindi which I still can read and write. Later on I learnt some Persian. When I went to Europe I learnt German and Dutch. I know both the languages quite well. While in Europe. I also took some lessons in French. And of course, English has been the second language all these years. I wish I could learn Russian and Chinese but could not find time.

Defence Journal: Do you have any hobbies and how you relax after a strenuous day?

Dr. A.Q. Khan: I used to go for fishing, fly kites and play hockey in my young days. Then I played volley ball at the university. Now it is so difficult to do these things. I now do some walking and play with our dogs and cats and it is very relaxing. I also read quite a bit. We go to bed very late, usually after midnight, as my wife is also always doing something, knitting, reading, etc.

Defence Journal: Thank you, Dr. A.Q. Khan.

CHAPTER - 9

PAKISTAN'S NUCLEAR PROGRAMME: CAPABILITIES AND POTENTIALS OF KAHUTA PROJECT*

Pakistan is a fast developing country and, therefore, its energy requirements are increasing day by day. We have used almost all our hydel resources to generate electricity. Unfortunately, despite much efforts, we have not found substantial reservoirs of oil in the country. Some people argue and suggest that now we should try to master solar energy and use it for our requirements. Solar energy acquisition was tried very hard by many developed countries during oil crisis, but it could not, and still cannot, be produced economically. Now except for a few experimental set ups, like heating of houses, cooking, etc., no remarkable achievement has been possible in this field. The other option left is to acquire nuclear technology. Fourteen years ago our government established the Engineering Research Laboratories, now called Dr. A Q. Khan Research Laboratories, Kahuta at Rawalpindi with the task of setting up a uranium enrichment plant to produce nuclear fuel used in light water nuclear power reactors to be installed in Pakistan for generating nuclear power. In the following few minutes I am going to describe the early part of our work and our efforts during the past 14 years to make Pakistan self sufficient in this most important and invaluable technology of uranium enrichment so vital for our nuclear fuel requirements.

The Kahuta Plant has put Pakistan on the world nuclear map

---

* This lecture was delivered at a meeting organized by Pakistan Institute of National Affairs, on September 9, 1990, at Lahore, Pakistan.

and has laid a solid foundation for our self sufficiency in future in the peaceful uses of nuclear energy. The enriched uranium (3-3.5%) being produced at Kahuta will be used as fuel in our future nuclear power reactors. It will save the country hundreds of millions of dollars and ensure our independence from political pressures and blackmail.

The use of the two atomic bombs by the USA against Japan laid the foundation for a mad nuclear arms race which is still going on. The Russians, genuinely suspicious of the American intentions, went all out to have their own atomic and hydrogen bombs. This was followed by Great Britain, France and China.

While these nations were, on the one hand, busy manufacturing and stockpiling nuclear bombs, simultaneous attempts were underway to use the same immense power of the atom to produce power. The USA, the USSR, Canada and the UK succeeded in making nuclear reactors for this purpose and there was a widely publicized campaign for atoms for peace. However, knowledgeable and sane people never overlooked the fact that there was grave danger of nuclear weapons proliferation with the spread of peaceful uses of nuclear energy. After all, there is only a weak, transparent screen between the two. Once you know how to make reactors, how to produce plutonium and to reprocess it, it becomes a rather easy task to produce nuclear weapons.

Concerted efforts by the Third World countries supported by some genuinely worried Western countries like Sweden, Ireland, Holland, Switzerland, etc. led to a consensus on the urgent need of an international agreement to stop the spread of nuclear weapons. This resulted in the establishment of the now world renowned Nuclear Non Proliferation Treaty or the NPT in 1970. About 130 countries have so far signed it despite its highly discriminatory nature, as it allows the nuclear weapon powers to accumulate and enhance their stockpiles of nuclear weapons while putting severe restrictions on even the peaceful utilization of nuclear power by the have nots.

In 1964 the People's Republic of China became the last

nation to join the nuclear weapons club before the NPT came into existence in 1970. China has serious security problems from both the USA and USSR and had no alternative but to go nuclear to safeguard her integrity, independence and sovereignty. Things had settled down nicely and there was a status quo in this matter when on May 18,1974 India shattered this delicate balance and tranquillity by exploding a nuclear bomb in Rajasthan.

BACKGROUND OF THE KAHUTA PROJECT

The sad part of the whole story was that unlike China, India had no such serious security problems. It had a friendship treaty with the USSR and it violated a sacred trust by clandestinely using a Canadian reactor, CIRUS, and American heavy water to make this weapon. Nothing damaged the NPT so much as the Indian nuclear explosion.

As far as Pakistan was concerned the whole story now started. As a result of the Indian betrayal of trust, the Canadians abruptly cut off all nuclear cooperation with us. Fuel and heavy water were refused for KANUPP and internationally made solemn agreements were turned into useless litter. We were penalized for a mischief done by India. All efforts by the Government of Pakistan to impress upon the Canadians to honour their solemnly made pledges failed. Pakistan was left high and dry.

To complete the humiliations of a developing and Third World country, the French backed down from the agreement made under aegis of the IAEA for the supply of a reprocessing plant. It was an international agreement made between two sovereign states with the IAEA as a referee. The Americans succeeded in arm twisting the French and the French, who normally have great pride, went back on their international agreement. The reprocessing plant was going to be under IAEA safeguards and there was not the remote possibility of misusing this facility for non peaceful purposes, though those who had advised the government of Pakistan to buy it were under other illusions.

It was at this stage that Pakistan took up the challenge and decided to go alone and be self-reliant in nuclear technology. In July, 1976, our government decided to go all out to master the enrichment technology and to ensure our reliance on our own fuel for all further light water nuclear power reactors. The Engineering Research Laboratories were set up on the 31st July 1976 to undertake the enormous task of putting up an indigneous enrichment plant. Mr. Ghulam Ishaq Khan, currently President of Pakistan, was appointed Chairman of the Coordination Board.

I had just returned from Europe after almost 15 years. I had studied at the famous Technical University of West Berlin, at the prestigious Technological University of Delft, Holland and at the famous and old University of Leuven, Belgium. I had worked for a number of years in Holland and had specialized in the uranium enrichment technology. I was young, had a doctorate of Engineering in Physical Metallurgy a most suitable discipline for handling sophisticated technological projects, had relevant experience and was down to business. I gathered together a team of highly dedicated, efficient and patriotic scientists and engineers and went all out to finish the job as quickly as possible. As one can imagine, it was not an easy task. The scientists and engineers whom I recruited had never heard of a centrifuge, even though some of them were Ph.D's.

A country which could not make sewing needles or even ordinary durable metalled roads was embarking on one of the latest and most difficult technologies. Only seven countries in the world USA, UK, France, USSR, China, Germany and Holland possessed this technology. Of the whole nuclear cycle, enrichment is considered to be the most difficult and most sophisticated technology. It was a real challenge to me and to my colleagues. The problem was very clear to us. We were not going to find out new laws of nature but were dealing with a very difficult and sophisticated engineering technology. It was not possible for us to make each and every piece of equipment or component within the country. Attempts to do so would have killed the project in the initial stages. We devised a strategy by which we would go all out to buy everything that we needed in the open market to lay the foundation of good infrastructure and would then switch over to indigenous production as and when we had to.

My long stay in Europe and intimate knowledge of various countries and their manufacturing firms was an asset. Within two years we had put up working prototypes of centrifuges and were going at full speed to build the facilities at Kahuta. We had selected Kahuta for two prime factors in our mind. The site should be out of normal traffic for security reasons and it should be near the capital for full support and quick decisions.

More important than these two factors was the consideration for the provision of facilities for our scientists and engineers. We never repented our decision and it is solely due to the selection of this site and my presence in the capital that we managed to rush through our programme for more than three years before the Western countries got wind of it and embarked upon concerted and coordinated efforts to kill our infant programme.

They were mistaken. We had done our homework quite well. We had considered this eventuality and were fully equipped to deal with it. My long stay in Europe and good knowledge of their way of thinking and of their psychology was an invaluable assett, while the Government especially our President, Mr. Ghulam Ishaq Khan, who had been all assistance to us, had kept faith and trust in our efforts and sincerity. I never hesitated to take any action which I thought to be in the best interest of our programme.

Tremendous pressure was brought on us. Our economic aid was cut off by the USA and embargo was put on such small things as rubber O-rings, magnets and margin steel tubes. We faced these problems with boldness and increased our efforts to finish the job as quickly as possible.

Once it was known that we were working on the enrichment technology, the Western press mounted a most vicious and unfounded propaganda against our programme. A case was initiated against me in Holland for writing two letters from Pakistan to two of my former colleagues. The letters were interpreted as an attempt to obtain information which the Dutch Public Prosecutor described as classified. I never received any answer to my letters, but was prosecuted without my knowledge and in my absence.

The information I had asked for was ordinary technical information available in published literature for many decades. I had requested for it as we had no library of our own at that time. I submitted certificates from six world renowned professors from Holland, Belgium, England and Germany that the information requested by me was public knowledge and was not classified. I filed an appeal against this unjust case and the High Court of Amsterdam quashed the proceedings and the verdict of the Lower Court was annulled. Justice eventually reigned supreme. On June, 16,1986, the Dutch Government finally dropped all the charges realizing that enough was enough. There was no substance in the case.

ENRICHMENT OF URANIUM FOR NUCLEAR POWER

Now I come back to our experience in the enrichment field. As I described earlier, it is the most difficult of the all technologies in the whole fuel cycle. If you can crack this nut the rest should fall in place without much effort, provided it is tackled competently and sincerely. The centrifuge technology involves top notch expertise in metallurgy, mechanical engineering, chemical engineering, process technology, electronics, automation and control, nuclear physics, vacuum technology, etc. An ultracentrifuge runs at 70,000-80,000 r.p.m and one can imagine the problems arising from demands on materials, the tolerances, bearings, imbalance of the rotating components, etc.

It is a Herculean task and an ultracentrifuge is undoubtedly a mechanical miracle. Naturally, the Western World was fully aware of these problems and was sure that an underdeveloped country like Pakistan could never master this technology. We proved otherwise. We not only succeeded in mastering this most difficult technology, but also in putting up a plant which symbolized our national pride and competence. While a lot of biased and unfounded propaganda was directed against us, in this regard some of our dear friends in Pakistan played a big role. The Western World never talked about their own hectic and persistent efforts to sell every thing to us. When we bought inverters from Emerson, England, we found them to be less efficient than we wanted them to be. We asked Emerson to improve upon some parameters and we suggested the method. As was later pointed out in the notorious BBC film, "Project 786—The Islamic Bomb", the requested modifications got the wind out of the Emerson people.

At the same time we received many letters and telexes from abroad and people chased us with figures and details of equipment they had sold to Almelo, Capenhurst, etc. They literally begged us to buy their equipment. We bought what we considered suitable for our plant and very often asked them to make changes and modifications, according to our requirements. One should realize that all this equipment was, what we call conventional technology. It was normal chemical process and vacuum technology equipment which had a thousand and one uses in other disciplines.

Notwithstanding the fact that we were handicapped by not being able to hold open discussions with foreign experts or organizations, we attacked all the problems successfully. Our scientists and engineers not only designed and ran good centrifuges but designed the cascades, worked out the header piping system, calculated the pressures, developed the control philosophy, and developed software and hardware for it. It was a hundred percent Pakistani effort and success story.

An enrichment plant needs a lot of precautions or fail safe

systems. We designed them all. We welded thousands of feet of aluminium pipes of the header, and of the feed and collection systems. Once the Western propaganda reached its climax and all efforts were made to stop or block even the most harmless items we said enough was enough and started indigenous production of all the sophisticated electronic, electrical and vacuum equipment.

Kahuta is an all Pakistan effort and is a symbol of Pakistan's determination to refuse to submit to blackmail and bullying. It is not only a great source of personal satisfaction to me but is also a symbol of pride for my colleagues.

Usually, in setting an industrial plant, the sequence is idea, decision, feasibility report, basic research, applied research, construction of a table mode, construction of a pilot plant, engineering chain of steps and usually takes a very long time, especially if your are dealing with one of the most difficult and sophisticated technologies of the world. We took a very bold step and started with all the steps simultaneously.

While preliminary work was being undertaken at Rawalpindi and procurement was being done for the most essential and sophisticated equipment and material, we were manufacturing the first prototypes of centrifuges, we were setting up a pilot plant at Sihala and were preparing blueprints for and starting the construction of the main facility at Kahuta. It was a revolutionary and bold step and it virtually ensured our success in a record time.

PAKISTAN ATOMIC ENERGY COMMISSION AND NUCLEAR POWER PLANT

The scientific community of Pakistan is genuinely concerned over the performance of the Pakistan Atomic Energy Commission. The Commission promised to fabricate indigenous reactors fixing a target of 8 reactors by 1990 and 16 more by 2000, for the production of 1000 megawatts and 1400 megawatts of nuclear energy respectively. But apart from the turnkey project of KANUPP not a single kilowatt of additional nuclear energy has been added so far to the national grid.

The PAEC should realize its accountability to the nation and discharge its responsibility with scientific acumen and a spirit of patriotism. A shift in policy from heavy water reactors to light water power reactors may be an answer to the situation. Failures in scientific experimentation should make us wiser rather than obstinate. When we all know that purchase of heavy water is a continuous problem of KANUPP and costlier proposition too, there is no sense in throwing billions of dollars of a poor country down the drain and yet remaining dependent on Western Bloc. The potential of our nuclear programme of energy production lies in a policy shift for right choice of techniques. The earlier our scientific leadership in the Pakistan Atomic Energy Commission realizes this stark reality the more it would be in national interest.

The PAEC may be well advised to fabricate or manufacture even a small research reactor to use the enriched uranium produced by us. Some persons amidst our scientific community are indulging in petty public showmanship to convince the nation that no reactor or fuel can be manufactured within the country. If India can why can not we? Had PAEC people done their job, we would not have been exposed and subjected to world wide mischievous propaganda against us.

In any large and difficult undertaking there are rough times to go through and of course success may not come till one is dead, but these things (difficulties, embargoes, failures, etc.) do not matter if one is in earnest. My colleagues and I were in earnest and by the grace of Almighty God, and through our sustained and untiring efforts, were lucky to see the success in our life time. My interview of February 10, 1984 to Mr. Tariq Warsi of the daily "Nawa-e-Waqt" put an end to all speculation and gave the nation the first happy tidings since the ugly debacle of East Pakistan in December 1971.

I would like to emphasise here that the success of the Kahuta plant is due to the enormous sacrifices made by the families (parents, wives, children, etc.) of the scientists, engineers and non technical staff working at the plant. It was only due to their understanding, love, affection and encouragement that all those working at Kahuta could concentrate fully on the enormous task entrusted to them. The engineers and scientists did a wonderful task, a task any nation would be proud of.

Time and again it has been solemnly declared by our national leaders, including the President, the Prime Minister and Foreign Minister, that ours is a solely peaceful nuclear programme. In late 1985 the late President, Gen, Zia-ul-Haq, went so far as to make the following proposals to India on the floor of the United Nations :

a) To declare South Asia a nuclear weapon-zone;

b) To sign the NPT simultaneously;

c) To sign a bilateral nuclear non proliferation treaty;

d) To agree to an international inspection team to visit and inspect each and every nuclear facility in each of the two countries; and

e) To renounce mutually the use of nuclear weapons.

While both India and Pakistan are fully justified in pursuing their individual nuclear programmes and not allow themselves to be blackmailed or bullied by other countries it is in the larger interest of their millions of people that they remove mutual distrust and come to clear, unambiguous and fail-safe understanding regarding the manufacture and use of nuclear weapons.

The Pakistan enrichment experience has demonstrated that if a nation is sincere and determined to achieve a certain goal she will do it and will do so much sooner than anticipated. What we achieved in five years at a much lower cost was considered by others unattainable by us in 50 years. If goal oriented and sincere efforts had been made by the PAEC they could definitely result in our own reactor in the coming years. It is still not too late and Pakistan can again show that it can meet any challenge when it comes down to national pride and honour.

Our efforts in the enrichment field have been most challenging, most adventurous most hazardous but most satisfying and gratifying. My colleagues and I are really proud of our contribution to the scientific and technological progress of our beloved country in this most important field. We are sure that our efforts and achievements will always be remembered by a proud and grateful nation and they will always be source of inspiration to our future generations.

CHAPTER - 10

PREPARING FOR THE 21ST CENTURY*

The 20th century has been full of complex problems for human survival and development of peace. If past mistakes and present follies are to be avoided, humanity must learn to seriously prepare and scientifically plan for the 21st century right now. The 21st century being only eight years away very little time is left to pre-empt its anticipated problems and forestall its foreseeable crises. Only then can we hope for progress in peace during the coming decades. Both, individuals as leaders and as followers, and institutions have a major role to play in the socially responsible process of sensibly preparing and democratically planning for the 21st century at local, national and regional levels. They must, however, have the proper facilities and be adequately empowered to do so successfully. This at best is most likely to occur during peace and under democracy.

Speaking specially of Pakistan, there is no dearth of talent and human and material resources. The prime prerequisites for progress and development are value based science and technology education, capital investment and depoliticisation of the educational environment. Investment capital, whether domestic or foreign, is shy of a disturbed law and order situation. These are problems which we must tackle firmly on a top priority basis.

Science fiction inventions like computers, robots, supersonic air crafts, space shuttles, space communications and nuclear

---

* A speech delivered at the PFI Seminar held on May 25, 1991 at Islamabad, Pakistan.

energy represent super sophisticated technologies. Whether it is a sewing needle or a satellite, nothing can be made without a proper understanding of its appropriate technology. Developed countries provided funding for the advancement of science and technology on a crash programme basis. Japan spent US$ 90 billion on R&D in 1991 and the USA about $130 billions for the same purpose. The results are visible to all. Pakistan must also conduct a comprehensive science and technology assessment for the next decade. We must work out our national goals keeping in view our natural resources, energy and the environment, as well as defense by dealing with material issues related to strategic materials, reduction of energy costs in production, recovery and recycling of scrap, all in the context of an awakened public awareness of the fitness of national and global resources.

In order to enter into an era of high technology we should first advance in each and every field of science and technology. Other nations have established strong national programmes in these fields, whereas we are still planning our Science and Technology priorities. We must realize that we will be nowhere in the battle for international competitiveness if we do not become aware of the present needs. We should put more emphasis on engineering sciences. We must create a dependable fund of local expertise in the technologies vital and essential for our industrial progress. I may, however, add that we in Pakistan are not oblivious to our responsibilities. There is now a growing awareness of the need to set up research facilities and institutions of higher learning in the field of science and technology in both public and private sectors. The Society for the Promotion of Engineering Sciences and Technology SOPREST, a private and nonprofit organization, headed by Mr. Ghulam Ishaq Khan, President of Pakistan, has undertaken the establishment of an advanced institution of engineering sciences and technology, namely the Ghulam Ishaq Khan Institute of Engineering Sciences and Technology at Topi near Tarbela in the N.W.F.P. The institute is our brain child, was conceived decades ago, and was seeded by the generous donation of the BCCI Foundation. I have the honour of being the Project Director of this important project. The construction work was started in April last year and we hope that the institution will start functioning in October 1993. The aim of this institute is to provide engineering and technological education of the highest possible academic standards at under graduate and post graduate levels in five important disciplines, viz Applied Physics and Mathematics, Computer Sciences, Electronics and Electrical Engineering, Mechanical Engineering and Metallurgy and Materials Science. The objectives are two fold-firstly to improve the quality of life of the common man in Pakistan and secondly to guide our industrialists in the development of import-substitution and exportable products through the application of science and technology. The institute will be a milestone in the field of science and technology.

In order to make sure that our country competes with others in advanced technologies we need to give due attention to the metal industry in Pakistan. An advisory committee of experts should be constituted for identifying and undertaking projects of national interest. This step, I believe, will provide great strength and stimulus to our industrial base for the future. There is a pressing need for developing a comprehensive technology policy for Pakistan, which must be an integral part of the overall economic and development planning of the country. Such a policy must encourage the adoption of an aggressive and forward looking stance towards technological modernization. It would help strengthen the industrial level incentives of modernization and R&D and facilitate transfer of technology by encouraging technical agreements. It would also contribute towards research and development as well as in the creation of trained and highly skilled manpower.

CHAPTER - 11

ADVANCED MATERIALS - II*

The theme of today's symposium, "Advanced Materials" has become an issue of vital interest to the future development of Pakistan. Many new engineering materials, as we know, have been added to the array of iron and steel products available to manufacturers since the dawn of the iron age. As a result, the iron age has evolved into the materials age. The materials age encompasses a broad enterprise. The vitality and the usefulness of the field of advanced materials are becoming evident everywhere. The award of prizes of fundamental advances in materials research by the Nobel Committee for three consecutive years 1985, 1986 and 1987 is a clear reflection of this recognition. A variety of advanced materials composites, engineering ceramics, rapidly solidified alloys, synthetic structured materials on modulated structure, monocrystalline metals, supeconductors, shape memory alloys, are now emerging from laboratory curiosity status to new device applications. In short, success in translating advances in materials science and engineering into new and improved materials is unparalleled. There have been gratifying broad applications of advanced materials. The raison d'etre of materials, however is their exploitation in practical application, from space satellites to aircraft and space vehicles manufacturing and allied weaponry, textile machinery to automobiles, sports equipment to chemical plants, and also in areas with immediate impact on human welfare, such as

---

* Keynote address delivered at `The Second International Symposium on Advanced Materials', 18-20 September, 1991, Islamabad, Pakistan.

biomaterials suitable for artificial organs, biochemical senors, vascular grafts and ophthalmological devices.

Science fiction inventions, like computers and robots, supersonic aircraft and space shuttles, satellites, space communication and nuclear energy, represent super sophisticated technologies which would not have been possible had metallurgists not invented advanced materials. Whether it is a sewing needle or a satellite, nothing can be made without a proper understanding of materials. Of all the "M"'s involved, viz manpower, materials, machines, methods and money, in the industrial and technological development of a country, materials and how to shape and use them is the most important factor.

Materials, thus, stand out not only as a pervasive part of the natural world, but they are generally useful to mankind and therefore invaluable to society. This confluence gives rise to a persistent driving force for probing materials ever more deeply and for using them ever more wisely. It is both a lofty challenge and a proud responsibility for materials science and engineering. The challenge has been taken up very seriously by the governments of industrially developed countries such as USA, the EEC countries, Japan, China and the USSR. The total funding provided by these countries, on a crash programme basis, amounts to about 20 billion US dollars.

This clearly indicates that the developing countries consider advanced materials a field of strategic importance. In the light of the information, a country like Pakistan must also conduct a comprehensive materials research and technology assessment for the next decade. In the first instance, we must have an initial recognition of materials science and engineering as a distinct area of endeavour. Then we must work out our national goals keeping in view our natural resources, energy, and the environment, as well as defence by dealing with materials issues related to strategic materials, reduction of energy cost in production, recovery and recycling of scrap, all in the context of an awakened public awareness of the finiteness of the national and global resources.

In order to enter an era of high technology we should advance ourselves in each and every field of science and technology. Other nations have established strong national programmes in science and technology, whereas we are still planning our science and technology priorities. We must realize that we will stand nowhere in the battle for international competitiveness if we do not become aware of the present needs. We should put more emphasis on engineering sciences. We must create a dependable fund of local expertise in technologies vital and essential for our industrial progress. I may, however, add that we are not oblivious to our responsibilities. There is now a growing awareness in Pakistan of the need to set up research facilities and institutions of higher learning in the field of science and technology in both the public and the private sectors. The Society for the Promotion of Engineering Sciences and Technology (SOPREST), a private and non profit organization, of which Mr. Ghulam Ishaq Khan, President of Pakistan, is the President, had undertaken the establishment of an advanced institution of engineering sciences and technology namely the Ghulam Ishaq Khan Institute of Engineering Sciences and Technology , at Topi near Tarbela in the N.W.F.P. I have the honour of being the Project Director of this important project. The construction work was started in April this year and we hope that the Institute will start functioning in October 1993. The aim of this Institute is to provide engineering and technological education of the highest possible academic standards at undergraduate and post graduate levels in five important disciplines including metallurgy and material science. The objectives are two fold, firstly to improve the quality of the life of the common man in Pakistan and secondly to guide our industrialists on the development of import substitution and exportable product through the application of science and technology. The Institute will be a milestone in the field of science and technology.

Before I conclude, let me address a special word to the worthy Primer Minister. In order to make sure that our country competes with others in special alloy production, we need to give due attention to the metal industry in Pakistan. An advisory committee of experts may be constituted for identifying and undertaking projects of national interest. This step, I believe, will provide great strength and stimulus to our industrial base for the future. There is a pressing need for developing a comprehensive technology policy for Pakistan, which must be an integral part of the overall economic and development planning of the our country. Such a policy must encourage the adoption of an aggressive and forward looking stance towards technological modernization, help strengthen the industrial level incentives of modernization and R&D and facilitate the transfer of technology by encouraging technical agreements and also control towards research and development as well as trained and skilled manpower.

CHAPTER - 12

ATOMS FOR DEVELOPMENT*

The underdeveloped world today is facing a serious problem of population blast which has created other related problems, like those of food, housing and means of livelihood. These problems are likely to aggravate and to result in unrest among the people and the nations.

Pakistan is one of the worst hit countries in this regard. Its population has increased from over 30 million in 1947 to almost 130 million in 1992, due partly to the influx of refugees from neighbouring countries but mainly on account of a very high birth rate and a marked decline in the death rate. Pakistan's population is growing at an alarming rate of 3.1 per cent per annum. This rate is much higher than the average rate of increase of 2.2 percent in South Asia. With current growth rate of population, Pakistan would have 150 million people by the end of this century and cross the 200 million mark by the year 2010.

If this rate of growth continues, Pakistan's population will be doubled in about 23 years while other developing countries and developed nations might take 34 and 111 years respectively to double their population. Over population in our country is in addition to the already existing national problems. We are amongst the world's poorest countries which are deprived of basic necessities of life such as health, education, adequate housing and even hygienic drinking water facilities. Besides, the investment rate in our country is too small to maintain a

---

* This article was published in `Pakistan Banker', Lahore, Pakistan, Vol. 3, No. 1, 1993.

balance in supply and demand required to meet and run the existing facilities.

BOTTLENECKS TO DEVELOPMENT

Against this enormous increase in population, the resources of the country are static. No appreciable source of energy has been discovered inspite of strenuous efforts made during the last four decades. The country is miserably deficient in all natural resources of energy, viz, coal, gas, oil, firewood and also the hydro electricity. Our existing sources of oil and natural gas do not provide us with more than 1/3rd of our present requirements and these, too, are not likely to last for more than 30 years to come. The hydel power produced by us is also about one half of our requirements and the possibility of its increase in the years to come is bleak.

The question of providing employment to the ever increasing population is also worrying the planners of our country. We are unable to keep every one on job which is causing unrest among the general masses. Gone are the days when one member of a family used to earn and provide food, clothing and shelter to the family of 5 to 10 members. Now every adult member of the family has to earn to make the family self sufficient. The needs have increased. The concepts of life have changed and, for that, more money is required to satisfy needs.

To meet the growing needs of the people and to provide them work we have to step up the pace of industrialisation. We can not depend upon imports from abroad as they consume most of our foreign exchange. So we have to become self sufficient in all walks of life.

To feed the ever increasing number of mouths and to give employment to the increasing masses we need to set up new industries. These industries cannot, however, be run without proper fuel. Huge amount of foreign exchange is being spent every year on purchase of fuel like coal and oil to keep running the industries already set up in the country.

ELECTRICITY – THE PATH BREAKER

Electricity was considered to be the answer to the deficiency of natural fuel like coal, gas and oil. However, electricity cannot be produced by itself. It can be generated through two sources viz, thermal power stations and hydel power houses on dams. The first source again entails investment of huge sums in the form of foreign exchange as such stations can be run only on coal, gas or oil. The second alternative also requires huge investments as the machinery has to be imported from abroad not only for generating electricity but also for constructing dams. Although, the running cost of these hydel power houses may not be much yet the initial cost will be in trillions, rather than billions of rupees.

There also are some other sources of energy. They are the solar energy and the bio gas energy. Unfortunately, however, these two sources can only supplement the existing energy sources to a very small extent. They cannot make up all the deficiency already existing not to speak of the needs of tomorrow. Some people argue that we should try to master the solar energy and use it for our energy requirements. Solar energy acquisition was tried by many developed countries during the oil crisis but it could not, and still cannot, produce energy economically. Except for a few experimental set-ups, like heating of exhibition houses, cooking, etc., no remarkable achievement has been possible in this field. The other option left is to acquire energy through nuclear technology.

ENERGY THROUGH NUCLEAR TECHNOLOGY

While the superpowers, on the one hand, were busy manufacturing and stockpiling nuclear weapons, simultaneous attempts were made to use the same immense power of the atom to produce power. The USA, the USSR, Canada, and the UK succeeded in making nuclear reactors for this purpose and there was widely publicized campaign for "Atoms for Peace". Electricity from the atom was first produced as early as in

1954, when the world's first pilot nuclear power reactor was commissioned in the USSR. In less than four decades, about 450 nuclear power plants were in operation in 26 countries producing about 336,000 MW of electricity accounting for 17% of the the world total electric power generation. Countries like France, Sweden, Taiwan, Belgium, etc. are generating over 50% of electricity required by them through nuclear energy. Pakistan at present, however, produces only 137 MW of nuclear energy which is almost negligible.

It is imperative for developing countries to increase and enhance their energy resources in order to expedite their industrialization, as nothing can be done without power. Pakistan, therefore, began to plan for the establishment of an Atomic Energy Commission. The main objectives for the establishment of the Pakistan Atomic Energy Commission as envisaged at the time were to:

a) Plan for the establishment of a full fledged Atomic Energy Agency in Pakistan;

b) Explore and identify sources of radioactive minerals; and

c) Recommend possible uses of nuclear energy.

PAKISTAN'S PEACEFUL NUCLEAR PROGRAMME

The Atomic Energy Committee was established in 1954 under the Ministry of Industries and Pakistan participated in the first United Nations Conference on "Atoms for Peace", held in Geneva. Although at that time Pakistan was politically unstable, it was still striving hard for its development in various fields. In 1956 this Committee was converted into the Atomic Energy Commission and Dr.Nazir Ahmad was appointed as its first Chairman. He fully utilized the available resources for educating Pakistanis in the field of atomic energy and also started negotiations with the USA to have an atomic research reactor. In October, 1958, Martial Law was imposed and General Muhammad Ayub Khan became the Chief Martial

Law Administrator. A separate Ministry for Fuel, Power and Natural Resources was established for the first time and Mr. Z.A. Bhutto was given its charge.

The Pakistan Atomic Energy Commission was reorganized in 1960 and Ishrat Hussain Usmani, a nuclear scientist, was appointed as its new Chairman. At that time Dr. Abdus Salam was Scientific Advisor to General Muhammad Ayub Khan. Dr. Usmani put the Commission on a solid footing. At the outset, stress was laid on the establishment of research, development and training facilities within the country, which resulted in the first national atomic research institute under the name of Pakistan Institute of Nuclear Science and Technology (PINSTECH). It was envisaged to establish in this Institute, under one roof, all the laboratories related to atomic energy. The services of Mr. Edward Durrel Stone, an internationally known architect, were availed of and the construction of facilities for an American made swimming pool-type 5MW reactor began in 1960. This reactor was supplied under the "Atoms for Peace" programme and started functioning on 31st December, 1965. The design, installation and operation of this first Pakistani Atomic Research Reactor (PARR-1) was successfully carried out by a small Pakistani team. Lately, this 5MW reactor has been converted into a 10 MW reactor.

In 1965 the government negotiated a deal with Canada for the Karachi Nuclear Power Plant (KANUPP) and singed a contract with the Canadian General Electric Company for the design, construction and installation of a CANDY type reactor. This project was funded by the Canadian International Development Agency whereas the technical assistance was provided by the Canadian Atomic Energy Establishment. The construction started in 1966 and was completed in the middle of 1971. The reactor started functioning on August 1971 and was formally inaugurated on 18th November, 1972. This is the first and the only power reactor in Pakistan with a nominal generating capacity of 137 MW.

In 1971 Mr. Bhutto, who had become Prime Minister of

Pakistan after the establishment of Bangladesh, decided to strengthen Pakistan's peaceful atomic energy programme and appointed Mr. Munir Ahmad Khan as the new chairman of Pakistan Atomic Energy Commission. Dr. Usmani was appointed Secretary to a newly established Ministry of Science and Technology.

During the period 1972 -1991 PAEC managed to keep KANUPP operating without outside assistance and to build a nuclear fuel fabrication facility in Kundian when Canada refused to supply the nuclear fuel. This was not a small achievement. Nevertheless, taking advantage of our early entry into nuclear power technology, the PAEC could have achieved greater success had it planned a strategy for advancing nuclear power with indigenous effort. Instead of producing an indigenous reactor, we signed now to secure nuclear power reactors on turn key basis. Thus the advantage we had from our early entry in this field was unfortunately lost due to lack of success in our reactor production programme.

Since 12 March 1991, Dr. Ishfaq Ahmad has been working as Chairman Pakistan Atomic Energy Commission. The government has recently singed an agreement with China for the supply of a 300 MW reactor. This might serve the purpose of a shot in the arm for pursuing the much needed nuclear power. At same time the PAEC is also strengthening the institutions dedicated to the production of more nuclear power reactors with indigenous efforts.

LONG TERM SPREAD EFFECTS

There is no doubt that nuclear technology supplements the conventional technology and helps develop the industrial base of a country. The mechanical, electrical and chemical engineering services and process get revamped, updated and enlarged. A highly specialized base is created in the fields of electronics, computer technology and automation. Laser data processing systems and ballistics replace the old order. The electronics and control mechanisms usher in an era of high technology. The industrial foundation and the technical know how put the country on a road to progress. The research and development effort trains its demographic resources. No wonder then that General de Gaulle was forced to say, "A nuclear weapons programme gives a technical rub off that makes you compete on the world market in a thousand other ways".

Pakistan's present nuclear energy programme has not only the potential to ease the country's power supply situation, but it has also some achievements in the agricultural sectors. For this purpose, we have developed nuclear techniques to get improved varieties of crops which are not only high yielding but also resistant to disease and pest attack. The role of nuclear energy is very prominent in the health sector also. A notable breakthrough in this field is the indigenous production of radio isotopes used for diagnostic purposes. With the help of nuclear energy, radio therapy procedures have also been developed to contain and cure cancer growth in the human body. In the light of the above facts, it is clear that Pakistan's interest in the nuclear technology is solely for the enhancement of its economic and industrial development; the best economical short cut to bring prosperity and development in the country.

An economic boom can only happen on a strong foundation of uninterrupted supply of energy. Pakistan's peaceful nuclear programme is basically aimed at achieving self reliance in our energy requirements for industrial development and economic and social progress of the country. In order to achieve these objectives, our peaceful nuclear programme must continue. This is in our country's best interest.

CHAPTER - 13

ADVANCED MATERIALS - III*

The greatest event in the world today is not the awakening of Asia, or the actions of one or another superpower, but the advent of change in the working conditions, thinking and structure of our society. Increased automation and sophistication in process technology has brought about a global industrialization which has been elemental in uplifting the economic and social well being of the masses. Materials science and engineering has also played a key role in bringing about this transformation in our society. The innovative use of materials has led to better medical care, enhanced safety in infrastructure projects, faster and safer transport, as well as the provision of more leisure facilities to the common man.

Global industrialization has demanded more efficiency in the application of resources to achieve industrial competitiveness. Smart use of advanced materials holds the key to this perception. Materials with new and improved properties with new methods of processing give industries a considerable leverage in competing in the world market. Advanced materials have been instrumental in promoting several areas of research and development of new materials to fulfill numerous research and industrial needs.

While the use of new materials cannot be sufficiently emphasized, there also exists an important intellectual challenge to discover new ways of thinking about them. Jabir-ibn-Hayan, an 8th century Muslim scientist, once said,

---

* Keynote address delivered at 'The Third International Symposium on Advanced Materials' 20-24 September, 1993, Islamabad, Pakistan.

"Scientists delight not in the abundance of materials; they rejoice only in the excellence of their experimental methods." Insight into the behaviour, properties and characteristics of existing materials in various environments will go a long way towards the progress of materials science and will ultimately lead to a useful technology.

The progress of science depends on new techniques, new hypotheses and new theories, probably in that sequence. Today, we have very powerful and precise analytical techniques for chemical, physical and microstructural evaluation of materials. The processing and optimization of properties of advanced materials demand innovative application. This includes materials used nearly in all the multi disciplines such as aerospace engineering, applied physics, artificial intelligence, biomedical engineering, computer science and engineering, electrical engineering, geological sciences, marine engineering and structural engineering.

I sometimes smile when I recall the good old days while working for my Master's degree, when micro structures observed at an optical scale level were considered to have enough details to establish the material's properties. Now I see my young colleagues in the laboratories taking high resolution micrographs and still keeping the door open for going beyond the atomic scale resolution.

Looking into the future of materials at this juncture, where the 21st century is knocking at the door, one can predict that the future will see expanded joint efforts to develop technologies needed to synthesise, atom by atom, today's advanced materials to produce new property combinations. As we are beginning to explain engineering properties such as intrinsic brittleness or ductility of crystals by quantum mechanics, one can foresee that mathematical modelling will quantitatively define a material's properties. Mathematical modelling and knowledge based processing with the help of ever increasing computing power will accelerate the development of advanced materials in future.

Dr.A.Q.Khan (N.I) with the World Squash Champion, Mr. Jehangir Khan on March 23, 1989 on the occasion of Conferment Ceremony of Pakistan Civil Awards at the Presidency. Both the dignitaries were awarded Hilal-i-Imtiaz.

Dr.A.Q.Khan (N.I) addressing a seminar on the "Current State of Nuclear Technology and Problems Faced by Pakistan in its Acquisition", at the EME College, Rawalpindi on August 10, 1990.

Dr.A.Q.Khan (N.I) meeting with the students of Jinnah Preparatory School in Satellite Town, Rawalpinid on the Parents Day 1990.

Dr.A.Q.Khan (N.I) sharing views with Hakim Mohammad Saeed the Chancellor of the Hamdard University during his visit to the madinat al-Hikmah, Karachi on February 14, 1991.

Dr.A.Q.Khan (N.I) alongwith Hakim Mohammad Saeed and colleagues, visiting the Library at the Hamdard Madinat al-Hikmah, Karachi on February 14, 1991.

Dr.A.Q.Khan (N.I) with the Prime Minister of Pakistan. Mohammad Nawaz Sharif at the Inaugural Session of the Second International Symposium on Advanced Materials, September 15, 1991.

Dr.A.Q.Khan (N.I) photographed with Mr. Jansher Khan, the World Squash Champion at the Peshawar International Airport on November 21,1992

Dr.A.Q.Khan (N.I) standing with the President of the Kazakh National Academy of Sciences, Prof.K.A. Sagadiev, after being conferred upon honorary fellowship of the Academy on June 21, 1995.

Dr.A.Q.Khan (N.I) with Mr. Wasim Sajjad Chairman Senate after presenting a Painting "Hard and Bloody Path to Independence - 1947" for the Senate Hall on November 11,1995.

Dr.A.Q.Khan (N.I), Prof. Dr.A.Raouf, Mr.Farooq Ahmed Khan Leghari President of the Islamic Republic of Pakistan and the Chancellor of the Institute, Mr.Ghulam Ishaq Khan & Mr.H.U.Beg at the G.I.K. Institute on March 26, 1996.

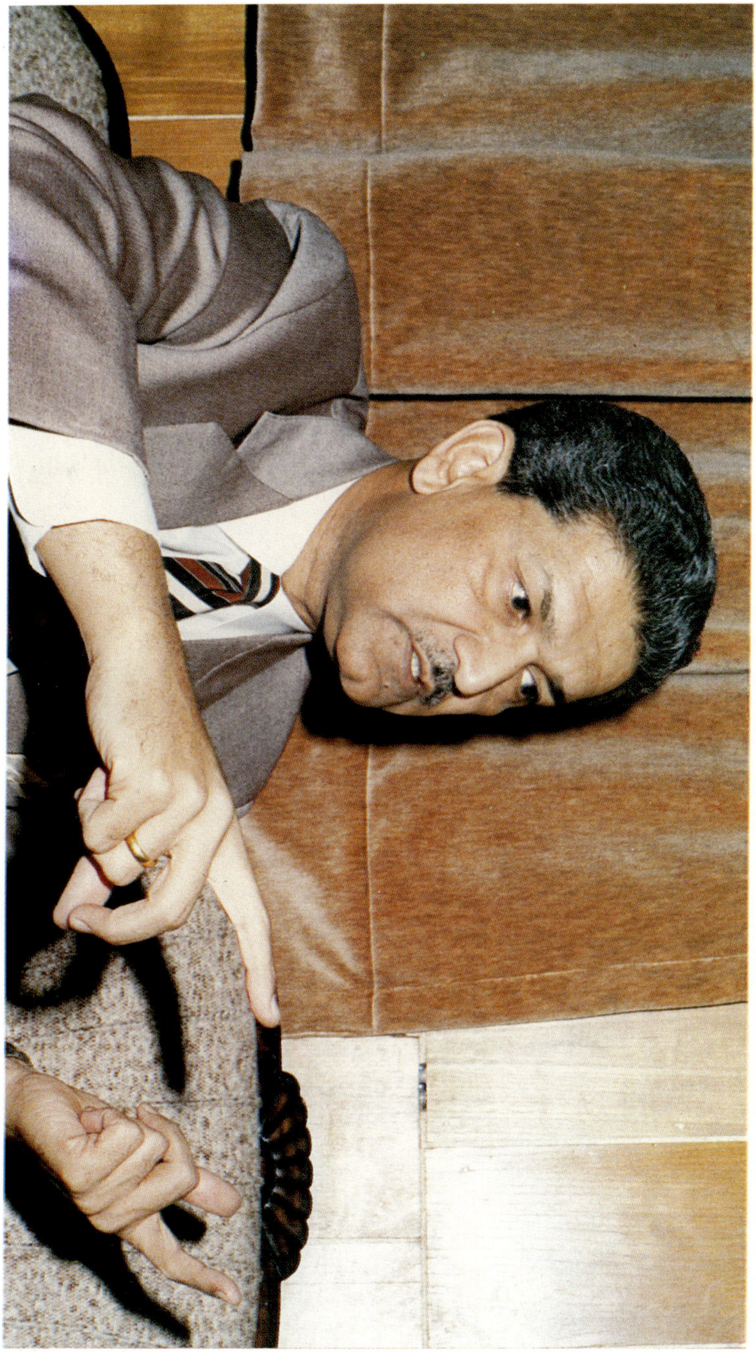

General view of a commercial Centrifuge Plant

Composite materials, including the metal matrix composites and the polymermatrix composites, will dominate for at least a quarter of the next century as the materials of very high strength to weight ratio. Weight reduction in many civil as well as in military applications, such as passenger aircraft, space ships, army vehicles and advanced submersibles is beginning to emerge as an important factor to be considered in future application. Composite materials provide as much as 30-40% weight saving while providing an equivalent level of performance.

Engineering plastics are promising materials of the future. There will be an increasing demand for resins that flow better, freeze faster, eject easily and cause less damage to the moulds. New techniques such as high pressure moulding, co-processing such as co-injection moulding, and sandwich moulding will offer unique advantage to the processor and user. Engineering ceramics will also acquire a respectable position in the list of advanced materials of the future. World research on the science and technology of super conductivity will see a greater use of engineering ceramics in many practical applications.

Surface engineering and coating technology will have an extended role to play in the future to face the unfriendly environment. New developments in organic metal and ceramic coatings will provide protection to the underlying substrata exposed to harsh environment. Another field of significant importance for the future is the study of crystallographic orientation of crystallites in a material engineering texture. Texture investigation is being used to study the kinetics of all kinds of solid state processes as well as to produce a material with particular anisotropy including isotopic material. Texture analysis using electron, neutron, and X-ray diffraction methods will go a long way in the processing of materials with much improved engineering properties.

One of the greatest challenges of the 21st century will be the availability of educated, trained, and skilled manpower to handle the challenges of industrial research and development of advanced materials. We are not oblivious to this need of the future and in this connection a non governmental organization viz the Society for the Promotion of Engineering Sciences and Technology, has undertaken the task of establishing an advanced Institute of Engineering Sciences and Technology at Topi. The civil works and other necessary infra-structures are nearing completion. The Institute will start its first under graduate classes in October this year. This Institute has been designed to provide engineering and technological education of the highest standard to both under graduate and post graduate students in five important disciplines including metallurgy and material science. As Project Director of this important Institute, it is my earnest desire that scientific and technical education takes roots in this country and I invite you all to give us a helping hand to achieve our cherished goal. We want close cooperation between this Institute and your institutions.

CHAPTER - 14

MAGNETS AND MAGNETIC MATERIALS*

The first use of materials occurred when a human being first picked up a stick or stone to be used as a weapon, a tool, or a source of fire. Since then the development of civilization has been intimately linked with the ability of human beings to work with materials, beginning with the Stone Age and ranging through the era of Copper and Bronze, then Iron Age, and recently the Age of Advanced Materials.

Looking at the wider spectrum of engineering materials, the linkage between development of civilization and materials reflects that the standard of living in any society is determined primarily by the goods and services that are available to its people. In the context of today's industrial scenario "goods" are the products of most of the major manufacturing industries either materials or fabricated from materials. The exceptions are food, beverage, chemical and fuel industries. Even within these industries materials play a key role. Global life style of modern times is recognized by the rapid transportation of goods and persons and by the rapid transfer of bulk information. Recent use of light weight, high strength alloys in transportation system (e.g. jet aircraft) and semi-conductors in computers and computer based communication satellites are just a few examples to highlight the fact that the materials have the potential to revolutionize our life style in very profound and practical ways. Further, leading and emerging economies of the world such as Japan, Germany and Korea, underline the

---

* Based upon the Keynote address, delivered at `The First National Workshop on Magnets and Magnetic Materials' held in Islamabad, Pakistan on April 20, 1994.

political significance of materials.

We are now in a period when materials are evolving more rapidly than at any time in history. This is evident in the large number of innovative materials that have become commercially available over the past two or three decades. Materials, thus continue to play their role as "pace-setter' for the development of civilization, but now the process works at a greater pace. Magnetic materials, the topic of this workshop, are no exception in this regard, particularly in the context of modern engineering history. We know that these are not a major type of material by volume but are extremely important for conventional as well as advanced engineering applications.

Most of us know that a magnet is a piece of material which attracts iron. It has been known to human beings for more than 4000 years under its trade mark "Magnet stone". Chinese used to have a freely pivoted needle made of Magnet stone for navigation in ancient times.

A magnet is a permanent source of potential energy and hence indispensable for electric industry. A magnet has a wide range of applications, in manufacturing motors, generators, lifters, levitation trains, microwave tubes, loud speakers, transformers, magnetic sensors and relays, just to mention a few. Even in household, magnets play an important role; ferrite magnets, being cheap, are used as shutters in doors of almirahs and of kitchen instruments or as lifters/attractors in toys. More recently, it has been established that pigeons find their orientation with the help of some built in magnetic waves, whose nature is not yet known.

Although magnets are known for more than 4000 years, it is only since Faraday, who in the middle of the 18th century discovered that by moving a magnet in a copper coil a current is induced in the coil , a new era emerged. Since then tremendous efforts have been made in the development of magnetic materials for the production of superior quality magnets. In the advanced countries, and since the discovery of the rare earth based magnets by the end of sixties, a substantial amount of money is being invested in the development and production of superior rare earth based magnets.

During the last two decades, Taiwan, South Korea and India have made great progress in the exploitation of oxide magnetic materials for application ranging from simple home appliances to space technology. One can hardly keep pace with the new sophisticated developments and applications of dielectric and magnetic materials coming in the market every day. Raw materials falling under these two categories are of strategic importance for the material security of any country. Unfortunately, here in Pakistan we have not explored or exploited our natural resources for the benefaction of oxide materials or perhaps even identified their existence under the good earth of our geographical boundaries, alone manufacture any component of dielectric and magnetic properties. This shows serious lack of foresight, vision and direction by the scientific community in our country and we have to spend precious foreign exchange to import magnetic and dielectric components for all our needs from abroad. India, our neighbouring country, established dielectric component industry in the late 1960s and early 1970s, hard ferrites in mid to late 1970's, soft ferrite industry in early 1970s and microwave ferrite in early 1980's which are now mature industries there. It should be noted that 30% of all magnets sold in England are manufactured in India. Is this not a dismal situation in our case that we do not manufacture even simple types of magnets commercially?

While on a global scale, the rate of technological advancement is enhancing progressively, our national scenario is not very enviable. We, as a nation, seem to be oblivious of the gravity of this situation. It is indeed very sad to realize that in a country where highly talented manpower is available, quality control, and research and development activities are almost non existent, thus causing an unacceptable brain drain.

We know that the present government has a deeper appreciation of the fact that for a sustainable economical growth, technological development is a prerequisite. Technological development cannot be achieved without trained manpower, proper infrastructure, and provision of necessary engineering materials. To raise trained manpower which could meet the challenges of modern times certain reforms in the existing educational systems are needed. We know that the people's government is already committed to bringing necessary changes in the present educational system which would place more emphasis on scientific and technical education. I may, however add that we are not oblivious to our responsibilities. There is now a growing awareness in Pakistan of the need to set up research facilities and institutions of higher learning in the field of science and technology in both the public and private sectors. I am confident that the group of experts who have gathered here today will be happy to extend their help and support to the government in implementing its policies in education, science and technology. I am also confident that the deliberations of this workshop will stimulate enough interest to initiate research and development work in the very important field of magnetic materials.

CHAPTER - 15

STATUS OF HIGHER ENGINEERING EDUCATION AND RESEARCH IN PAKISTAN*

Development in science and technology is the basis of all progress being made in the modern age. Unprecedented advancement in this sphere during the last half of a century or so has changed the very out look of the world we live in. The impact of technological developments covers all aspects of human life. The pace of development in this field is becoming increasingly fast and this fact accounts for the ever widening gulf between the developed and the developing people of the world.

In order to raise the level of socio-economic progress in the underdeveloped countries, a number of developmental models have been applied to these societies. Thus spread of education has been at the core of all such plans, but empirical evidence proves that mass literacy per se is not the sole remedy for the ill of underdevelopment. Sri Lanka is a conspicuous example. It is a country with one of the highest literacy rates in the world, around 88 per cent, but it has little to show in terms of overall socio-economic development. One basic reason for this is their failure to groom a corps of high educated scientific and technical manpower. This is in stark contrast to Asian Tigers, where high literacy rates have been backed up by an army of scientist and technicians who are constantly translating the progress made in the laboratories into industrial development.

---

* Keynote address delivered at the Regional Meeting on Cooperation with Central Asian Republics in the Field of Higher Education held in Islamabad, Pakistan from September 26 to October 2, 1994.

Engineering is a practical and physical expression of theoretical research in various disciplines of science. Engineers build a nation. The more skilled they are, the stronger the country is. In a word where national power determines the order of the nations, development of science and technology in general, and of engineering in particular, has become crucial for the survival and progress of a country.

With lines clearly drawn between the developed and underdeveloped countries, the latter have grown into consumer only societies. Import-based economies of the Third World have not only accentuated the dominance of the West, but have also been responsible for undermining the process of domestic technological and industrial growth. Education hardly gets the attention it deserves from the decision makers and higher engineering education is a rare commodity. Especially, the Muslim world is badly hit by this malady.

The average literacy rate in the Muslim countries is about 37% and the number of scientists and engineers produced by them is barely above 50,000 (1). Ironically, Israel alone has the same number of R&D manpower. The share of Muslim world in the cumulative R&D activity round the globe is negligible. Countries like Russia (with more than one million scientists), U.S.A. (about one million) and Japan (half a million) are far ahead, both in qualitative and quantitative terms (2). On the whole the developed North has 92% of the total population of scientists. Research is also a rare activity in the Muslim world which contributes only 500 science articles to the one million published every year (3). The number of scientific books published in the Muslim world is also proportionally low.

ENGINEERING EDUCATION IN PAKISTAN

Pakistan is no exception to the rule. In fact, contrary to the earlier promise exhibited in the field of science and technology in the 1950s it has a bleak record in this all important field. Official estimates put the literacy rate in Pakistan at about 34%

though if universally recognized criteria are applied, the real rate comes down to 27% (4). Out of this literate population, very low number of students graduate to higher levels of education. According to official statistics, there are only 154 university students in a population of 100,000 Pakistanis. Of these, only 50-60 are science students (5). India, on the other hand, has twice that number and there are more than 300 university students in the same population size.

Pakistan spends about 2 percent of its GNP on education and most of it is wasted due to mismanagement. This is only half of the financing prescribed by the international agencies like UNESCO. The percentage of GNP being allocated to the education sector stands out as a decisive determinant for the number and quality of the out put of the educational institutions. The amount spent on R&D activities and scientific education is even less. In 1981, for example, expenditure on basic research work was estimated to be US$ 3.929 million but no amount was allocated for applied research (6). In comparison, India was spending US$ 76.44 million on basic research during the early 1980s out of which the share of the engineering sciences alone was US$ 36.12 million (7). Even now the Pakistan Government allocates less than 0.5 of the GNP towards such activities which is well below the required financing. According to 1990 statistics, Pakistan spends at least 16 times less on this sector than the annual expenditure of an average university in the U.S.A (8). Therefore, it is not surprising, though unfortunate, that Pakistan Science and Technology manpower consists of only 6,000 people. The size of the engineering community in Pakistan is also very small. Up to 1991, Pakistan Engineering Council (PEC) had registered 39,254 engineers. More than 30,000 of them are qualified in the filed of civil, electrical and mechanical engineering.

The state of engineering education in Pakistan is the direct result of the overall educational scenario. There are six engineering universities in the country working in the public sector - University of Engineering & Technology, Lahore, University of Engineering & Technology Jamshoro, NED University of Engineering & Technology Karachi, NWFP University of Engineering & Technology Peshawar, University of Engineering & Technology Taxila and National University of Science and Technology (NUST), Rawalpindi. The last two Universities have recently been chartered. Other public Universities like the University of the Punjab, also impart engineering education in some disciplines while a few institutes have been newly established by the private sector.

The University of Engineering and Technology UET, Lahore, is considered to be the foremost engineering institution in the country. It was established in 1961 as a result of the upgrading of the Maclagan Engineering College which had existed since 1923. Six major faculties are functional at the university. Included are those of civil engineering, electrical engineering, chemical, mineral and metallurgical engineering, architecture & planning and natural science, humanities and Islamic studies. Various colleges and engineering institutes including the Textile College Faisalabad, are also affiliated with the university. The total budget allocated to the university for the year 1994-95 is Rs 97.213 million. In addition to it, the university is also generating itself about Rs. 38.470 million by offering self financing education to the prosperous students, etc. The university has a capacity of enrolling more than 6000 students in the above mentioned faculties for graduate and post graduate programmes including Ph.D. An annual system of examination has been adopted. The bachelors programme is of 4 years duration while those of M. Sc. and M.Phil. are for two years each. It has also developed liaison with a number of private and public organizations for scholarships and fellowships. The more desirable linkage of technological cooperation with the industry has not been utilized to the maximum, thus creating few opportunities for the university and industry to benefit from each other.

The NED University, Karachi, was established by upgrading

the NED Government Engineering College, the oldest institution of its kind in the country functioning since 1922. The process of upgrading was assisted by the World Bank and was completed in 1972. Covering an area of 100 acres, the NED University has Dawood College of Engineering, P.N. Engineering College, Government College of Technology and Civil Aviation Academy, Hyderabad in its fold as affiliated institutions. The university offers bachelors degrees and M.Sc programmes in the disciplines of civil engineering, electrical engineering and mechanical engineering. A semester system is followed. An amount of Rs. 58.589 million is allocated by the Government of Pakistan for the year 1994-95, while about Rs. 6.814 the university hopes to generate through its own resources. The NED University spends about 3 percent of the total budget on research and development work (10). Due to the fact that the university is situated in the largest city of Pakistan and that the competition for enrollment is tough, a relatively better quality of output can be expected from the NED but inadequate funds, especially for research purpose can be singled out as major impediment.

Established in 1952, the Engineering College in Peshawar initially functioned as engineering faculty at the Peshwar University. Its status was raised in 1980 and it was renamed as NWFP University of Engineering & Technology. The university awards graduate and post graduate degrees in the fields of civil, electrical, mechanical mining and agricultural engineering. There are, about 2000 students enrolled at the University, including foreign students. The Federal Government of Pakistan has allocated Rs. 55.660 million to the university for the year 1994-95 out of a total estimated budget of Rs. 60.06 million (10). Changing from an annual system to a semester system has produced some good results, but it suffers from the same ill that have become the hallmark of all the state sponsored engineering institutions, subsidised education within limited budgetary allocation, inadequate facilities for research and absence of healthy liaison with the industrial sector.

The ordinance to establish Mehran University of Engineering & Technology was promulgated in 1977 through which the former Sind University Engineering College was given its present status. The initial proposal was for it to function at Nawabshah, but for reasons of expediency the main campus was moved to Jamshoro where better facilities were available. The term system has been introduced at the university, which offers graduate and postgraduate courses up to the masters level in certain fields of engineering. Besides the Mehran University College, three other technological colleges are located at university. The total budget estimate for the year 1994-95 is Rs. 153.580 million, whereas the Government of Pakistan has granted an amount of Rs. 74.857 million (10). Its main target is the relatively backward area of the interior Sind.

The University of Engineering & Technology, Taxila, has also been upgraded from the status of college to that of a university in the 1990s and its budget is 21.330 million for the year 1994-95. The National University of Sciences & Technology NUST has been recently chartered with an aim to maximizing the utilisation of the already existing educational facilities of the army colleges which offer undergraduate programmes in some engineering disciplines. These include Military College of Engineering, Risalpur, Military College of Signals, Rawalpindi, College of Electrical and Mechanical Engineering, Rawalpindi and the National Institute of Transportation. Besides streamlining, consolidating and enhancing the educational work at these colleges, the university is chartered to start its higher level engineering degree programmes at the M.Sc. level. The hitherto non existent Ph.D research in various branches of engineering will also be offered at the university in the future. The establishment of this university has opened the doors of these engineering institutions for civilian students as well.

With the exception of this, all the public sector engineering universities are located in specific target areas for the recruitment of students. The level and quality of eduction varies from one university to another. Education at this level is subsidised and the institutions are heavily dependent on the Government for their survival. This factor does not only undermine the autonomy of these universities, but also hampers their smooth running, as these educational institutions lack uniformity as far as their systems of education and examinations are concerned. Adhocism is prevalent and no proper procedure of coordination and cooperation exists among them. This implies that only R&D work which is being done does not have a cumulative effective effect on the overall state of engineering technology in Pakistan. They also lack an efficient and progressive linkage with the domestic industrial sector. With the exception of a few scholarships, the role of industry in R&D activities has been negligible.

Other than these public universities, there are some centres of engineering education in the private sector as well. These are the Ghulam Ishaq Khan (GIK) Institute of Engineering Sciences and Technology, Topi, NWFP; Syed University, Karachi; Institute of Textile Engineering, Karachi and Institutes of Computer Science established by the Foundation for Advancement of Science and Technology (FAST) at Lahore and Karachi. Moreover, several other private institutes are disseminating engineering education of varying degrees.

The GIK Institute has been set up by a non governmental organization known as the Society for the Promotion of Engineering Sciences & Technology (SOPREST). The Institute started functioning in 1993 and so far two batches of 150 students each have been enrolled. Its activities will be in full swing next year after the introduction of postgraduate programmes. M.Sc. courses are planned to start in October 1995, while Ph.D level research will be introduced in early 1996. The GIK Institute will thus be the first private chartered institution in Pakistan to offer higher engineering eduction. Currently, the faculties of metallurgy and materials engineering, mechanical engineering, electronic engineering, computer science and engineering sciences are running under-graduate course programmes. One of the main objectives of the institute is to develop a healthy liaison with the industry besides disseminating engineering education of the highest level. As it is being run in the private sector, it is likely to be free of the hazards that are confronted by most of the universities in the public sector.

STATE OF HIGHER ENGINEERING EDUCATION

Higher engineering education in Pakistan is just shambles. Though the above mentioned public and private sector universities and institutes are running under-graduate programmes with relative success, the higher stages of learning are badly lacking basic infrastructure, required manpower and other essential facilities. The quality of teaching at universities like the UET Lahore, and the NED University, Karachi, is satisfactory at the under-graduate level but laboratory equipment and its maintenance is an area which leaves much to be desired. This inadequacy of facilities in the laboratories persists with more intensity at the higher level of engineering education.

Besides the basic infrastructure, our post graduate engineering students are badly handicapped in terms of project research programmes. Project level research is virtually non-existent and the output of our universities is below par even by average standards. There is hardly any facility for the repair and maintenance of sophisticated and advanced laboratory equipment. Syllabi at these engineering education institutions also need to be revised. Not only is there an urgent need to update the cirrculum, but it should also be given an applied research orientation. The engineers graduating from these universities do not have the opportunity to raise the level of their technical skills to meet the requirements of the industry and higher level research.

Participation by the private sector in the R&D activities at the Pakistani engineering universities is completely missing. Examples of joint projects undertaken by these universities and industry are very few. This contributes to the miserable state of higher engineering education in Pakistan as post graduate education is void of any incentives for engineers.

The major universities of Pakistan, like the UET, Lahore and the NED University, Karachi, do offer M.Sc. and Ph.D programmes for their students, but the out put is negligible. No more than 20 to 30 students graduate at the masters level every year. Figures about Ph.D from Pakistani universities are also very depressing. Out of a total of 377 Ph.Ds awarded up to 1988, not a single one was in any of the engineering disciplines, (11).

STATUS OF ENGINEERING AND TECHNICAL RESEARCH IN PAKISTAN

Pakistan is a country with a population of 120 million and a literacy rate of about 30%. At the time of independence from the British rule in 1947 the region which now comprises Pakistan had five universities, with only one university with a tradition of good research in various scientific disciplines. Majority of the researchers and senior academicians were Hindus, who migrated to India. The vacuum was filled by a few local and some scientists who migrated into Pakistan from India. During the first ten years following the old British model, four research laboratories under the newly formed Pakistan Council of Scientific and Industrial Research, were established at Karachi, Lahore, Quetta and Peshawar. The main objective was to develop the R&D programmes and technological know how to utilize the local resources for the socio economic needs of the country. Pakistan Atomic Energy Commission was also instituted under which a centre was established to conduct research on the peaceful uses of the atomic energy including power generation.

In the course of about thirty years, the Government has

established about 130 research centres, laboratories and institutes. They are managed by the Ministry of Defence, Ministry of Production, Minisitry of Industries, Ministry of Communications, Ministry of Railways, Ministry of Petroleum and Natural Resources and Ministry of Water & Power. However, some of the defence related laboratories work as autonomous organizations.

These centres and laboratories could be placed broadly in three of categories of excellence in sciences at the universities, general purpose and defence related R&D organizations and institutions. Major technological and engineering based institutions in the public sector are ;

a) Defence-related institutions/organisations

* Air Weapon Complex
* DESTO
* Dr. A. Q.Khan Research Laboratories
* Heavy Industries Taxila (HIT)
* KAMRA
* Margalla Electronics
* National Institute of Optometrics
* Pakistan Ordinance Factories
* Pakistan Atomic Energy Commission
* Precision Engineering Complex (PIA)
* SUPARCO

b) General purpose R&D instituions/organisations

* Centre for Advanced Molecular Biology
* Fuel Research Centre
* Heavy Mechanical Complex
* Leather Research Centre (PCSIR)
* Metal industry R&D
* MVRDE
* National Building Research Institute
* National Centre For Technology Transfer
* National Institute of Electronics

* National Institute of Power
* National Institute of Silicon Technology
* National Physical Standards Laboratory
* National Agricultural Research Centre
* OGDC
* Pakistan Scientific Technical Information Centre
* Pakistan Council of Appropriate Technology
* Pakistan Council of Research in Water Resources
* Pakistan Council of Scientific & Industrial Research (PCSIR)
* PCSIR Laboratories Complex, Karachi.
* PCSIR Laboratories Complex, Lahore
* PCSIR Laboratories, Peshawar
* PCSIR Laboratories, Quetta
* Pakistan Council of Science & Technology
* Pakistan Mineral Development Corporation
* Pak Swiss Training Centre (PCSIR)
* Pakistan Steel
* Solar Energy Research Centre (PCSIR)
* WAPDA

The state of affairs concerning the on going research and development work in private sector is not very encouraging. Though it has made remarkable progress in production of non ferrous alloys, steel, cement, sugar, textile, electrical and electronics goods, R&D is virtually non existent.

Thus the status of R&D work in engineering, both in the private and the public sector, is pitiable when we compare it with other developing nations. India, for example, figures among the top eight countries in the world as far as the space satellite launching capabilities are concerned. Their centralised R&D Centre streamlines the research and development activities going on all over the country, sets targets for different research and industrial organisations and evaluates their performance. Moreover, the fact that they have pursued indigenization of technology as a matter of policy, rather than depending on imports alone accounts for their high level of development in various fields of strategic importance despite rampant poverty and huge population.

In Pakistan, on the contrary the situation is very depressing. The number of research and development institutions in the country is very small and even those which are present fail to come up to the mark, both in terms of input and output. Personal efforts and a few miracles here and there are the only achievements we can boast of. There has been no organised endeavour at the national level to streamline R&D activities in the field of science and technology in general and in the advanced engineering and technologies in particular. Government negligence and overall socio-political environs can be identified as the major reasons for miserable state of affairs that we have at our hand right now.

The conditions in which our scientific community is surviving and making efforts to do whatever can be done, also need to be mentioned. There should be a more conducive atmosphere for them to indulge themselves in scientific research and development. In addition, they must be allowed to carry out their R&D projects without the thwarting bureaucratic interference so that they may direct their energies towards the work they specialise in.

PROBABLE AREAS OF MUTUAL COOPERATION BETWEEN PAKISTAN AND THE CENTRAL ASIAN REPUBLICS

The Muslim Central Republics have just come out from Kremlin rule during which period they were part of one of the most advanced and scientifically developed empire of the 20th century. The industrial and R&D infrastructure which they possess is a big advantage for these countries. However, the nature of the problems which they are facing is also unique. A process of regional cooperation among the Central Asian Republics and between Pakistan and these republics would help to raise the standards of higher engineering education in both parts of the region. Close linkages between the institutions across the territorial boundaries are necessary, not only to promote a cooperation based research culture, but also to develop ties between their respective engineering communities.

It is a very good omen that in the first Regional Meeting on Cooperation with the Central Asian Republics in field of Education, the highest strata of the scientific community in Kazakhistan, Kyrghystan, Tajikistan, Uzbekistan, Azerbaijan and Turkmenistan is present. Their views on the issues under discussion will certainly be very important in initiating the process of cooperation in this field.

The most desirable area for cooperation between the Central Asian Republics and Pakistan should be mutual engineering manpower exchange programmes. Geographical proximity and religious harmony are two facts which should encourage and facilitate such contact at the academic and professional level. The excellent infrastructure of the Central Asian Republic's higher engineering institutions and the format of education can be utilised to make up for some of the shortcomings of our higher engineering education.

Regular and well channelised exchange of information on developments in theoretical and applied engineering should also be coordinated. This practice would keep the regional engineering communities in touch with one another and enhance the prospects of maturing the idea of developing indigenous approaches and methods to the problems peculiar to this region.

Workshops and conferences with representation from the engineering community of all the regional countries is another area which needs to be tapped. Such ventures will open up new opportunities to share views on a number of technical and research problems facing them. Joint teacher's and student's training programmes can also be very useful as synthesis of different experiences would benefit the participants immensely.

1. At the governmental level, agreements to initiate the process of cooperation in the area of higher engineering education should be signed so that this option could be effectively utilised. Private organisations in Pakistan could also be involved in such ventures. This would incorporate industrial productivity with higher education and improve the state of both these sectors.
2. There are a number of critical decisions which should be taken swiftly so as to ameliorate the state of higher engineering education in Pakistan. A strong political will and commitment on the part of the Government.
3. Honest and rational planning.
4. Allocation of sufficient resources for higher engineering education.
5. Careful selection and extensive advanced training for teachers.
6. Proper attention to the provision, repair and maintenance of laboratories and their equipment.

The changing realities of international politics and the geostrategic location of Pakistan and the Central Asian Republics demand close ties among the Muslim countries of the region in all fields, especially those related to economic development. Expertise in engineering guarantees rapid and efficient build up of industrial and economic structures of a country. In order to move ahead towards the goal of self sufficient countries like ours should expedite the process of cooperation in key areas like that of higher engineering education.

The proposal designed to establish linkages at the academic and professional level should not be hindered by bureaucratic obstacles. For the proper execution of plans in these fields of cooperation, the governments of our countries will have to exhibit a strong political will and commitment in this regard. The goals of the exercise should be clearly defined; a constant evaluation of the approved projects is a must for their successful implementation.

More than half a century ago the philosopher mathematician Professor Alfred North Whitehead had already warned about the consequences of slackness in the development of science and technology and I quote.

> "In the conditions of modern life, the rule is absolute - the race which does not value trained intelligence is doomed. Today we maintain ourselves, tomorrow science will have moved over yet one more step and there will be no appeal against the judgment which will be pronounced on the uneducated".

This warning is still very real. If we do not take quick and appropriate measures we will be left behind, so far behind that we will never be able to join the science caravan of the developed nations.

REFERENCES

1. See "Report on High-level S&T Manpower", Pakistan Academy of Sciences, Islamabad. (1990) p. 2.
2. Ibid. pp. 2-3.
3. Atta-ur-Rahman, "Higher Education Science and Technology: A matter of National Survival", University of Karachi. p. 4.
4. Ibid. pp. 7-8.
5. "Report on High-level S&T Manpower", op. cit. p. 5.
6. "Technology Atlas Project: A framework of Technology-based Development", Vol. 3, United Nations Economic and Social Commission for Asia and the Pacific. pp. 182-183.
7. Ibid.
8. Rahman, op. cit. p.5.
9. Paksitan Engineering Council's Annual Report for 1990-91.
10. Facts and figures about Pakistani Universities have been taken from the "Handbook of Universities of Pakistan", published by the University Grants Commission.
11. M.M. Zafar, Nilofar Arshad and M. Arshad, "Status of Science & Technology with Special Reference to High Quality Manpower - A Brief Account" *Science, Technology and Development,* Vol. 8, No. 2, March-April, 1989. p. 11.

CHAPTER - 16

THE NEW ROLE OF MEDICAL PROFESSION*

I feel honoured and consider it a personal privilege to be with the elite of the medical fraternity on the auspicious occasion of the awarding of Fellowships at this prestigious institution which has, over the years, developed into a centre of excellence.

The college is a unique institution dealing with a number of diverse disciplines with a professional scientific approach to the problems and offering solutions to alleviate human suffering.

Science has taken great strides in the second half of this century influencing all fields of human activity. Medical science, in particular, has experienced a sharp departure from conventional norms and practices. Astounding discoveries and introduction of new technologies have changed the very outlook of the profession and has made it possible for practitioners to save millions of lives by the judicious application of their professional knowledge and dedication.

Unfortunately, the 20th century scientific revolution is not without its adverse repercussions. It is a double edged sword. If, on the one hand, millions of people can be given a new lease of life, it has been amply demonstrated that millions of human beings can also perish merely at the push of a button! It is up to the scientists and the users of these technologies to direct them in such a way as to benefit humanity, not to harm it. A great responsibility rests upon our shoulders to use science as a tool to improve the condition of human life.

---

* Address delivered at the convocation of the College of Physicians and Surgeons, Karachi, Pakistan on January 9, 1995.

You are fortunate in the sense that, as doctors, your application of science is directed mainly towards saving lives and alleviating suffering. Today is a great day for those of you who are recieving their diplomas certifying their proficiency in the respective disciplines. But this is just another milestone in your long journey through your career in which you would face great challenges and achieve professional prominence. There will hardly be a moment of respite as the scientific progress and advancement in the modern era is too fast for you to be complacent. If you would not make the required effort, you will soon find yourself lagging far behind the others which you could ill afford given the already highly inadequate medical facilities in our country.

Your profession needs consistent and continuous hard work. Moreover, it should be also performed in a legitimate and ethical way. In the present world, material forces have commercialized even the noblest of professions and I regret to observe that the noble medical profession is no exception. Your profession is a unique field of science in which the human factor is predominant. Everybody knows that your reward cannot be measured in terms of monetary gains only; the gratitude and blessing you receive from a poor patient are often more rewarding than anything money can buy.

It is equally important to remember that it is too easy to get lost in a maze of electronic gadgetry whereas a word of hope, a benign gesture of encouragement and a cheerful smile will help evoke a better, healthy response from a despondent patient. This is all the more important in our surroundings where modern medical equipment is not always available except at a few institutions.

It is needless to emphasise that in medicine, as in any other branch of science, further progress is not possible without research. We live in an extremely competitive world. I am sure that those who, by dint of their hard work, have passed the FCPS examination are second to none in their chosen field. Pakistani doctors, where they are working, are as good as their foreign colleagues and their competence and insight is widely acknowledged.

As materials scientist, I have impression that the practitioners of this profession, especially our surgeons, are not fully utilizing the newly developed biomaterials. Though stellar achievements, such as the Jarvik artificial heart, have gained wide publicity in the media, a large number of engineers and surgeons are making significant, though lesser known, advances in this field. Recent research in biomaterials is directed towards fulfilling the need for adequate implant materials better suited to the human body than the ones already in use. A survey among the youths of USA reveals that no less than 126,000 persons underwent hip implant in that country alone. The main reason for this large number of implants is the tremendous improvement in the development of longer lasting biocompatible materials. High level of self-adjustment ability, functional adaptability and self healing ability of the biomaterials, as compared to other materials used for this purpose, account for the advancement of these materials.

The innovative applications of metals, ceramics, polymers and other advanced materials provide an opportunity for those unfortunate men and women of all ages, who suffer from bodily deformities or loss of limbs and bones, to mitigate their handicaps. Zirconium based compositors, for example, have been found to be very useful in the development of prosthetic devices. Likewise, metallic plasma sprayed coating on the high cycle fatigue of titanium alloys have also been indentified as the potential method of reducing the chances of loosening of the implant material. This rapid progress in biomaterials has rendered the use of polymethylmethacrylate bone cement for implants obsolete. The long lasting porous coated implants are now giving the patients a brighter chance to live a full life.

I am confident that this batch of physicians and surgeons will not rest on its laurels. And I hope that they will not only keep themselves abreast of the on going process of development in their respective areas of specialization, but will also endeavour to prove their mettle by making new discoveries and introducing innovations. As a scientist, the lesson I have learnt from my professional life is that there is no substitute for experience, diligence and perseverance. You must remember what the Quaid-i-Azam prescribed for the youth of the nation to excel in life - "Work, work and more work". It is the only key to success.

I am also aware of the serious problem a number of fresh doctors and surgeons are facing in Pakistan. There are not enough jobs for most of them. Whereas the physicians can probably start their practice with some simple equipment, the surgeons are at a disadvantage that they cannot start their profession without a proper operation theater which requires substantial amount of money. It is almost criminal on our part to force them to give up their noble profession and join the bunch of civil servants who do not enjoy a good reputation in our country. I would request the Government to provide some easy, secure loans to these physicians and surgeons to stay in their own professional field and serve the needy and suffering population.

I congratulate all those fellows who have earned their diplomas by going through the examination and urge them to go forth and serve the needy and suffering people. I also felicitate our honourable guest Fellows on whom this honour has been conferred in recognition of their high scholastic and academic achievements.

Finally, I would like to thank the College of Physicians and Surgeons, Pakistan, for giving me the opportunity to visit this prestigious institution and to meet such a galaxy of distinguished medical men from all over the world. I once again congratulate the recipients of FCPS Diploma and wish them all the best in their career.

CHAPTER - 17

RESTRICTED AREAS OF SCIENCE & TECHNOLOGY AND WAYS TO DEVELOP SUCH TECHNOLOGIES IN THE MUSLIM WORLD*

Science and technology is not the exclusive domain of a race or people. The very word `restricted' reflects the self assumed monopoly of the West over certain branches of science and especially, its efforts to curtail the development of the Muslim World which the Western powers unjustifiably see as a potential threat to their monopoly. Development made by certain Muslim states in the restricted technologies does not trickle down to others because of international pressure and lack of coordination and cooperation among the Muslim countries. The achievements of the Muslim scientists working in their own countries do not create a cumulative effect on the overall scientific and technological progress of the Muslim world because of the absence of an efficient and coherent mechanism of technologies developed by them. Thus, scientific and technological development in the Muslim world is visible in patches, not in the form of continuous, cumulative pattern.

In addition to much needed indigenous scientific and technological development, the larger process of scientific and technological integration of the Muslim world should also be initiated. The scientific and technological integration of the Muslim countries could well prove to be the stepping stone leading to the fervently sought and urgently required, political unity. In order to attain this objective, inter Muslim states

---

* Speech delivered at the International Conference on Science in Islamic Polity in the Twenty First Century from March 26 to March 30, 1995 at Islamabad, Pakistan.

structures should be instituted with the specific function of harmonizing, coordinating and progressively channelising the activities of the scientists engaged in scientific and technological research and production activities.

GLOBAL SCIENCE & TECHNOLOGY RELATIONSHIPS

The world today stands divided along the line of development. There are people who term themselves developed and regard the rest as either developing or, in a rather discriminatory sense, underdeveloped. The scientific and technological development that the West boasts of, stands on the foundations of progress, made, initially by the colonical powers by the exploitation of raw materials and human resources in their colonies. At the same time, the industrial revolution swept across the European and American continents, leaving the colonised people lagging behind by centuries because they were only used as raw materials for the development of the colonial powers.

The process of decolonisation, catalysed by World War II, reshaped the very nature of the world. The number of states multiplied and the erstwhile dominated natives became independent. Most of the Muslim countries, as they exist now, emerged on the globe as sovereign political entities during that period. A new international economic system under the auspices of Keynesian economists was established and, politically, the international community was divided roughly in accordance with their allegiance with the two centres of power that surfaced as an aftermath of W. W. II—the West, led by the USA, and the East led by the USSR. The latter has disappeared while the former is still surviving to tighten its grip on the world. The superiority of the West was, in fact, ingrained in the post colonial political and economic structures and the rest of the world was relegated to the status of mere portage whose dependence on the Western powers raised doubts about the very validity of the independence phenomenon.

The Muslims in particular had to bear the brunt of these unequal, asymmetrical relations among nations. Not only have they been at the receiving end of numerous political, cultural and military assaults of the West and its local accomplices, but they have also suffered from the developed world's discriminatory policies in every sphere of life. They are being denied access to the scientific and technological developments which are the hallmark of the modern age. This pigeon holing of science and technology in Western societies has further diminished the prospects of the Third World in general, and the Muslim nations in particular, while entering into the next century as developed and progressive nations. The very word restricted technologies exposes the parochial approach of the Western mind which, in the post cold war has quite unjustifiably developed the fear of Muslims as a potential threat to its monopoly.

The most conspicuous among these so called restricted technologies are the ones related to computer technology, software development, aerospace, electronics, chemical & biochemical technologies, and defence production, especially those which can be directly or indirectly used in nuclear and missile programmes. The Muslim countries, particularly those which have shown a potential for making rapid progress in science and technology, have been strictly labeled as prohibited areas for the transfer of advanced technologies. This brazen quarantine is further extended to include the flow of scientific and technological information and education. It is widely known fact that students from countries like Pakistan, Iraq, Libya and Iran are not accepted for higher studies in nuclear physics and other related disciplines at universities in the US while no such restrictions are applicable to students of other nations.

There are only formal multilateral agreements among the developed countries which put them under an obligation not to transfer certain restricted technologies to the less developed or developing countries; one was agreed upon by the London Group of Suppliers (The London Club) and the other is the Missile Technology Control Regime (MTCR). Besides the major industrialized powers like the USA, Great Britain, France, Italy, Belgium, the Netherlands, Germany and Canada, the London agreement of April 16, 1987, also includes Japan. This group prohibits the transfer of nuclear technology and any related material to non nuclear weapon states.

I would like to pause here for a moment to focus on this strange categorization of states. Is it logic and common sense to let a few have this advanced technology which can decide the fate of all humanity and call them members of Nuclear Club, while others live in fear under this hegemony? One of the major arguments propounded by these states in support of this nuclear "apartheid" is the supposedly irresponsible behaviour expected from the less developed, fragile and relatively small states in case they obtained nuclear weapons. If history is anything to go by, then the only irresponsible, downright inhuman instance of the abuse of nuclear technology has been perpetrated by no other country than the leader of the non proliferation drive itself - USA. Besides, this rationale is humiliating and insulting to the majority of the mankind living outside the West.

Another restricted area of technology pertains to missiles. The Missile Technology Control Regime (MTCR) works along the same lines. Though the threshold of MTCR safeguards for missiles is 300 km with a payload of 500 kg, yet transactions well below this are obstructed by the Western countries. The recent M-11 issue involving Pakistan and China is an example in point. In addition to the ballistic missile technology, the MTCR tends to put restrictions on technologies and materials which can, directly or indirectly, be used in missile production. These restrictions obviously not only leave countries like ours defenseless, but also have other grave implications, such as putting restrictions on technologies used for socioeconomic development.

It is also pertinent to note that while diplomacy in international politics is supposed to be conducted in black and white, there is a lot of ambiguity in the Western attitude, especially towards Muslim countries. In areas of science and technology where no legal or statutory grounds are available for enforcing embargoes, the West, and the USA in particular, has resorted to the use of covert manipulation in a number of cases involving transfer of advanced technologies through bilateral agreements. Unfortunately, the Muslim countries have been the main victims of such restrictive policies. Even if a Muslim country is trying to acquire a technology for developmental and peaceful purpose only, it is considered guilty of trespassing the prohibited areas.

The denial of access to modern technologies by the Western countries thwarts the process of overall socioeconomic development as well. Nuclear energy, for example, is urgently needed where conventional sources of power generation are either limited, or fail to reach the required level of supply. Similarly, computer technology has become a must for advancement in all areas of human progress. Computers are now household gadgets but a wall of misplaced apprehensions on the part of the West prevents an equitable and smooth flow of new computing techniques to the developing countries. Moreover, the advanced countries have shown a marked tendency towards being discriminatively selective in providing new technologies to other countries. Again, the Muslim countries are, invariably, left out.

THE MUSLIM WORLD AND SCIENCE & TECHNOLOGY

The Muslim world spreads from Indonesia in the east to Morocco in the west. There are about 52 independent Muslim states in addition to a number of Muslim minority groups scattered in various states. With a total population of around 1.2 billion, Muslims occupy more than 27 percent of the world territory. Geographically, the Muslim world is like a girdle round the mid rib of the world. They are blessed with almost 80 per cent of the world's fuel oil and palm oil reserves, contributing 60 percent of world crude oil production which makes up 70 percent of the oil trade, 80 percent of natural rubber, 67 percent of spices and 75 percent of jute. They also possess strategically important deposits of gas, coal, silver, gold and other mineral ores. However, most of the Muslims live in agricultural societies and the majority is still waiting for the fruits of the technological revolution to reach them.

A large number of Muslim states are also party to bilateral regional and international conflicts which have the potential of precipitating into armed conflicts. According to statistics, the Muslim territories have been involved in more than 250 crises and conflicts since 1945. The geostrategic location of the Muslim countries further enhances their needs in terms of defence. Yet this is the area in which the technologically advanced countries exhibit the worst form of discrimination against them.

Pakistan has been constantly pressurised by the Western countries to forego its defence concerns vis-a-vis a historically hostile and expansionist India and to unilaterally sign the NPT. This would have grave implications for the very survival of the country. On the other hand, it is interesting to note that those same countries have been overtly and covertly helping India to develop its nuclear and missile capabilities by providing material, equipment and technology. It is an open secret that fuel for the Indian Tarapur reactor was supplied by the USA till 1983 and, after that, by France, the same country which, in 1976, backed out from an agreement to provide a reprocessing plant to Pakistan. Iran's nuclear programme is also a target for a vicious campaign unleashed by the West despite the fact that it is signatory to the NPT and, as a top official of the IAEA recently confirmed, no violation of the treaty has ever been reported. A top US official quoted in the papers to have justified the pressure applied on Iran on the basis of apprehensions that Iran might opt for using its programme to develop nuclear weapons. The Muslim countries are being punished for supposed intentions.

Pakistan, Egypt, Turkey, Algeria, Iran and Libya are the Muslim countries identified to have broad based nuclear research programmes. Another Muslim country accused of having stepped on this prohibited path was Iraq, whose nuclear installations were destroyed by two Israeli air attacks, an incident which caused little concern among the self appointed custodians of international law. What Israel has been doing does not bother the West a little bit. South Africa also made nuclear weapons but the West did not take any actions against it.

I feel highly depressed to observe that the response of the Muslim world to the growing need for development in these areas of science and technology has so far been less than adequate. As a matter of fact, it has been rather pathetic as has been the case with other S&T disciplines. The overall science and technology scenario in the Muslim world is not heartening. While 92 percent of the S&T manpower of the world is working in the industrialised countries, the share of the Muslim countries is negligible. The Muslim countries have less than 100 research scientists and engineers per million as compared to the advanced countries figure of 3000. Given their territorial expanse and demographic size the share of the Muslims in the world overall scientific and technical activity is also minimal. They only invest a fraction of the total investment made in the S&T areas all over the world, less than one percent, while 97 percent of the finances are invested by the industrialised countries. Scientific journals, periodicals and other publications, which are considered valid indicators of the quantity and quality of the research activity, publish more than a million research articles every year in the developed countries. The Muslim S&T community, spread over 52 nations states, contribute only about 2000 publications in a year nearly half of them coming from the semi-developed 18 countries and only a few of them pertaining to the above mentioned so called restricted areas of science and technology. Though there are a number of reasons for this bleak scenario, I would like to mention briefly some of the major factors responsible for the dismal performance by the Muslim countries in the field of science and technology in general and the sensitive areas of S&T in particular.

LACK OF POLITICAL WILL

Most often, the debate on the acquisition and/or development of restricted areas of S&T spills over into political issues. Most of the regimes ruling the Muslim territories have shown a tendency to drag their feet in the acquisition of restricted technologies for various reasons. Besides fears of a backlash from the Western powers, the internal structure of governmental procedures pushes the projects of developing these crucial technologies to the lowest priority. Except for a few countries, the majority of Muslim states find it hard to break away from their self imposed restrictions and fears.

LITERACY

The average literacy rate among the Muslims of the world is estimated to be a meagre 37 percent. This is an embarrassingly low figure if we compare other developing nations of the third world. The statistics of scientific and technological education for the Muslim communities are even more pathetic. Merely 35 percent of the students study science at the secondary level which drops down to 25 percent at the higher secondary or college level. Only about 20% of university students are enrolled in scientific disciplines. Unless this sector of socio-economic development is focused upon, the development of science and technology in the Muslim world would remain a dream only.

INADEQUATE RESEARCH & DEVELOPMENT FACILITIES

Research and development activities are of central importance for scientific progress. For a country like ours, a considerable level of R&D is crucial for attaining the goal of self reliance which is badly needed in the wake of the restrictions imposed by the technologically advanced countries. The total R&D expenditure of the Muslim countries amounts to about 0.1 - 0.4 percent of their GNP which is only a pittance as compared to the developed countries R&D expenditure. The latter spend 2 - 3 per cent of their GNP on promoting research and development. Moreover, defence research and development (DR&D) consumes about 50 percent of the amounts earmarked for R&D in the West. Among the Muslim countries, only Pakistan, Egypt, Indonesia and Turkey have been relatively keen to pursue defence related R&D activities and have shown great potential for defence production.

WEAK INDUSTRIAL INFRASTRUCTURE

The industrial sector of a state is an indicator of the level of modernization and its capability to advance. It is also an expression of the S&T development made by that country. The Muslim world, which had already missed the industrial revolution, seems to do little about catching up with the leaders of the world. Looking at the relatively developed Muslims countries one finds that they owe a great deal of what little development they have to the infrastructure inherited from their colonial rulers, which they later built upon. However, for most of the Muslim World, this aspect of socio economic development is found lacking in quality and quantity, and the wealthier Muslim countries have import based economics and little attention is paid to setting up a solid industrial base.

FINANCIAL AND MANPOWER LIMITATIONS

Both these problems faced by Muslim countries are mainly due to their own policy planning. But now, it is time that we divert our resources and invest more in S&T projects and the training of manpower. Estimates made by the ISESCO put the required minimum number of competent scientists and technologists needed by the Muslim world at 1.4 million and we fall short of this figure by at least 5,000,000. The major reason behind this shortfall is, of course, the absence of financial incentives for the students going for S&T research and education. If we are to have any chance of competing with the developed world, our priorities have to be sorted out and the Muslim world needs to spend a higher proportion of its GNP in these areas rather than the negligible amount it spends now.

WAYS AND MEANS OF DEVELOPING RESTRICTED S&T AREAS IN THE MUSLIM WORLD

The development taking place in the world around has provided sufficient evidence that the dawn of the 21st century will find the Muslims placed at the centre of a number of strategically important issues. It needs no elucidation that the position of any country in the comity of nations is determined by its relative economic and military power. It is a fallacy for the Muslims to think that they can move ahead with dignity at their present level of dependence on the advanced countries for the defence and security of their homelands. We will have to take a realistic and objective view of the situation and must endeavour to change things for the better sooner than later.

Much will depend on the performance of the Muslims in the fields of science and technology, as progress in these fields has become the criterion of gauging a nation's strength or weakness. Unless we achieve a considerable level of self sufficiency in the areas denied to us by the West, we will keep suffering from financial, political and military dominance. We know that the restricted technologies are among the most expensive ones and efforts to acquire them from abroad consume a large percentage of our finance. The Western control over these technologies also determines their supremacy in the political and military spheres. No matter how efficiently we utilize partially transferred, second rate technologies, we cannot break free from these shackles unless a vigorous effort is launched to master these technologies ourselves.

While some of the Muslim countries are making serious efforts to make headway in this direction, there has been no significant collective effort on the part of the Ummah to venture into the restricted areas of S&T. There are at least a dozen organizations in the Muslim states which could be utilized as an effective and solid base for furthering this cause. These include the Islamic Foundation Scientific and Technological Development IFSTAD, the Islamic Institute of Defence Technology, the Islamic Space and Upper Atmosphere Research Centre, the Inter-Islamic Network on Space Science and Technology, the Arab Institute of Aerospace Technology, and the Arab Organisation for Industries which is meant exclusively for military industries. With the exception of the first two, the others have largely been inactive or suffer from lack of funds and attention. Moreover the prescribed limitations of their functions and self imposed restrictions prevent them from playing positive role in enhancing the level of the Muslim Ummah's capabilities in these strategically crucial areas of science and technology.

There have, however, been some indigenous ventures undertaken by Muslim countries like Pakistan, Malaysia, Indonesia and Turkey, which have gone a long way in breaking the myth of Western monopoly over scientific and technological progress. But the process of scientific evolution is a cumulative process where progress cannot be made in isolation. There have to be networks for regular and efficiently managed exchange of information and expertise. That, unfortunately, is badly lacking as far as these particular areas of science are concerned. In contrast, the Western countries are pooling their talents and money and are reaping the benefits of their wise policies.

Some academicians have aired the proposition of establishing an Islamic Atomic Energy Commission. For the time being, only Pakistan has an operational nuclear power plant. Pakistan hardly meets 0.1 percent of its energy requirements from the nuclear energy produced by that plant having a capacity of 137 MW. Such a Commission would certainly provide a proper organisational mechanism and platform for the exchange of knowledge and monitoring of the recent developments in this field for the mutual benefit of the Muslim countries. It would also make it possible for the Muslim world to learn to utilise alternative sources of energy. I would like to emphasise here that the honourable survival of the Muslim world lies in joining hands for acquiring this mode of energy production which would also have its political and military advantages. The only way to neutralise or withstand the pressure exerted by the West is to make ourselves self sufficient in technologies which are either totally restricted or rationed to us.

Another very ambitious plan to set up an Islamic Bank of Strategic Materials IBSM was proposed by the late Gen. Ali Nawab of Pakistan in 1979 at the conference titled "Defence and the Muslim World" held in London. That proposal envisages the formation of a bank to facilitate the processes of defence production in the Muslim countries by channelising strategic materials resources. However, the Muslim states are still looking for a level of integration where a plan like this could be implemented.

I would also like to stress that the existing organisations should be made effective and the scope of their areas of competence should be enhanced. But, at the same time, we need to organise the efforts of the muslim scientists and researchers to have a cumulative effect on the overall progress of S&T in the Muslim countries. For this purpose, I would suggest the importance of joint ventures in enhancing the level of coordination and cooperation among muslim scientists.

Such ventures would give an opportunity to scientists from different background to work with each other and benefit from the research done in one another's countries. Joint projects also imply the pooling of finances and effective utilisation of these resources. In the case of the said technologies, it is all the more important for muslim countries to join hands and shake off the curse of dependence. It does not by any means, imply that the Muslims close their doors to the Western technical know how because, after all, that is where most of the recent scientific knowledge comes from. However, we should get rid of the burden of dependency and pursue our own agenda of shaping our future and muster up enough strength to see it through.

As most of the restricted areas of S&T are directly or indirectly related to defence products, I would like to propose that the defence research and development (DR&D) institutions and industries of the Muslim countries are engaged in joint defence production and military cooperation at the bilateral level, there is a need for a broader base, more comprehensive and cohesive organisation to perform R&D work for the indigenous development of sophisticated and restriceted technologies and to translate it into industrial products.

Hard incentives and proper working conditions are also required to bring back the Muslim scientists and engineers working in the West. We should not overlook the fact that it will not be easy for this highly skilled corps of scientists and technicians to leave the attractive and lucrative careers they are pursuing in the advanced countries unless the governments of the Muslim countries provide them with a conducive atmosphere to exercise their skills and expertise. This again leads us to the question of finances. It is not that there is a dearth of financial resources, in fact, some of the Muslim states are among the richest in the world. The fact is that S&T expenditures are not attended to satisfactorily and most of the times they receive a low priority. Once again, I emphasise that we should spend a much larger proportion of our GNP's for the promotion of science and technology which is a key factor for socio-economic development

I also feel that the Muslim countries should establish many more advanced and well equipped educational institutions to lead our younger generation into the next century. This is one aspect of S&T development where non-governmental agencies and the private sector can play a role equal to, if not better than, the governments of our countries. The promotion of quality S&T education is essential if we want to move ahead from the traditionally slow progress of the Muslim World in this sector. When the educational institutions in the Muslim World start competing with those in the developed countries, then the scientists produced by them would first reduce and then eliminate the dominance of the West and would contribute to the elevation of the status of science and technology in the Muslim countries.

CHAPTER - 18

ADVANCED MATERIALS - IV*

The greatest event in the world today is the increased automation and sophistication in process technology which has brought about a global industrialization and has been elemental in uplifting the economic and social well being of the masses. Materials science and engineering has played a key role in bringing about this transformation in our society. The innovative use of materials has led to better medical care, enhanced safety in infrastructure projects, faster and safe transport, as well as the provision of more leisure facilities to the common man.

Global industrialization has demanded more efficiency in the application of resources to achieve industrial competitiveness. A smart use of advanced materials holds the key to this perception. Materials with new and improved properties and with novel methods of processing give industries a considerable leverage in competing in the world market. Advanced materials have been instrumental in promoting several areas of research and development to fulfil numerous research and industrial needs. Recent optical fibers and personal computers would not have been possible without the availability of advanced materials.

Composite materials, including metal matrix and polymer matrix composites, will dominate for at least a quarter of the next century as the materials of very high strength to weight ratio. Weight reduction in many civil as well as in military

---

* Keynote address delivered at 'The Fourth International Symposium on Advanced Materials', 17-21 September, 1995, Islamabad, Pakistan.

applications such as passenger aircraft, space ships, army vehicles and advanced submersibles is beginning to emerge as an important factor to be considered in future applications. Composite materials provide as much as 30-40% weight saving while providing an equivalent level of performance.

Magnetic materials, on the other hand, play a vital role both in industry as well as in our daily life. One cannot imagine a single machine or instrument in industry, or even in our daily life, without a magnet. To fulfill the future demand of miniaturization of satellites and space ships, computer hardware and data storage, etc. the size of the magnets should be a small as possible with higher magnetic strengths. In the 1930s when the first generation of the AlNiCo magnetic material was discovered it was thought to be a miracle because it had 10 times more magnetic strength than the best available magnetic material at that time. Now a magnetic strength of 60 mega gauss orders had been recorded for rare earth magnets, thus decreasing the size of machines by 10 orders of magnitude and still work is going on to achieve higher magnetic strengths by smaller magnets.

Engineering plastics are other promising materials of the future. There will be an increasing demand for resins that flow better, freeze faster, eject easily and cause less damage to the mold. New techniques such as high pressure molding, co-processing such as co-injection molding, and sandwich molding will offer unique advantages to the manufacturer and the user. Engineering ceramics will also acquire a respectable position. Technology of super conductivity will see a greater use of engineering ceramics in many practical applications.

Looking into the future of materials at this juncture, now, when the 21st century is just around the corner, one can predict that the future will see expanded joint efforts to develop the technologies needed to synthesize, atom by atom, today's advanced materials to produce new combinations of properties. As we are beginning to explain engineering properties such as intrinsic brittleness or ductility of crystals by quantum mechanics one can foresee that mathematical modelling will quantitatively define properties of materials. Today trial and error is no longer a practical method of design and the objective is achieved by the application of proven design theory and the use of construction materials selected from a wide range of available materials. The recent advances in scientific computation and visualization have made it possible to develop models that accurately simulate a variety of net shape forming, casting, and powder metallurgy process. The modeling of casting for example, can be used to predict defects, temperature gradient, solidification velocity, and dissolved gases, and to predict macro – and micro-porosity, microstructure, cell size, grain size, and dendrite arm spacing. Advanced graphics and animation display internal features such as temperature, porosity, microstructure, isolated pools of liquid metals, fluid flow and turbulence. Certainly, the mathematical modeling and knowledge based processing with the help of ever increasing computing power will accelerate the development of advanced materials in the coming years.

Before I conclude, I would like to draw your attention to the fact that science, scientists, and technocrats play a pivotal role in advancing our technology, our economy, and the building of our State. Science has become a very powerful and productive force in the world. It has become rich as well as dominating. Unfortunately, a substantial part of science and technology is being masked with secrecy to the disadvantage of many nations, especially in the Third World. This is a stark reality which we have to live with. However, this and similar gatherings provide us a platform to share and disseminate knowledge for the betterment of humanity.

I am fully aware of the limited resources of our country, but unless and until we invest in science, technology and education we will remain a backward and underdeveloped country. For a better future we must do much more than we have done so far in terms of financial investment.

CHAPTER - 19

PROSPECTS OF PROMOTING SCIENCE AND TECHNOLOGY IN THE ISLAMIC DEVELOPMENT BANK IDB MEMBER COUNTRIES*

Standing at the threshold of a new millennium as mankind prepares to bid farewell to the current century, the latter will long be remembered by humanity as an era of advanced development, rapid change and of unprecedented progress. It has been a century in which civilization transformed so amazingly that our world became vastly different from the one inhabited by our forefathers; when human knowledge explored new frontiers, research broke new grounds, and the marvels of man's skills and expertise surpassed any other reference to human history.

The twentieth century has been the century of SCIENCE AND TECHNOLOGY (S&T) and as we enter a new millennium, mankind is guided by none other than these two wonderful twins, namely, Science and Technology.

POSITION OF S&T IN TODAY'S WORLD

The quest for knowledge, creativity and innovation is amongst the noblest attributes of civilized societies and science born out of man's curiosity to know nature is thus mankind's most prestigious shared heritage.

1) Economic Importance

The emerging realities of the post Cold War era have made it

---

* The lecture was delivered at the Islamic Development Bank's Headquarters at Jeddah, Saudi Arabia, on May 19, 1996.

clear that the policies of the states are no more being carried out in pursuance of a particularism but with the fall of communism economic interests, prospects and concerns compel the governments and peoples of the world to forge common grounds. Today it is a country's strong infrastructure based upon latest scientific research and sophisticated technology, that lures foreign investors and potential buyers. The recently concluded Asia Europe Meeting and the forming of the Asia Pacific Economic Forum are the best examples in this context.

The occupational colonialism of yester years has been replaced by economic colonialism of today as the world stands clearly divided into developed and developing countries, specifically on the basis of the former's superiority in science and technology.

2) Strategic Importance

Not just one aspect of growth, but a vital phenomenon and vivid reality of our times, the two sine qua non for real and sustained economic growth have changed the whole concept of geostrategic interests. Today, a strong economy based upon strong S&T infrastructures, provide the only guarantee to self reliance, yielding international credibility, national harmony and hence true independence and fool proof security. Rene Maheu, former Director General of UNESCO once said and I quote; "Unless it has its own scientists and technicians, no country can call itself free". From Japan to Singapore, Asia bears the testimony of this observation.

THE IDB MEMBER STATES

Possessing an unlimited pool of human and material resources, the 57 Islamic countries of the world are best suited to promise prosperity for their people by any account. Out of these, 50 states are currently members of the Islamic Development Bank. Thus, with such an overwhelming majority of the Muslim World, IDB offers a unique opportunity for a meaningful cooperation among states, home to one third of the world's population with a strength of around 1.2 billion people.

With 12.25 million sq. miles of area and 27% of total global territory, it is from the Muslim World that the world is provided with as much as 40% of the needed raw materials, 60% of world crude oil production that makes up 70% of the trade, 40% of the natural gas, 80% of natural rubber, 75% of jute. etc.(1)

IDB MEMBER STATES' PRESENT SCENARIO

It is ironical that the resources of the Muslim World have not been utilized wisely to provide a suitable base for progress and development and the Muslim World has on the whole failed to devise any such mechanism. Thus, despite being the proud owners of the world's most precious resources, it is forced to take a back seat when it comes to a share of the fruits of progress.

The economic scenario of the IDB member states paints a bleak picture when reference is made to the World Bank's classification in this regard. Table 1 shows that only 4 IDB members are included in the category of high income economies against all the countries of the Organization for Economic Cooperation and Development OECD. Just 6 are considered as upper middle income economies, 19 as lower middle income economies and the rest, 21 in all, being regarded as low income economies.

A comparison on the basis of Table 2, which shows the per capita GNP of these countries, reveals the disappointing economic status of the Muslim World. Socio-economic conditions in the Muslim World vary greatly and there are no signs of homogeneity in this respect. While countries like Brunei, UAE and Kuwait have per capita GNP of above US$ 14,000, as many as 18 Muslim States have figures less than or equal to just US$ 500. Countries like Somalia and Guinea Bissau even exist below the poverty line with their GNP at only US$ 200.

The total GNP of all the Muslim countries was not more than US$ 900 billion in 1993 (1), which amounted to just 5% of the world's total. On the other hand, the 15 member states of the European Union, much smaller than the Muslim World in terms of area and population, have more than US$ 6861 billion (2), seven times more than the whole of the Muslim World!.

REASONS AND REPERCUSSIONS

The reason for the above is primarily because of our bankruptcy in the fields of Science and Technology. This backwardness is the bottom line for the economic exploitation, ignorance, cultural subversion, and internal and external dissensions being faced by the Muslim World. It is indeed unfortunate to determine that we cannot irrigate our lands, feed our masses, develop our infrastructures and even fight our wars without the help of the developed nations. The Muslim World is forced to toe the line of the advanced world as the latter's technical expertise and scientific skills allow it to exclusively dominate international affairs. Our resources are being robbed by the advanced nations, our governments virtually becoming hostage to international agencies and from Afghanistan to Bosnia and from the Middle East to Somalia our lands being converted into lucrative markets of the western manufactured arms.

We are forced to watch this in utter helplessness. In fact the Muslim World today faces yet another challenge with the introduction consumption efficient technologies as the purchasing power of oil today is less than half of that in the mid 1970's and a quarter of that in early 1980's. Oil prices in 1994, roughly US$ 16 per barrel, were lower than at any time since 1973 (3). The oil market was reported to be closer to gut than shortage because of 3-4 million barrels per day of unused production capacity (4). This in turn is putting a downward

Table 1

Classification of IDB Member Countries' Economies by Income, 1995

INCOME GROUP	LOW INCOME	MIDDLE INCOME		HIGH INCOME
		LOWER	UPPER	
	Afghanistan	Algeria	Bahrain	Brunei-
C	Albania	Azerbaijan	Gabon	Darussalam
	Bangladesh	Cameroon	Libya	Kuwait
O	Benin	Djibouti	Malaysia	Qatar
	Burkina Faso	Indonesia	Oman	U. A. E
U	Chad	Iran	Saudi Arabia	
	Comorose	Iraq		
N	Egypt	Jordan		
	Gambia	Kazakhstan		
T	Guinea	Kyrgyz Republic		
	Guinea-Bissau	Lebanon		
R	Mozambique	The Maldives		
	Mali	Morocco		
I	Mauritania	Palestine		
	Niger	Senegal		
E	Pakistan	Syria		
	Sierra Leo	Tunisia		
S	Somalia	Turkmenistan		
	Sudan	Turkey		
	Uganda			
	Yemen			
Total = 50	21	19	6	4

Source: Global Economic Prospects and the Developing Countries, a World Bank Book, 1995.

TABLE 2

Per Capita Income And The Precentage Of GNP Being Spent On Education And Defence

S.No	Country	Per Capita Income (in US $) 1991	Defence Spending (%age of GNP in U$) 1990	Education Spending (%age of GNP in US$)
1	Afghanistan	200	15	
2.	Albania	(1987) 1,300	4.1	
3.	Algeria	2,020	(1992) 1.8	9.1
4.	Azerbaijan	1,670		
5.	Bahrain	6,910	6.0	5.4
6.	Bangladesh	220	1.6	2.2
7.	Benin	380	2.1	
8.	Brunei Darussalam	14,220		
9.	Burkina Faso	350	2.8	4.9
10.	Cameroon	940	2.1	3.3
11.	Chad	220	5.6	
12.	Comoros	500		4.3
13.	Dijbouti	480		2.5
14.	Egypt	610	11.1	6.0
15.	Gabon	3,780	4.5	5.7
16.	Gambia	360		5.2
17.	Guinea	440	(1988) 1.2	1.4
18.	Guinea Bissua	190	(1987) 3.3	2.8
19.	Idonesia	610	(1992) 2.0	0.9
20.	Iran	2,320	(1991) 15.0	4.1
21.	Iraq	3,020	18.0	5.1
22.	Jordan	1,120	9.5	4.4
23.	Kazakstan	2,470		
24.	Kyrghyz	1,550		
25.	Kuwait	(1989) 16,150	(1991) 21.0	5.0
26.	Lebanon	880	(1992) 8.2	
27.	Libya	(1989) 5,310	(1992) 1.1	9.6
28.	Malaysia	2,490	(1992) 5.0	5.5
29.	The Maldive	460		6.9
30.	Mali	280	3.2	3.3
31.	Mauritania	510	4.2	
32.	Morocco	1,030	(1992) 4.2	4.0
33.	Mozambique	120	(1987) 8.4	
34.	Niger	300	0.8	3.1
35.	Oman	5,000	(1992) 16.0	3.7
36.	Pakistan	400	(1992) 6.4	2.0

Table 2 (contd.)

37.	Palestine			
38.	Qatar	9,030	(1989) 8.0	3.4
39.	Saudi Arabia	6,200	(1992) 13.0	5.8
40.	Senegal	720	2.07	
41.	Sierra Leona	210	3.0	1.4
42.	Somialia	120	10.9	0.4
43.	Sudan	480	13.0	4.8
44.	Syria	1,110	(1992) 5.0	4.4
45.	Tunisia	1,150	(1992) 3.5	6.0
46.	Turkey	1,820		1.8
47.	Turkmenistan	1,700	0.8	
48.	Uganda	260	4.7	3.4
49.	United Arab	15,770	20.0	1.8
50.	Yemen	540		

Source: 1) World Bank Report, 1994
2) World Almanac, 1994.

pressure on oil prices. OPEC, which comprises of an overwhelming majority of the Muslim countries, is finding it hard to sustain this pressure. There are also rumours that some Muslim countries are now selling the oil under the table of lower price than the market rates.

POSITION OF S&T IN THE MUSLIM WORLD

Nowhere in the world is the field of Science and Technology being ignored more than in the 57 Muslim countries. The lack of infrastructure, colonial era bureaucratic set ups and lack of political and national commitment in terms of science and technology in these countries have worked prohibitively in placing S&T on national agendas.

1) Educational Status

The literacy rates shown in Table 3 adequately indicate that more than half of the Muslim population is forced to live in the darkness of illiteracy and ignorance. What preference is being given to the education sector by us can best be judged by the fact that an average of nearly 4% of our GNP is spent on education against that of 7% on defence (Table 2). This educational spending ranges from the lowest at 0.4% in Somalia to the highest of 9.6% in Libya against the defence spending of 10.9% of the former to 1.1% of the latter. The total number of universities in the Muslim World, irrespective of their quality, is not beyond a mere 400(5).

Whereas, according to a latest survey, only three out of every hundred adults were found being unable to attend any school in the industrialized world, in the Muslim World as many as 77% of the population, aged 25 and above, had never been to any school. This figure is even higher than that of the rest of the Third World countries where it was found to be 64%. The report further reveals that the Muslim world has the lowest school going population, that is 47 per 100 children aged 5-19, the highest student teacher ratio which is 88 students per teacher, lowest enrolment in higher education,

Table 3

Vital Statistics of the IDB Member Countries

S.No	Country	Area in sq. miles	Population (000) (1992 est)	Literacy Rate (% age)
1.	Afghanistan	251.773	16,095	29(1990)
2.	Albania	11,100	3,285	72(1990)
3.	Algeria	918,497	26,666	52(1991)
4.	Azerbaijan	33,400	7,450	97(1993)
5.	Bahrain	268	551	77(1992)
6.	Bangladesh	55,813	199,000	47(1992)
7.	Benin	43,483	4,997	28(1993)
8.	Brunei Darussalam	2,226	369	95(1995)
9.	Burkina Faso	105,869	9,653	18(1992)
10.	Cameroon	179,714	12,658	65(1992)
11.	Chad	495,755	5,238	30(1991)
12.	Comoros	838	493	15(1989)
13.	Dijbouti	8.950	390	48(1991)
14.	Egypt	386,650	56,386	44(1990)
15.	Gabon	103,446	1,106	70(1991)
16.	Gambia	4,127	902	30(1993)
17.	Guinea	94,984	7,783	35(1989)
18.	Guinea Bissua	13,948	1,074	36(1991)
19.	Indonesia	735,268	195,000	85(1990)
20.	Iran	636,293	61,183	54(1990)
21.	Iraq	167,924	18,445	60(1991)
22.	Jordan	37,737	3,557	70(1989)
23.	Kazakstan	1,049,200	17,101	97(1993)
24.	Kyrghyz Republic	76,646	4,567	97(1993)
25.	Kuwait	6,880	1,318	71(1989)
26.	Lebanon	4,015	3,439	75(1991)
27.	Libya	679,359	4,485	64(1991)
28.	Malaysia	127,316	18,410	80(1991)
29.	The Maldives	115	226	93(1989)
30.	Mali	478,764	8,641	25(1991)
31.	Mauritania	419,212	2,059	30(1991)
32.	Morocco	172,413	26,708	50(1990)

Table 3 (contd.)

33.	Mozambique	303,769	15,469	14(1989)
34.	Niger	489,189	8,052	28(1991)
35.	Oman	82,030	1,587	20(1989)
36.	Pakistan	310,403	121,664	35(1991)
37.	Palestine	--	--	--
38.	Qatar	4,247	484	76(1991)
39.	Saudi Arabia	839,880	16,900	62(1990)
40.	Senegal	75,750	8,205	10(1988)
41.	Sierra Leone	27,925	4,456	21(1991)
42.	Somalia	248,300	7,235	24(1990)
43.	Sudan	966,757	28,305	27(1991)
44.	Syria	718,498	13,730	64(1991)
45.	Tunisia	63,170	8,445	62(1990)
46.	Turkey	301,381	59,640	81(1991)
47.	Turkmenistan	188,417	3,838	97(1993)
48.	Uganda	93,354	19,386	52(1993)
49.	United Arab Emirates	32,000	2,522	68(1989)
50.	Yemen	203,796	10,394	38(1990)

which is just 8 per 100 in the age group, 20-24. In most of the Muslim African countries, it is below 1% of the adult population(5).

2) Status of R&D

a) **Number Of S&T Manpower :** Very few Muslim countries have created basic institutions in this regard. In the absence of any state policy in the realm of science and technology, many of our Muslim brethren, I am afraid, have not the slightest perception of the issue. Our S&T systems are inadequate to enable the efficient utilization of available resources and the modernization of existing production systems. The R&D facilities provided to our scientists and technicians are minimal. At present, the Muslim world has the lowest number of S&T manpower in the world, which is liberally estimated to be around 8 million. In fact, owing to its development needs, this number is required only as high class scientists, 10% of whom should be engaged in R&D, by the year 2000 (6), if we wish to enter the next century in a dignified manner.

On the R&D side, there are, as another study reveals, only 45,136 scientists and engineers working in all Muslim countries combined, compared with 34,800 in Israel alone, or 400,000 in Japan (7). Today, almost 94% of all R&D scientists are working for the developed world where there are 3000 scientists for every million people. For the Muslim world, the figure is less than 100 per million (1).

This continuous lack of interest in science and technology on our part has led to an overwhelming majority of our exceptional talent to emigrate to the developed world. It is estimated that in North America alone more than 30,000 Muslim scientists are engaged in research oriented jobs while the total number of such manpower rendering services abroad is more than 1 million (6). Today we stand deprived of our talented scientists, engineers, doctors, skilled technicians and craftsmen because we have not been able to provide them the needed support and enough room to carry out their jobs in a conducive atmosphere.

b) **Budgetary Allocations :** According to an estimate of the OIC Standing Committee on Science and Technology Cooperation, the advanced nations undertake almost 97% of the global expenditure on scientific research and technological development. The Muslim Ummah on the other hand, spends not more than 1% of the global R&D budget.

What importance is being attached to R&D by the developed nations is apparent from Japan's budget for this year. This country' s commitment to the promotion of science and technology is evident from the fact that the total R&D budget of different agencies and ministries is approximately US$ 18.66 billion, which is around 3% of the total Japanese budget (8) The total R&D expenditure by the Muslim World is not more than US$ 4.5 billion, which is less than 0.5 % of our total budget.

c) **R&D Works And Publications :** The obvious outcome of the above mentioned findings is the almost non existent level of R&D out put in the Muslim world. The survey conducted by the Philadelphia based Institute of Scientific Information finds that in the 25 top countries of the world ranked on the basis of the origination of research papers and articles the United States tops the list, India is eighth and Israel fifteenth with not a single inclusion of any Muslim country. This is further stressed by the fact that out of the 100,000 science books and 2 million research papers published every year, the contribution of the Muslim world does not exceed the figure of a mere one thousand (9).

Owing to my personal interest in Materials Science, I would like to draw the attention of the august gathering to the state of affairs in this particular subject while I am sure, the position in the other disciplines of Engineering and Applied Sciences is no bigger than this. According to a study undertaken by my colleagues some time back, the contribution of the rest of the world in the number of papers published in different specific fields of research in Metallurgy and Materials Science, was more than 42158 (10). The Muslim world, on the other hand, portrayed a very disappointing picture with the publication of just 240 papers (Table 4). This was the joint effort put up by 18 Muslim countries while the others stood nowhere in any R&D activity in this respect (Table 5)

The subject wise break up, shown in Table 4, shows that in many vital areas of this exceptionally important field, there has either been no contribution by the Muslim countries or this contribution has been negligible. Table 5, on the other hand, shows that the major share in this respect came from three countries, namely Egypt, Turkey and Saudi Arabia.

MEASURES FOR ENHANCEMENT OF S&T IN THE IDB STATES

When the Muslim world's top scientists and policy makers gathered in Islamabad on March 30, 1995 to concentrate on Science in Islamic Polity in the Twenty First Century their deliberations were summed up in the adoption of a declaration that depicted not only their realization of the importance of S&T in the modern world, but also the challenges being faced by the Ummah in this context. Thus, while it noted with concern the lack of critical mode of thought and scientific spirit among the Muslims (11), it also recommended a number of

TABLE 4

Papers Publisher In Metallurgy & Materials Science During 1988 By The Muslim Countries And Rest Of The World

Sr No	Section	Muslim Countries	Other
1	Constitution	7	1452
2	Crystal Properties	11	1595
3	Lattice Defects	2	678
4	Structural Hardening	--	367
5	Physics of Metals	6	779
6	Irradiation Effects	3	528
7	Metallography	--	305
8	Testing & Control	4	1497
9	Analysis	7	629
10	Mechanical properties	30	4826
11	Physical Properties	9	738
12	Electrical & Magnetic Phenomena	9	1649
13	Chemical & Electro-Chemical Properties	5	1335
14	Corrosion	79	3071
15	Ores & Raw Materials	3	270
16	Extraction & Smelting	5	1842
17	Refining & Purification	2	216
18	Physical Chemistry	1	414
19	Ferrous Alloy Production	3	1612
20	Non Ferrous Alloy Production	1	384
21	Foundry	6	2339
22	Working (Forming)	3	2729
23	Machining	7	1277
24	Powder Technology	7	1386
25	Joining	7	2527
26	Thermal Treatment	--	1686
27	Finishing	7	1475
28	Metallic Coating	8	1504
29	Engineering Components & Structure	4	794
30	Composites	1	704
31	Electronic Devices	--	394
32	General& Non Classified	1	442
33	Special Publications	1	715
	TOTAL	240	42158

TABLE 5

Papers Published During 1988 From Muslim Countries
In Materials Science

Sr. No.	NAME OF THE COUNTRY	NUMBER
1.	Egypt	73
2.	Turkey	54
3.	Suadi Arabia	44
4.	Pakistan	14
5.	Kuwait	14
6.	Iraq	42
7.	Jordan	8
8.	Indonesia	3
9.	Iran	3
10.	Morocco	3
11.	United Arab Emirates	3
12.	Bahrain	2
13.	Yemen	2
14.	Algeria	1
15.	Malaysia	1
16.	Somalia	1
17.	Qatar	1
18.	Kenya	1

remedies, ranging from a change in attitudes to the setting up of proper mechanism. The most significant among such mechanisms was:

`To establish Ummah level Centres of Excellence in different Muslim countries in areas of higher science and technology...' (11) Nothing is more essential for us today than the establishment of such distinguished academic centres of research and development. Such institutions would not only polish our raw talent to be transformed into highly skilled manpower but could concentrate on our vital problems and propose effective remedies in order to cope with the challenges of our times. Establishment of such centres is needed in a number of fields where they can be of invaluable help in drawing up strategies.

Critical Areas Of Concern

1) Agriculture

The Muslims World, as pointed out earlier, is supposed to be providing the rest of world with as much as 40% of the needed raw material. How unfortunate then it is to note that ours is the region with the acute shortage of food. At present 30 out of the total member states of the OIC which face serious food shortages pay a bill of almost 30 billion dollars for their food imports. This seems quite absurd as we are the proud owners of the most fertile lands from the Nile delta to the Indus basin and on to the vast Kazakhstan fields.

The crux of the problem lies in the fact that no concerted effort has ever been made towards enhancing our production by engaging in modern scientific methods. 60% of the Muslim World population is employed in the agricultural sector. Research in this sector, thus, is vital not only to achieve agricultural development, but also to release labour for other industries. Development of indigenous technologies to suit our needs and redress our existing problems are badly needed.

Though there are a number of universities and institutions in the Muslim world associated with the agricultural sector, their output in terms of research and production of skilled manpower is, by and large unsatisfactory because of the lack of resources and absence of cohesion of approach. Thus, there is an urgent need for a broad based research centre in this sector to focus on devising ways and means to eradicate the menace of famine and drought and to enhance the productive capacity.

2) Industrial Sector

Progress in the absence of a powerful industrial sector based upon the smooth flow of needed raw material and skilled labour is meaningless in today's world. The overwhelming progress of the East Asian nations has proved that even in the absence of sufficient indigenous production or raw materials, strong industrial infrastructure can guarantee unprecedented prosperity.

The Muslim world has unmatched potential to progress if we can develop our industrial sector based upon the local supply of raw materials. This can be successfully achieved if we develop local expertise and technology to convert the existing raw materials into finished goods.

The Muslim World, however, badly lacks this capability. Though some industries based upon local raw materials have been established in many countries, such as Pakistan (textile industry) but in the absence of sufficient skilled labour and development of technology, these have not been totally successful in capturing world markets.

3) Defence Technology

Probably no other nations are more dependent on the advanced countries as the Muslims are when it comes to security and safety. While most of the Muslim countries lack the infrastructures to develop even conventional arms, there has continuously been intense pressure from the advance world to hinder the Muslim World from acquiring some advanced capability in this regard.

MEASURES TO BE TAKEN BY THE MUSLIM COUNTRIES

The above mentioned sectors demand our urgent attention and this is only possible if there is a firm commitment on our part. The Muslim countries will have to put their S&T house in order on a priority basis as a first step towards acquiring technology. Only then can they hope to gain strength at home and respect abroad.

1) Commitment on Part of the Respective Governments

Firm resolve in practical measures and not just lip service is required from our government. This spirit of our governments must be reflected by undertaking the following steps

a) **Framing of National S&T Policies :** A specific strategy must be drawn up by the respective governments, keeping in view local needs and requirements. Such policies must underline specific goals, target areas and stipulated time frames.

b) **Evolution of a Scientific Culture in the Respective Societies :** Governments dedication to S&T must be reflected in giving S&T top priority as the vitally debated social issue. This is to be achieved by employing every possible communication channel. A general awareness is to be created bringing S&T at the top of the national agendas.

c) **Establishment of well coordinated National S&T Institutions :** Agencies with the task of coordinating and supervising the functioning of different S&T organizations must be established. This will enable a streamlining of efforts in this regard, avoiding duplication and wastage of precious resources.

d) **Priority be given to Scientists and Technicians :** Such institutions be put under the able guidance of able technical minds. It must be ensured that these are free of bureaucratic control and constraints. These institutions must not become typical public works departments, overcrowded by non-technical, clerical staff. Even those at the top echelons of government, entrusted with the responsibility of executing such policies, must have solid scientific education and well established R&D management experience.

e) **Assurance of Sufficient Resources :** The government must ensure the continuous supply of adequate resources and S&T related projects must be put above financial constraints.

2) Restructuring the Basic Educational System

a. An all out effort must be made to achieve maximum level of literacy in a minimum possible time.

b. Redrawing the existing out dated curricula right from the initial stages, improving the education of pre college students be given top priority.

c. The education system must be managed by trained people.

d. Down to earth technical, polytechnic type education should be the priority.

3) Higher Education

a. Well equipped educational institutions, offering R&D facilities in basic as well as applied sciences, be established. This is one aspect of S&T development where non governmental agencies and private sector can play a vital role and an effective public-private partnership be achieved.

b. The standard of engineering education be managed in a manner that not only responds to the industrial demands of the country, but also breaks new frontiers for the future.

c. The R&D programmes of the existing institutions must be improved. This includes improvement in their infrastructure from libraries to laboratories and improvement in faculty selection and training.

d. Post-graduate and post-doctoral programmes be taken much more seriously. The present trend of the universities in not carrying out such programmes efficiently must be checked vigorously. It should be assured that a maximum number of students are enrolled in such programmes. However, until this capability is developed within the country, it is necessary to send a large number of teachers abroad for Ph.Ds. This is yet another area where the private sector can play a significant role by sponsoring such candidates, thus ensuring benefit from their specific research in the respective industry.

There is much to be done in a short span of time. The Muslim world has already missed one opportunity of development and progress by ignoring the industrial revolution of the sixteenth century. We simply can not afford to repeat the same mistake at this critical hour of our existence. A revolution in thought and perception is required and a joint resolve from every one of us is what is the need of the hour.

Joint efforts by the Muslim countries, in the shape of mutually beneficial ventures, are urgently needed. This will not only save our resources but will enable us to break new grounds of common interest. We must bear in mind that the process of scientific evaluation is a cumulative process where progress cannot be made in isolation.

There exist islands of hope in the Muslim world as we can benefit a lot from the higher level of expertise of the Central Asian States. Malaysia, Indonesia, Turkey, Iran, Pakistan and Egypt also have enough potential to be exploited through joint ventures.

On the other hand the different agencies of OIC Standing

Committee on Scientific and Technological Cooperation COMSTECH approved a plan of action back in 1983, envisaging self reliance in S&T in the Muslim World within twenty years. It must evaluate its performance in this regard as more than half of the time has already passed and we have not been able to devise even the basic mechanism let alone the target goal. Besides COMSTECH, there are more than a dozen organizations of OIC. However, there are only a few on S&T which include: Islamic Educational, Scientific and Cultural Organization ISESCO, Islamic Foundation for Science, Technology and Development IFSTAD, Islamic Institute of Technology. Besides these, COMSTECH has also helped in the establishment of the Islamic Academy of Sciences ACS and six other Inter Islamic Science and Technology Networks. In addition, several other institutions, like the Muslim Scientists and Scholars Forum (MSSF) and the Institute of Science Studies in Islamic Polity (ISSIP) were also recommended by COMSTECH at the International Conference on Science in Islamic Polity in the Twenty First Century, held at Islamabad, Pakistan, from 26th to 30th March 1995. It is, however noted with regret that there has not been any vital output from these organizations nor have these bodies, so far, been able to achieve any breakthrough in the promotion of S&T activities in the OIC countries.

Agencies like Islamic Development Bank and OPEC can also play a very healthy role by aiding the developing Muslim countries in their efforts to develop their infrastructures. In this respect, I am pleased to note that the IDB is already engaged in some healthy contributions. It is currently providing financial assistance to R&D activities in the Muslim world through its `Merit Scholarship Programme' and its monetary help in undertaking projects like the GIK Institute of Engineering Sciences & Technology at Topi (N.W.F.P., Pakistan), is praiseworthy.

A more vigorous approach however is needed both on the part of the Bank as well as the Muslim World. Instead of spoiling our resources on mere bureaucratic and clerical set ups, we must opt for more dynamic ventures. The GIK Institute can be presented as a role model in this regard. If we are able to establish such research oriented institutes throughout the Muslim World on the basis of public-private partnerships with an active assistance from donor agencies like IDB, OPEC, OIC Fund and COMSTECH, offering the highest degree of scientific and technical education, we can expect a major breakthrough as early as in the first decade of the next century. This will not only stop the continuous brain drain but will also enable us to compete with the Western world in a befitting manner. Our scientists, engineers and technicians will have more room for R&D activities and we will be able to develop indigenous capabilities as far as S&T is concerned.

This and much more can only be achieved if there is determination on our part if the resources are spent to achieve strength for the Muslim Ummah and not spoiled in enmities against each other, and if we are able to evolve a common concept of Ummah among ourselves in practical terms. The highest wisdom, Koran-e-Hakim, the last word of the Almighty reveals and I quote: "God changes not as to what concerns any people until they change in respect to what depends upon themselves"

A joint approach and unity among the Ummah, thus can alone promise a bright future for us as and, above all, disillusioned new generations.

BIBLIOGRAPHY

1. A.Q. Khan, `Restricted Areas of S&T and Ways to Develop Such Technologies in the Muslim World; Proceedings of International Conference on Science in Islamic Polity in the Twenty First Century, COMSTECH, Islamabad, Pakistan, 1995, pp. 309-315.
2. `EUROSTAT NEWS RELEASE' Asia EU Dialogue, Jean Monnet Building, L- 2920 Luxembourg.
3. Christopher Flavin, `Oil Production Up' Vital Sign, 1995, World Watch Institute, Washington, USA, pp 46
4. Christopher Flavin & Nicholas Lessen, `Oil Shock' Power Surge, W.W. Norton & Company, 1994, p.46.
5. Ghulam M. Haniff, `Scientific Manpower for the Twenty First Century' Proceedings of International Conference on Science in Islamic Polity in the Twenty First Century, COMSTECH, Islamabad, Pakistan, 1995, pp.238-254.
6. M.A. Kazi, `Scientific and Technological Cooperation in the Muslim Countries' COMSTECH, Islamabad, Pakistan, 1989, pp.11-12, 53.
7. Ghulam M. Haniff, `The American Journal of Islamic Social Sciences' Vol.9, No.4, 1992. pp.5151-532.
8. David Swinbanks, `Money Woes Fail to Weaken Japan's Support for Science' Nature, Vol. 379, January 11, 1996, p. 105.
9. Atta-ur-Rahman, `Higher Education; Science and Technology in Pakistan' 1994, p.4.
10. M. Afzal Khan, Nazeer Ahmad and A.Q. Khan, `State of Science and Technology in the Muslim World' J. Pak, Steek, Vol, 9, No 5&6, 1990, pp.23-30.
11. Declaration adopted on March 30, 1995, at `The International Conference on Science in Islamic Polity in the Twenty First Century' organized by COMSTECH, Islamabad, Pakistan.

Other References

1. World Bank Annual Reports, 1994, 1995. The World Bank Publication, Washington, D.C., U.S.A.; 20433.

2. Human Development Report, 1994, The World Bank Publication, Washington, D.C; U.S.A., 20433.

3. `Global Economic Prospects and the Developing Countries, 1995' The World Bank Publication, Washington, D.C., U.S.A. 2033.

4. `Cooperation South' (UNDP Publication, Oct. 1995).

5. The World Almanac and Book of Facts, 1994, Funk & Wagnalls, One International Boulevard, Suite 444, Mahwah, New Jersey 07495-00017, U.S.A.

6. S.M.A. Shah, `Science, Technology and the Developing Countries' Pakistan Association of Scientists & Scientific Profession PASSP Publication No.2, 1993, Pakistan.

CHAPTER - 20

DR. A. Q. KHAN RESEARCH LABORATORIES, KAHUTA: TWENTY YEARS OF EXCELLENCE AND NATIONAL SERVICE*

It was twenty years ago, to be precise on July 31, 1976, when the first real seeds of Pakistan's nuclear programme were sown. That date marks the turn in our beloved country's destiny as it was on this fateful day that the Engineering Research Laboratories, an autonomous organization was formed, by order of the late Prime Minister Zulfikar Ali Bhutto. The aim was to establish a Uranium Enrichment Plant and provide Pakistan with nuclear capability. In the record time of six years Pakistan was put on the nuclear map of the world and a solid foundation was laid for our self-sufficiency in future for the peaceful uses of nuclear energy.

I had just returned from Europe after almost 15 years. I had studied at the famous Technical University of West Berlin, at the prestigious Technological University of Delft, Holland, and at the famous and old University of Leuven, Belgium. I had worked for a number of years in Holland and had specialized in the Uranium Enrichment Technology. I was young, I had a Doctorate of Engineering in Physical Metallurgy (a most suitable discipline for handling sophisticated technological projects), had published a large number of important research papers in international journals, had relevant research and industrial experience and was, above all, obsessed with patriotic feelings, thus being well equipped to embark upon "Mission Impossible."

---

* Parts of this article appeared in sections of Pakistani press on July 31, 1996.

The late Prime Minister Zulfikar Ali Bhutto set up a Coordination Board, consisting of Mr. Ghulam Ishaq Khan, Mr.A.G.N Qazi and Mr. Agha Shahi (Sahibzada Yaqoob Khan became a member after the retirement of Mr. Agha Shahi), with full government powers and instructions to provide me all assistance to achieve our goal in the shortest possible time. Their task was to coordinate the activities of our Project and that of the PAEC and to ensure that the progress was properly maintained. Formed directly under the control of the Prime Minister, the Project was seen by many as the obsession of a single person, viz. Zulfikar Ali Bhutto. Premier Bhutto was labelled as being desperate to have one.' He had warned the world as far back as 1969 that, "All wars of our age have become total wars and it will have to be assumed that a war waged against Pakistan is capable of becoming a total war. It would be dangerous to plan for less and our plan should, therefore, include the nuclear deterrent. India is unlikely to concede nuclear monopoly to others. It appears that she is determined to proceed with her plans to detonate a nuclear bomb. If Pakistan restricts or suspends her nuclear programme, it would not only enable India to blackmail Pakistan with her nuclear advantage, but would impose a crippling limitation on the development of Pakistan's science and technology. Our problem, in its essence, is to obtain such a weapon in time before the crisis begins. If India builds the bomb, we will eat grass or leaves, we will go hungry. But we will get one of our own. We have no alternative."

When the Indians exploded their nuclear device on May 18, 1974, Mr. Bhutto said, "It is a fateful development. A more grave and serious event has not taken place in the history of Pakistan. The explosion has introduced a qualitative change in the situation between the two countries. Pakistan will not succumb to nuclear blackmail."

After the Pokharan Test, Mrs. Indira Gandhi wrote to Mr.Bhutto, "There are no political or foreign policy implications of the test. India still adheres to its policy of using atomic energy solely for peaceful ends." Mr. Bhutto wrote back to Mrs. Gandhi, "It is a question not only of intention, but of capabilities. It is well established that the testing of a nuclear device is not different from the detonation of a nuclear weapon. Given the indisputable fact, how is it possible for our fears to be assuaged by mere assurances, which may in any case be ignored in subsequent years. Governments change as do national attitudes. But the acquisition of capability, which has direct and immediate military consequences, becomes a permanent factor to be reckoned with."

His prompt initiative to acquire my services for this vital national cause, was yet another proof of his determination and foresight. No matter what people may say, think or propagate, while this venture of national integrity attains an adolescent age of twenty, it goes without saying that the miracle would never have been possible, nor could it have matured so rapidly to the present advanced level, had it not been actively nourished, patronized and supported first by Mr. Bhutto and then sustained single mindedly by former President Ghulam Ishaq Khan. The former Foreign Ministers, Mr. Agha Shahi and Sahabzada Yaqoob Khan, till their retirement, also provided us all possible moral support and did not succumb to any outside pressure to abandon the programme. The late General Zia stood firmly behind our programme. However, the services of the late Prime Minister to the nation have always been highly valued by me and it was because of this reason that I did not hesitate for a moment to appeal to the then President and Chief Martial Law Administrator, General Zia-ul-Haq, against his death sentence in 1979. It is most unfortunate, and a tragedy for Pakistan, that General Zia did not acquiesce to my request and to the many others made by well wishers of the country and executed Mr. Bhutto.

The two decades of the Kahuta Project have never been smooth sailing. Instead, it has been a story of an uphill task with every step being marred by a new set of intricate problems and obstacles. The world would never allow us to have it and we would never bow to surrender it. Confrontation was thus inevitable and we fought it to win at every front be it on the economic one, diplomatic brawls or the acquiring of the latest scientific and technological know how.

The seventies was a time of immense stress for Pakistan as the country was aspiring for the peaceful use of nuclear options in order to overcome its acute energy shortage but was being blatantly opposed by the world powers in pursuit of its legitimate right. It was a time when the arms race, embarked upon by the Americans after using the first atom bomb against the Japanese, had entered a crucial stage. The Group of Five - the five permanent members of the Security Council and of the Nuclear Club, namely the USA, the former Soviet Union, Great Britain, France and China was joined treacherously by India when it exploded a device on May 18, 1974 at Pokharan in the desert of Rajasthan. It made a qualitative change in the balance of power between India and Pakistan. This was also indeed a severe blow to the Nuclear Non Proliferation Treaty of 1970 as in pursuit of their ambitions, the Indians had heavily relied on the Western assistance given under the guise of peaceful uses of nuclear energy. The reactor that produced the desired plutonium for this explosion was a Canadian built one while the credit for providing the Heavy Water went to the Americans. But the West, finding itself utterly helpless to punish or halt New Delhi in its nefarious designs, poured its venom on Islamabad. The Canadians abruptly cut off all nuclear cooperation with us and even fuel and Heavy Water for KANUPP were refused despite the fact that it was under international safeguards. The French followed suit and to add to the miseries of a poor nation, backed out of their earlier commitment to provide a nuclear reprocessing plant thanks to arm twisting by Washington. The fact that the plant was supposed to be placed under the IAEA's aegis and that it was a legal and binding agreement between two sovereign states protected by international law meant nothing to the then French President.

This state of affairs could never be tolerated nor was it. We were not ready to pay the price of a crime that had not been committed. After being convinced that it was impossible to turn his cherished dream into reality under the then existing, rather conservative, set up of the Pakistan Atomic Energy Commission, I was given the go ahead signal by Premier Bhutto to go all out to master the enrichment technology indigenously and that too by employing the latest technique of ultra centrifuge, in order to fulfill all our national aspirations.

The task was gigantic and there were no visible means to accomplish it. We had no good industrial infrastructure and no reasonable base of advanced scientific manpower was available from where one could kick off. I had to start from scratch. But as they say, "Where there is a will, there is a way", so too our determination uncovered the path to our goal and within a short period of six years, the target was accomplished.

All scientists and engineers know that the enrichment technology is the most sophisticated of all the nuclear technologies. It was beyond our means to make each and every component or engineering device indigenously as doing so would have cost an enormous amount of time and we were sure that the Project would have been aborted at the very early stages because of this. We, therefore, rightly decided to buy whatever we could from the international market. With years of experience working on similar projects in Europe, my contacts there with the various manufacturing firms were an invaluable asset to me. This information proved to be of great help for the Project, as within three years we had put up working proto types of centrifuges and were going at full speed to build the facilities at Kahuta.

The dedication and commitment of my colleagues, young and old, deserve a special mention here as they enormously added to my strength and faith. Putting up a team of experts from a corps of new entrants to the arena was not that easy. Many of them had never heard of a centrifuge. But they had the faith and commitment that paid off in the end. They had smelt blood; they went for the kill.

Another factor that highly contributed to the swift completion of the project was the high level of secrecy maintained. The Project had to be undertaken under complete cover as the only key to success was to ensure that not a single word was heard or said about it. The selection of the site at an obscure place like Kahuta added to such efforts. With no charm for the outer world, the place would not draw crowds and security was easily maintained. Being so near to the capital, It was always very easy for us to take quick decisions and implement them without any delay. Now, after twenty years, when I look back I wonder how did we manage to hide it from the prying eyes of the Western world. There can be no doubt that, had they known about it at that time, the story of Kahuta would not have been there to be told. But by the grace of Almighty Allah, the collective dedication of the nation made it possible to master a most advanced technology, known to only 4 or 5 countries in the world, in a very short span of time. No one would believe that a country which was not capable of producing sewing needles, could do the magic. Later events show how all hell broke loose when finally the Kahuta story came out into the open. A most vicious propaganda campaign was launched against our programme by the Western press and pressure was exerted from all quarters. There were sanctions, embargoes and even character assassination. The case against me in Holland is a classic example in this regard. Flimsy charges were levelled against me and I was accused of having stolen nuclear secrets by acquiring some highly classified information. Apart from the fact whether I had acquired information and how classified it was, this case is a classic manifestation of the bias and discrimination that is being held by the advanced world against the developing countries. Later in the courtroom, certificates of six world renowned Professors from Holland, Belgium, England and Germany were submitted, stating that the concerned information was of an ordinary nature and had been fully available in publications for many years. The charges were subsequently quashed by the Amsterdam High Court. The Dutch Government graciously admitted that there was no substance in the case. The fact is that I had requested the said information from a friend as at that time we did not have a library or the relevant literature. I had full faith in the Dutch judicial system and I was not disappointed.

THE GIANT STEP

The gigantic pace with which the Kahuta Plant was established has always amazed and enthralled our people. I have been asked by countless people about this particular point as it is really hard to believe that something that took at least two decades in the most modern countries of the world, was accomplished in the record time of only six years here. As a matter of fact, the usual course of setting up a plant suggests that the sequence in this respect be idea, decision feasibility report, basic research, applied research, construction of a table model, construction of a pilot plant, engineering of the real plant and then the construction of the facility and its commissioning. We, on our part, revolted against this norm and took a very bold step in nuclear arena, starting all these steps simultaneously. While preliminary work was being undertaken in the old sheds at Rawalpindi and procurement was being done for the most essential and sophisticated equipment and materials, we were manufacturing the first prototypes of centrifuges. The pilot plant was being set up at Sihala while the blue prints for the main projects were being prepared as the construction on the main site at Kahuta geared up. This was the unique distinction of Kahuta and a revolutionary step by all means on our part. The French First Secretary, Focault, who was beaten up together with his Ambassador when he tried to sneak into the prohibited area, wrote to his CIA boss at Teheran, "Something strange is happening at Kahuta. Construction work is going on at a pace quite uncharacteristic of Pakistan. One can see day to day progress."

CENTRIFUGE TECHNOLOGY

Our experience in the enrichment field, the most difficult of all the technologies in the whole fuel cycle, deserves a special mention. Owing to the intricacies involved, the process calls for extra vigilance, immense patience and absolute proficiency. If it is handled properly, the rest falls into place without much effort.

As for the working of the technology, in an article in DAWN of September 5, 1986, the noted science writer, late Mr. Azim Kidwai admirably explained the whole of the Centrifuge process for a layman. It is reproduced below:

> "The two isotopes in natural uranium dug out from the earth and with which the world has been deeply concerned for the last 40 years or so, are: Uranium - 235 (U-235) and Uranium - 238 (U-238).
>
> Out of the two the real meat is U-235 that fissions and creates energy. It acts as the fuel in atomic reactors; it makes the atomic bomb (the so-called uranium bomb). The bomb dropped on Hiroshima was a uranium bomb.
>
> The atoms of other isotope, U-238 do not fission, do not split, and so, it cannot be used directly for the production of atomic energy. Nature has condescended to play a joke. The proportion of U-235, the meat, in the natural uranium dug out from the earth, is very low. It is only 0.7 per cent, that is , less than one percent (one in 140 parts).
>
> For production of energy, therefore the Uranium has to be "enriched" invariably. In other words, the percentage of U-235 has to be increased from less than one percent to higher proportions. That is known as enrichment. The enriched uranium used in atomic reactors has the U-235 content of 3 to 4 percent. For making a bomb, the bomb grade uranium has to have U-235 to the extent of 90 percent or above.

> Uranium can be enriched (that is, the percentage of U-235 increased) only by very cumbersome physical methods. The isotopes of uranium being chemically the same, no chemical method can work.
>
> The physical method invariably, has to exploit the meagre difference in the atomic weights of U-235 and U-238, a difference of 3 in 238. U-235 is just a shade lighter than U-238.
>
> That is why uranium enrichment is so difficult, so cumbersome, and so far has remained almost beyond the resources and expertise of developing countries (Pakistan being an exception.)
>
> The methodology used at Kahuta is the latest, least power intensive and very sophisticated. It is known as the ultra-centrifuge technique and is only one tenth power intensive as compared to the old traditional method called diffusion process that yield the enriched uranium for the bomb dropped on Hiroshima).
>
> The ultra-centrifuge rotates at terrific speed of 70,000 to 100,000 revolutions per minute. Any mix of lower and higher density put in it tends to separate towards the centre and the rim from where they are extracted through a highly sophisticated process."

The above description gives a clear indication of how complex the technique is and what a splendid job has been done, and that too indigenously, by Pakistani scientists. It may be noted that the centrifuge technology involves top notch expertise in metallurgy, mechanical engineering, chemical engineering, process technology, electronics, automation and control, nuclear physics, vacuum technology, etc. Since an ultra centrifuge runs at a phenomenal speed, i.e 70,000-100,000 R.P.M. one can imagine the problems arising from demand on materials, the tolerance, bearings, imbalance of the rotating components, etc. It is a Herculean task and an ultra centrifuge is undoubtedly a mechanical miracle. Naturally, the Western world was fully aware of the problems and was sure that an under developed country like Pakistan could never master this technology. We proved otherwise; we not only succeeded in mastering this difficult technology but also in putting up a most modern plant which symbolises our national pride and competence.

It is worth nothing that while spitting venom against Pakistan's peaceful nuclear programme what the advanced world conveniently tended to overlook was its own hectic and persistent efforts to win us as buyers of their equipment. One such episode, which is worth mentioning, is that of an English firm named Emerson.

When we bought invertors from them, we found these to be less efficient than we wanted them to be. We asked Emerson to improve upon some parameters and we suggested the method. As was later pointed out in the notorious BBC film, "Project 786-The Islamic Bomb", the requested modifications took the wind out of the Emerson people. At that time we received many letters and telexes from various European firms and people chased us with figures and details of equipment they had sold to Almelo, Capenhurst etc. They literally begged us to buy their equipment. It was a competition to woo us. They were willing to do anything for money, if the money was good.

We bought what we considered suitable for our plant and very often asked them to make changes and modifications according to our requirements. One should realise that all this equipment was what we call conventional technology equipment, which had thousand and one uses in other disciplines. Notwithstanding the fact that due to the secret nature of the Project, we were handicapped by not being able to hold open discussions with foreign experts or organisations, my colleagues and I successfully tackled all the problems.

OUR EXPERTISE AT ITS BEST

Our scientists and engineers not only designed and ran good centrifuges but designed the cascades, worked out the header piping system, calculated the pressures, developed the control philosophy and developed software and hardware for it. An enrichment plant needs a lot of precautions or fail safe systems. We designed them all. We welded thousands of feet of aluminium pipes for the header and for the feed and collection systems. Once the Western propaganda reached its climax and all efforts were made to stop or block even the most harmless item, we felt enough was enough and started indigenous production of all the sohisticated electronic, electrical and vacuum equipment. Thanks to our sustained efforts we are now fully self reliant in such sophisticated equipment as High Frequency Invertors, Uninterrupted Power Supplies (UPS), Flow Meters, Pressure Gauges, Fast Computers, all kinds of Nuclear Valves, Vacuum Pumps, etc. We also manufacture our own desublimers, autoclaves, uranium hexa-fluoride gas containers, laser separators, electron beam welding machines, balancing machines, etc.

Kahuta is an all Pakistani effort and it is a symbol of a poor but proud nation's determination and defiance to blackmail and bullying. It is not only a great source of personal satisfaction to me but it is also a symbol of pride for my colleagues. Together, we have come a long way from the days of nuclear enrichment to a wide variety of projects involving other defence productions and manufacturing of latest scientific equipment. In fact, there prevails a general misconception that our laboratories are only involved in nuclear activity. This, I consider highly unfair to the outstanding skills and potentials of our talented team. It has always been a great source of pride for me that the Almighty granted me the courage to channelize whatever talent we could gather into a large scale mechanism of national service. With a manpower of about seven thousand highly skilled and professional people, including more than two thousand Ph.Ds/M.Phils M.Ss/M.Scs/B.Es, KRL has now become a full fledged research and industrial complex. No longer it is restricted only to nuclear matters, but its potential is being utilized in other spheres of national development as well.

DEFENCE RELATED PROJECTS

It was General Charles de Gaulle, the French President, who, when asked about the usefulness of starting of his own nuclear programme in the presence of the American, British and NATO nuclear umbrellas had quipped, "A nuclear programme gives you a technical rub off that makes you compete on the world market in a thousand other ways."

Our nuclear programme has also proved to be highly beneficial for becoming self reliant in our national defence. While spelling out other achievements of the KRL towards achieving this goal for the country, our contribution in building highly sophisticated weapon systems deserves a special mention. The various sophisticated technologies perfected during the course of time has enabled us to undertake many defence projects of national importance. It has not only made us self reliant in various sophisticated weapon systems but has also enabled us to save huge amounts of valuable foreign exchange. Intense research is being carried out in this realm with the aim of fully equipping our gallant armed forces with the latest conventional weapons. In this respect special attention is being paid in employing latest high tech knowledge in the fields of engineering, electronics, opto-electronics and laser technology to develop the most sophisticated equipment. Some of the Weapon systems produced by us in addition to our main task viz the production of enriched uranium of the desired concentration and its processing are being described here.

1. Anza Surface-to-Air Guided Missiles

Keeping in view the rapid international development and the severe regional threat posed by Indian air power, KRL has geared up its activities in this vital arena for a long time. Development of different varieties of Anza bears testimony to this particular commitment. Named after the spear of the Holy Prophet (MPBUM) these are surface to air guided missiles falling into two different categories.

i. Anza MK-I :

Man portable and shoulder fired Anza MK-I is an IR homing air defence guided weapon system. It was delivered to the Pakistan Army in January 1990 and has since then been utilized by them and produced at KRL. A highly reliable lightweight missile, easily portable by single man, Anza MK-I is incorporated with an electromechanical impact fuse and a self destruction device for a warhead. It can be launched either in automatic or manual mode. Its cruising speed is 1.5 Mach and its effective range is 4200 meters.

ii. Anza MK - II:

An improved version of the MK-I, Anza MK-II has many more qualities in addition to those present in its parent system Anza MK-I. The first lot of Anza MK-II was inducted in the Pakistan Army in September 1994 while mass production began in October of the same year. Compatible with all the latest Surface to Air Missiles its main difference from the MK-I is its high speed (600 m/sec), high resultant and sustained velocity, high manoeuverability and its all aspect engagement capability. Its effective range is 5000 meters and it can engage high speed, highly manoeuvering targets with both fixed and rotary wings.

2. Baktar Shikan Anti Tank Guided Missile Weapon System

The Baktar Shikan is a second generation anti tank missile weapon system which uses the principle of optical aiming, IR tracking and automatically generated remote controlled and wire transmitted guidance signals. With its long range it has a greater penetration power and has powerful anti jamming capability. It is easy to operate and is capable of destroying all known tank targets at ranges up to 3000 meters with more than 90% hit and penetration probability.

3. Mine Sweeping Line Charges

Available in three different ranges of MSSL-60, MSSL-125 and MSSL-250 respectively, the Mine Sweeping Charges consist of a line charge rocket motor, DC battery and some accessories. These are projected across a minefield by a rocket motor and detonated by remotely operated power supply within seconds of landing. Used to clear paths of respective lengths through any minefield containing anti personnel mines with blast susceptible fuses, these allow safe passage for troops and have been highly successful in operation.

4. Multi Barrel Rocket Launchers

This Launcher has a calibre of 122.4mm and is used to fire fin-stabilized rockets with a range of about 25 kilometres. The launcher, which is either vehicle mounted or vehicle towed, can traverse through 180 degrees, thus giving it a higher rate of accuracy. With its 30 barrels in two groups, arranged in three lines of 5 each, the rockets can be launched singly or in salvo from within the cab. However the rockets can be launched at a distance of up to 60 meters away from the cab with the aid of a remote control unit connected to the vehicle by a cable. While the Multi Barrel Rocket Launchers are produced by us, the 502 Army Engineering Workshop mounts them on the launching trucks.

5. Laser Range Finder

It is yet another of the many proofs of the professional skill and expertise of the scientists and engineers at KRL. The Laser Range Finder is a highly useful device for accurately ranging both static and moving targets from 150 m to 10,000 m. In good visibility the range is up to 20 km. It is designed to have low power consumption, high reliability and meets all Military Standards.

6. Laser Threat Sensor

Laser Threat Sensor is an early warning device which is used to sense a laser beam aimed at it from any direction. The exact location of the threat (incoming beam) is indicated by nine LEDs, covering all directions above horizon. It has the capability to differentiate between a Laser Range Finder, Laser Target Designator or a Laser Target Tracker Signal. In addition, a provision of Sensor output signal, interfacing for appropriate counter measures, is also available. It can be used on stationary or moving objects of any size or shape.

7. Laser Actuated Target

Laser Actuated Target is used for training of gunners on modern tanks in a realistic environment. The output of the device is a clear visual indication up to 1km. Firing capability of the gunners can be improved with the use of this device. It saves ammunition and does not require any proper firing range. Laser Actuated Target is currently being used by the Pakistan Army.

8. Laser Aiming Device

Visible laser beam from the aiming device focuses on a target at the speed of light. This makes aiming swift and more accurate. Laser directed fire provides optimum hit accuracy. Invisible laser beam is also useful when concealment of own position is desirable. The fire can make use of night vision device for observing, aiming and firing at the target.

9. Digital Goniometer

Digital Goniometer is a device used to measure azimuth and elevation of a target. A general purpose gonimometer has been designed, developed and fabricated, which is especially useful for field military operation. The Digital Display gives readings directly in miles (without involving any vernier or sub scales) The operator can quickly point to the required target by using the convenience of Fine Adjusting Knobs. When the horizontal and vertical locks are released the device can even be used to monitor moving targets.

The table top construction of this goniometer allows the user to mount any sighting device such as telecscopes thermal imagers, video cameras and laser range finders.

Two spirit levels help the operator to level the device horizontally. The azimuth can be reset by using an reference or by using the precision magnetic compass mounted onto the goniometer.

10. Power Conditioners For Weapon Systems

KRL has designed and developed high performance Power Conditioners for following weapon systems.

a) TOW A6TM ATGM Weapon System

b) "Baktar Shikan" Weapon System

c) "ANZA" Training Missile System

The power conditioners have successfully completed extensive field trials by users and technical evaluation by inspection & Technical Development (ITD), GHQ. The users have recommended induction of equipment in Pakistan Army because of the ability of these power conditioners to enhance weapon system reliability, simplify logistics, rugged construction and being practically maintenance free. The equipment meets all applicable Military Standards (Mil Std) of Electro Magnetic Interference (EMI), Electro Magnetic Compatibility (EMC), environmental conditions and ruggedness.

11. Switched Mode Power Supplies

Special Purpose Hi Performance Switched Mode Power Supplies have been developed for the following defence systems:

a. LAADS Radar

b. Skyguard Radar

c. Air Defence Automation System

The power supplies designed and produced have not only enabled out of action vital defence equipment to be made serviceable, but also meet strict performance criteria. These power supplies have following vital characteristics:

a. Input over voltage protection.

b. Output over voltage protection.

c. Output short circuit protection

e. EMI/EMC incorporated

f. Line and Load Regulation better than 0.5%

g. Conversion efficiency better than 80%

h. Saleability to IP66 standard

j. Ruggedized to Mil Std 810D

K. Full backup support

12. Tow Missile Modules

Special electronic modules packages have also been developed and produced for TOW Missile Base Repair Workshop. These modules are neither available in the local market nor these can be imported.

13. Add-on Reactive Armour Kit

An Add-on-explosive reactive armour module is an energetic armour element able to release its energy in a very short time to react against the shaped charge jet. The module is developed indigenously in three different sizes to defeat modern shaped-charged warheads by making use of its chemical energy which is produced on detonation by the explosive sheet sandwiched between two armour plates set at an oblique angle with respect to the attack direction of the jet. When initiated by the high speed jet, the explosive sheet drives the metal plates outwards and these moving plates perturb and eat the mass of incoming jet, thus reducing its penetration into the armour.

Efforts have been made to limit the risk of accidental detonation by small arms fire, shell fragments, lightning strikes, etc. The problem of collateral damage, that is the combined detonation of a full warhead and the Add-on-explosive reactive armour module explosive sheet can lead to sympathetic detonation, damage or removal of surrounding modules and fixing is minimized to the maximum. These armour modules have been developed for armoured vehicles, artillery pieces and APCs.

14. Anti Tank Ammunition-armour Piercing Fin-Stabilized Discording Sabot (APFSDS)

As part of our continuous efforts to enhance the punching power of our armed force we have also produced thousands of high density penetrators for the Anti-Tank Ammunition. Because of their very special composition, enhanced kinetic energy and lethal penetrating characteristics, these penetrators are capable of destroying modern battle tanks, armoured vehicles and bunkers. While the special penetrators are manufactured by us, the Pakistan Ordnance Factories produce the final APFSDS shells and deliver to the Pakistan Army.

15. Anti-tank Mine Clearing Line Charge Plofadder-195 AT

Based upon the state-of-the-art technology for breaching mine fields, laid with anti-tank/anti-personnel mines, the Plofadder-195A is a highly effective mine clearing system which clears a safe passage 195 M long and 6 M wide in seconds allowing the movement of heavy armour by simply pressing a button. It can easily be transported to the launch site on an open topped armoured carrier or on a truck trailer and can be deployed on the minefield from a safe distance of 50 M by using a firing lead.

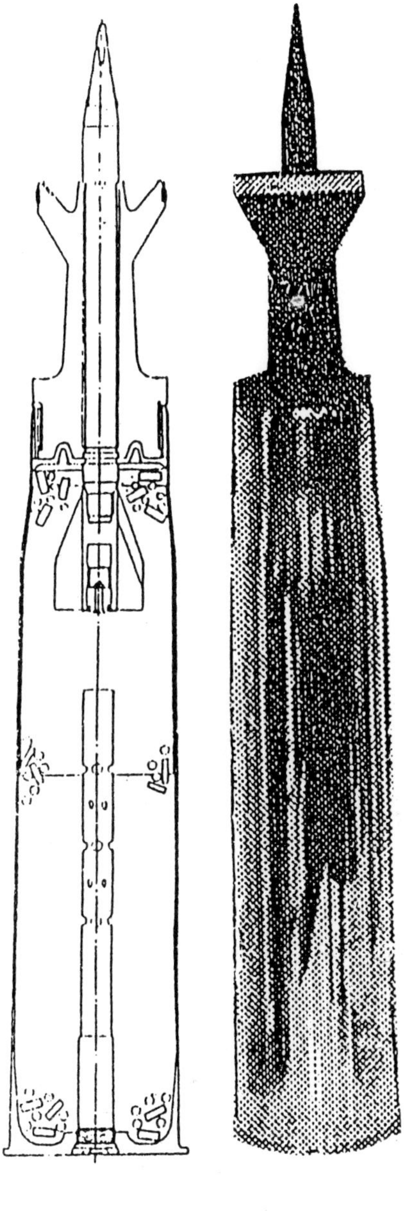

APFSDS Ammunition
(Heavy Metal Penetrant)

16. Remote Control Mine Exploder (RCME)

A highly reliable one, RCME is an electronic state of the art multi channel device to explode 16 different mines at user's option from a remote location without any wire link. As demanded by its application, the system is especially protected against accidental operation in response to spurious commands or noise signals. The system is extremely user friendly and simple in operation. Another of its distinctive features is that although all the systems operate at the same frequency, the coding system has been designed by using the most sophisticated techniques, practically eliminating any possibility of operation at false signal.

INDUSTRY BASED PROJECTS — THE DREAM OF SELF RELIANCE COMES TRUE

As pointed out earlier, I consider it a bit unfair to the exceptional skills of my colleagues at KRL to perceive our Laboratories as confined only to the nuclear arena. This one, might be our real prominence but surely is not all of our excellence as today KRL is fully contributing its share to build a self reliant Pakistan by producing the most sophisticated and latest electronic equipment, which is in great demand by the local industry and if purchased from abroad will cost the nation a huge chunk of precious foreign exchange. We at KRL, have embarked upon the bulk production of Kenvertors — the textile invertors — and UPS (Uninterrupted Power Supplies) which, when employed by the local industry, have set fine records of accuracy and cost efficiency. Apart from the numerous facilities offered by these equipment, their indigenous production promises a better and efficient after-sales service.

1. Thick Film Hybrid Circuits Technology

Thick film technology has established itself as one of the major manufacturing methods to produce microelectronics circuits. We, at KRL, besides having a printed circuit board production plant, are fully equipped with the most modern equipment for Thick Film Hybrid Circuits. The stages of design and manufacturing are carried out by a team of highly skilled and qualified engineers and scientists who keep a vigilant eye and ensure top quality throughout these stages.

2. Kenvertors — Textile Invertors

A remarkable achievement of our engineers, this indigenous production is aimed at providing the country's industrial sector with an effective and economical scientific tool. Not only will it provide the industrial sector, particularly the large textile, an easy access to the highly advanced technology but will also save huge sums of precious foreign exchange that is currently being spent on the purchase of such equipment from abroad.

This power electronic equipment has been developed by using the most advanced technique, of `Pulse Width Modulation' (PWM). This has enhanced the efficiency of the equipment and has also modified it according to the local needs. The Invertors, currently being used by the textile industry for spinning and likewise operations, are run at speed of 15,000 to 20,000 RPM. KRL Invertors are best suited to meet this requirement of the textile industry.

3. Un-interrupted Power Supplies (UPS)

In case of the UPS system produced by the KRL, the attainment of the `Off Line' facility with an ability to sustain a rated load as much as 500 VA, make them most suitable for the protection of electronic equipment, like computers, from any damage resulting from abrupt power failures and load shedding. While the `On Line UPS' system has already been developed by the Laboratories, which is being used by different sectors in the country in large numbers, this latest production is designed to keep the battery at trickle charge and has the ability to come on line within just 5 milli seconds. It also offers the facility to regulate the output.

4. Laser Pointer

A very useful helper during presentations and conferences, Laser Pointers produce a bright red colour spot in continuous or pulsed mode. These pointers, produced at the KRL are ideal for directing visual attention of audience during a lecture, demonstration or a conference for pointing at areas of interest on charts, graphs, slides, overhead images or video images.

HIGHER EDUCATION, RESEARCH AND DEVELOPMENT-KRL TAKES THE LEAD

One of the areas, that has always attracted my attention and has been on top of my agenda, is to develop solid scientific and technological base in the country. There is no gainsaying the fact that nowadays technology holds the key to a flourishing economy, formidable defence and expanding social sector, as development in the present world is another name of a country's solid science and technology infra-structure.

This is amply demonstrated in the world wide distinction between the developed and developing countries, the difference lying in their Science and Technology capabilities. Viewed from this angle, it is most unfortunate to note that, while Pakistan has been independent for 50 years, it badly lacks in terms of research and development and as we prepare to celebrate the country's golden jublee, we are still regarded as the back benchers in the world theatre.

It is thus that we find the Western world exerting undue pressure on us, forcing us to toe their line in international affairs — something totally unacceptable to any self respecting sovereign nation. Sovereignty, after all, is always absolute, be it in terms of political science or in exercising the legitimate right to acquire technology. But who else better than myself knows what it means when one goes to exercise this right. Thus, in my quest to foil any move aimed at our sovereignty, I have always longed to encourage our able scientists, technologists and engineers to come forward and play their due role in this crusade of national pride.

CONFERENCES, SYMPOSIA, SEMINARS — ANOTHER STEP FORWARD

KRL is proud to provide the scientists and engineers of the country a platform in the shape of numerous international, regional and national workshops, conferences, symposia and seminars to interact with the top scientists and engineers of the world, exchanging views, knowledge and the most advanced scientific information.

1. ISAM (International Symposia On Advanced Materials)

Perhaps no other scientific forum has gained the respectability and maturity that has been acquired by this unique colloquium on the complex world of advanced materials. First held in 1989, the Symposium is now a biannual feature of KRL and so far there have been four such gatherings, while preparations for the fifth one, to be held in 1997, are under way. At every meeting it has attracted a record number of top scientists, metallurgists and engineers from all over the world and so far we have been proud to play hosts to delegates from Austria, Belgium, Bahrain, China, Finland, Germany, India, Iran, Italy, Japan, Jordan, Kazakhstan, Malaysia, Mexico, Russia, Saudi Arabia, Spain, Sweden, the United Kingdom, the United States of America, Uzbekistan and the West Indies, besides a large number of local engineers and scientists.

What the utility of this international event has been can easily be judged by the proceedings of all these symposia, which are duly printed in a book form, and are providing a useful data base and reference for the ongoing research in the country. It has always been my endevour to initiate debate on our technological problems and find their solutions by healthy discussion. To quote my Keynote address at the 4th ISAM:

"The greatest event in the world today is the increased automation and sophistication in process technology which has brought about a global industrialization and has been elemental in uplifting the economic and social well being of the masses. Materials sciènce and engineering has played a key role in bringing about this transformation in our society & Material Science is the science of tomorrow and if we wish to excel in our future, we ought to be proficient in this extraordinary branch of science. This has been the motive of the Symposia and an effort on our part to encourage research in this field".

2. National Workshop On Magnets And Magnetic Materials

This workshop, which was held in 1994 was an enormous success in enabling the country's scientists to focus their attentions towards the vital area of magnets and magnetic materials - those materials, though not major by volume, but of extreme importance for conventional as well as advanced engineering applications. A magnet, which is a permanent source of potential energy, is a very useful and indispensable material for the electro-industry. Owing to its wide range of applications in manufacturing motors, generators, lifters, levitation trains, microwave tubes, loud speakers, transformers, magnetic sensors and relays, etc. an urge has always been there to encourage the local scientific community to concentrate on this vital subject. This aim was duly fulfilled by the Workshop, which has gone a long way in providing the latest information regarding production and applications of rare-earth based magnets and Alnico Magnets.

3. All Pakistan Software Competitions And Exhibitions

In view of the ever expanding role of professional computers in today's scientific arena and hence the growing demand for a variety of software the need was felt in the country to encourage the local software industry so as not only to save the precious foreign exchange currently being spent on its import, but also to take a lead in the world software market by exploring the chances of exporting indigenously developed software.

Thus, with the objective of encouraging indigenous software development and to write software package of high standard, KRL has been organizing this singular software gala for the last seven years. Not only have the number of entries, both in professional as well as student categories, increased over this period, but the standard of out put has also tremendously improved during successive exhibitions.

4. National Seminar On Power Electronics & Opto-Electronics

Held for the first time on June 18, 1996, this highly productive and well attended seminar turned out to be another milestone achieved by KRL and hence another feather in our cap. These two fields being specializations of electronics, their importance in today's scientific arena can very well be imagined. Power Electronics has intense application in Power Supplies, Invertors, UPS, Electronic Controls, Welding, Rotary and Linear Motors, Lifts, Escalators, etc. and Opto Electronics is the basis for Lasers, Night Vision Devices, Image Intensifiers, Thermal Imagers, Medical Equipments, Television, etc. It is, therefore essential to gain proficiency in this intricate branch of electronics. With this objective in mind this seminar was organized. It not only enabled the scientific community of the country to concentrate on the subject but also enabled them to have a clearer vision of the issue by free and frank discussions amongst themselves.

5. International Conference On Phase Transformations

Keeping in view the importance of phase transformations in the development of advanced materials, KRL organized this three day international Conference of Phase Transformations from September 1 to September 3, 1996, in Islamabad. Being the first international conference of its kind to be held in

Pakistan, it was yet another grand gathering of the world's renowned scientists, engineers and technologists who arrived from every corner of the world to attend this international moot. In this way, the conference certainly enabled the participants to establish a dialogue among the scientists and engineers of the developed and developing countries. Apart from other relevant issues, the conference concentrated on vital topics such as Equilibrium and Non-equilibrium Phase Transformations, Solidification and Solid State Transformations in Ferrous and Non-Ferrous alloys and Ceramics, Analytical Techniques to study the Phase Transformations and Mathematical Modelling and Computer Simulation of Phase Transformations.

6. National Conference On Vibrations In Rotating Machinery

The National Conference on Vibrations in Rotating Machinery, held from September 7 to September 9, 1996, was first of its kind and a major break through in the intricate field of Vibrations. The conference provided a forum for engineers and scientists in vibrations engineering all over the country and abroad to discuss new and advanced ideas in theory, computational or experimental approaches and applications of vibration engineering. Leading professionals in this field delivered keynote addresses on some very interesting themes on the subject, such as Balancing Technology, Vibration Measurement Analysis and Diagnostics, Squeeze Film Dampers, etc.

Plans For Future Scientific Colloquiums

The think tank at KRL is never short of ideas and when it comes to organizing research oriented gatherings, our scientists are always on the forefront. In addition to the above mentioned regular features, KRL will be hosting a number of other colloquiums on vital scientific issues like Vacuum Technology, Welding Technology, Machine Production Technology, etc. In addition, while we look forward for the holding of the grand ISAM-5 and 8th Software Exhibition & Competition in 1997, KRL plans to organize Conference on Vibrations in Rotary Machinery on the international scale in 1998. All these efforts are directed towards a single goal and that is our aim to provide satisfying answers to the ever emerging queries in the respective fields, enabling the engineers and scientists of the country to play their due role in national reconstruction and progress.

This clearly demonstrates the fact that at KRL, people are always busy in research, they are never short of questions and problems and hence we delight in playing host to such highly fruitful meetings.

GIK INSTITUTE OF ENGINEERING SCIENCES & TECHNOLOGY, TOPI, DISTRICT SWABI, N.W.F.P

During my crusade to build the Kahuta Project, apart from all the international pressures and strains, another problem that always haunted me was to make a team of highly skilled professionals ones who could rightly be called masters in their respective fields. While I may very proudly claim today that I did accomplish this task successfully and the nation now has a team of the finest skilled manpower at Kahuta, at the time of Kahuta's inception, such was not the case. Due to the substandard curricula and lack of research facilities at our universities and higher educational institutions and the immense brian drain that had forced our finest technical experts to settle and serve the West, it was really an uphill task to form a proper team. This I have always regarded as one of the prime reasons for our backwardness in the advanced world of science and technology and I always longed to bring a revolutionary change in the existing inefficient paraphernalia of higher education in the country. In the shape of the GIK Institute of Engineering Sciences and Technology, Topi by the grace of God, we have been able to serve our nation in this vital sphere as well.

I have been closely associated with Mr. Ghulam Ishaq Khan the former President of Pakistan, in establishing this fine seat of learning in advanced sciences and technology at Topi. In my capacity as the Project Director and under the guidance of Mr.Ghulam Ishaq Khan and with the active support of some of his former able colleagues, I have been able to play a key role in the construction of impressive buildings, setting up of well equipped laboratories and establishing the finest faculty. The institute is an exemplary educational and research base in the country which can rightly be compared with any top university in the world. The degree of seriousness at the campus can very well be judged from the fact that, while the first batch of under graduates will be passing out in the summer of 1997, the institute will be all set to initiate its post-graduate research classes at the same time. This will certainly be a great achievement in itself, keeping in mind the disappointing state of research in public sector universities.

An autonomous body, independently chartered and financed by the private sector and hence not a burden at all on the national exchequer, the institute has, with a surprising pace, grown to become a centre of excellence in engineering sciences. While attracting the best possible talent for its faculty, the prime target of the Institute is to ensure that the engineers/scientists graduating from it should be an asset to any organization. Through their education and training, its graduates will be able to tackle successfully any problem in their respective fields and will make positive contributions to the overall improvement of the scientific and technological status of the country.

REHABILITATION OF PEOPLES STEEL MILLS (PSM), KARACHI

The importance of metallurgical engineering to the development of a country cannot be sufficiently emphasized or stressed. The steel industry plays the most important role in this process. As a professional Metallurgical Engineer, I have been fully aware of this fact and that is why I pursued for almost 15 years to get the PSM revived and rehabilitated.

Originally planned as the only alloy and special steel plant in the country, this Mill was set up in 1968 with the name of 'Valika Steel Mills' in the private sector with the technical collaboration of M/S Nissho lwai Company of Japan. The Mill was nationalized in 1972 and was made a state enterprise in 1975. It was however, most unfortunate that in the next 4 years this fine and invaluable industrial enterprise was badly managed and literally thrown to the wolves. It was closed in 1979.

Knowing the importance of an alloy steel mill for the country, I tried very hard right from 1979 onwards to convince the successive governments to revive this useful plant. My efforts bore fruits when in 1993 Prime Minister Mohtarma Benazir Bhutto realized the importance of an alloy steel plant and made me responsible for the Balancing, Modernization and Rehabilitation (BMR) of the Peoples Steels Mills, Karachi. We are responsible for bringing this plant on line and then let it be operated as a purely commercial enterprise to meet the needs of the local industry.

In a short span of 2½ years, we have changed the shape of the mill and have given a new lease of healthy life to it. The previous obsolete and rotten structure and equipment has been replaced with a more modern and sophisticated infrastructure. The central power and utility systems have been restructured and reactivated. The melt shop has been completely revamped and modernized and is now equipped to produce various grades of stainless steels and high quality alloy steels.

The installation and commissioning of electric arc furnaces, ladle furnaces, a vacuum degassing furnace and a vacuum oxygen degassing furnace, together with a continuous caster, has turned the Mill into a modern high quality steel manufacturing facility. The trial production of alloy steels was successfully started on July 20, 1996.

The BMR programme has been carried out with the technical cooperation of the famous Austrian firm Voest Alpine with the backing of the world renowned steel manufacturing firm Boehler. When the downstream facilities are completed by early 1998, the PSM will produce about 45,000 tons of sheets, bars, tubes, etc. of various high quality grades of stainless and alloy steel for our industries and will help in the industrialization programme of our government. We are proud to have fulfilled our responsibilities.

SUPPORT TO EDUCATIONAL & SCIENTIFIC INSTITUTIONS

We are proud that the expertise of our Laboratories is the best in the country. It is for this very reason that different institutes, organizations and universities have reposed great trust in us. Whenever they confront any problem or are in need of financial and technical support, they approach us without any hesitation. Our doors are always open for those who think in the broader perspective of the national interest.

Science and technology is assuming an ever increasing importance the world over and in order to promote this noble cause in Pakistan, Dr. A.Q Khan Research Laboratories are extending financial and technical support to various universities, institutions and organizations both in the public and private sectors. Besides, we also render technical installation services of engineering equipments and also provide repair and maintenance services to these institutions free of cost. We consider it a national service.

Seminars, conferences, workshops, etc. are now becoming essential for any nation keen to progress. It not only brings together scholars, researchers and professors from different parts of the world to deliberate on issues of common interest but also nurtures new ideas. To participate in these seminars, etc. in foreign countries is sometimes hard for professors/scholars of different universities, organizations in

Pakistan due to financial stringency. If possible we help them, keeping in view the importance of scientific and technological development, KRL helps in organizing seminars, conferences and symposia in Pakistan. We also provide financial grants/donations to renowned professors to come to Pakistan to participate in such seminars, conferences, workshops, etc.

Most of the institutions, universities and medical centres of Pakistan are in dire need of computers, printers, uninterrupted power supplies, etc in order to cope with their day-to-day needs. KRL has always helped them with such equipment in order to make their activities more vigorous and efficient.

KRL is known for quality work and our engineers have expertise in installation and commissioning of various computerised control machinery. The installation and maintenance of Laser equipment for eye surgery in various hospitals and medical centres at Lahore, Karachi and Islamabad has also been carried out by KRL experts free of cost.

CONCLUSIONS

Kahuta, by all standards, is a story of our national pride and excellence. It illustrates the determination of a proud nation, whose march to self reliance and success could not be stopped by our adversaries, no matter how strong that force was, no matter how arduous the path was. I have been praised, honoured and showered with the overwhelming love and affection of our people for doing this job for our beloved country, but I sincerely believe that I for one, could never have accomplished this colossal task had it not been for the collective effort of all my colleagues, our Government and above all the sincere prayers of the whole nation. A scientist may deliver the goods; he cannot make society realize its preferences if the latter is not prepared to do so. This is the job of the politicians. Joel Primack has rightly said: "Although scientists as technical experts make important contributions to the federal policy making process for technology, the process remains basically political...."

The fact that Kahuta could mature to the present level is largely because of the strong political backing it received throughout its twenty years of existence. Never for once did any government back out of its commitment to KRL or bowed before the intense international pressure exerted to freeze or cap the project. In fact, as I pointed out in the beginning, it was initiated by Mr.Zulfikar Ali Bhutto, the country's first elected Prime Minister, who did not hesitate to lay his life for Pakistan's nuclear programme while facing bravely the on slaught of the West. His commitment to this Project was phenomenal and the foundation that he laid ensured the safe and successful completion of his dream. This was largely because of his strong and stable base among the masses and the democratic credentials that enabled him to face the brunt gallantly. Now that his daughter, Benazir Bhutto, is at the helm of affairs, the Project has a special soft corner in her heart. She has always supported us and provided us with every possible patronage and financial support to carry on with our invaluable work for our beloved country.

I would further like to emphasise that the success of Kahuta is due to the enormous sacrifices made by the families (parents, wives, children, etc.) of the scientists, engineers and non-technical staff, both civilian and armed force personnel working at the plant. It was only due to their understanding, love, affection and encouragment that all those working at Kahuta could concentrate fully on the enormous task entrusted to them. The engineers and scientists did a wonderful task, a task any nation would be proud of.

As far as I am personally concerned, I take great pride in acknowledging the great sacrifice made by my wife. Being a foreigner, she was in an extremely awkward situation at that time with no friends, acquaintances or relatives and then still looking after our two small daughters. She was always a pillar of strength and support to me and I have no hesitation in saying that but for her all out support, encouragement, understanding, perseverance and love, the story of Kahuta would have been different. There might not have been any Kahuta story to narrate, I am afraid to say. We paid a very heavy price for our patriotism in terms of our family life.

Whatever we have achieved we have achieved after great sacrifices and at high costs. It has given us international stature and has put Pakistan on the world nuclear map. We must safeguard it at all costs. The very fact that we have been invited to sit at the CTBT negotiating table in Geneva with the five nuclear states plus India and Israel is a clear manifestation of our achievements and our stature in the nuclear field. If asked later what they did in their life time for their beloved country, it will be enough for my colleagues to say, "I was a member of the Kahuta team."

Grateful and proud nations never forget their benefactors and heroes. The naming of the Engineering Research Laboratories (ERL) to Dr. A.Q. Khan Research Laboratories KRL, the conferment of the highest Civil Award of Nishan-i-Imtiaz on me and the conferment of various prestigious Civil Awards on my able colleagues is a clear manifestation of the appreciation of our work and achievements by our government and the country.

I am fully confident that our government and our armed forces will never compromise on this vital national project.

Pakistan Paindabad.

CHAPTER - 21

IMPACT OF RESEARCH ON HEALTH, EDUCATION AND COMMUNITY DEVELOPMENT*

It is a matter of great pleasure for me to be here on this important occasion and to address this distinguished gathering of eminent scholars in the field of Health Sciences. I am grateful to the organizing committee for inviting me this morning to inaugurate the 3rd Annual National Symposium of The Aga Khan University on The Impact of Research on Health, Education, and Community Development.

The establishment of this University in the private sector was a landmark in the history of higher education, particularly related to health, in Pakistan.

This is an appropriate moment for me to pay homage to His Highness the Aga Khan and his illustrious family, specially because we Pakistanis in general and our younger generation in particular, are oblivious of those great personalities whose sacrifices and contributions led to an awakening of the Muslims of the Indian subcontinent and the creation of Pakistan.

His Highness's grandfather, Sir Sultan Mohammad Aga Khan, was the President of the All India Muslim League for many years during the first quarter of the 20th century. It was the undaunted efforts of the Muslim League under his dynamic leadership that led to the reawakening of the political consciousness of the Indian Muslims and the creation of our beloved Pakistan.

---

* Inaugural Address by Dr. A.Q. Khan , HI,NI at the Third Annual National Symposium of the Aga Khan University on September 21, 1996.

Today, this country needs the selflessness and dedication of those great leaders for the very survival of our country.

Prince Aly Khan represented Pakistan at the United Nations, and even today people can recall the respect and admiration that his tenure brought for Pakistan. The invaluable services of H.H. Prince Sadruddin Aga Khan, younger brother of H.H. Prince Aly Khan and uncle of H.H. Prince Karim Aga Khan, as the United Nations High Commissioner for Refugees needs no elaboration.

It is therefore not surprising that His Highness Prince Karim Aga Khan should continue to extend the noble traditions of his ancestors.

The services of the Aga Khan Foundation and its multifarious programmes related to health and education are contributing immensely to the uplift and development of both rural and urban communities.

Let me now turn to the title of today's symposium, i.e. "The Third National Symposium of the Aga Khan University on Impact of Research on Health, Education and Community Development".

It seems to me that our first concern should be to address the importance of EDUCATION on Community Development. A sound education is the essential prerequisite for the development and prosperity of every community or nation. For years, we in Pakistan, have been holding meetings to find solutions to our declining educational standards. At the end of the day, it all adds up to absolutely nothing. Although the private sector has created small pockets of excellence in primary education, the majority of Pakistani children are bereft of such basic necessities like proper schools, qualified teachers, text books and allied paraphernalia that are necessary for their mental development. Concomitantly, the practice of cheating in examinations, intercession and bribery for admissions in schools and for passing examinations are the norms in our country today. The paper qualifications of individuals no longer reflect their ability or expertise. Therefore, when it comes to appointments for jobs personal connections and political pressure, rather than ability and merit, achieve the desired results for the fortunate and selected few. It is not surprising that instead of education, the man in the village prefers his son to stay within the family profession or to send him out as a child-labourer to earn money for the survival of his family, because education or ability is not a guarantee for a livelihood in Pakistan.

With this background, let us now examine the prospects of higher education and research. It should be intuitively obvious that research requires considerable expertise and command on the subject of interest. Above all, scientific research, health related or any other, requires absolute integrity, an ability to work hard, perhaps indefinitely, and a thirst for knowing the true nature of things. Within the reality of the existing social and political framework of cheating, intercession, favourtism and parochialism - are we educating our future generation to strive for excellence and to research into the true nature of things? The answer is emphatically no.

We do not seem to realize that due to the communication revolution, the world has truly become a small place. It may be possible for some of us to win a few points with political leaders by making false claims of remarkable discoveries, but no one can fool the international scientific community. The circle of top scientists in the world is a very small one and each one in any field is known to the others by virtue of the excellence of their scientific contributions. Dozens of laboratories jump to confirm and extend the discovery of another institution and competition is a cut-throat one. Recently even a Nobel Laureate had to resign from a very prestigious position because he failed to verify the accuracy of the claims made by scientists working under him.

Unfortunately, there seems to be no accountability in any sphere of activity in Pakistan. Irresponsible reporting in newspapers and periodicals lessen our credibility in the eyes of the international community. A recent case in point is an inaccurate report in the prestigious journal "Nature" that a laboratory in Pakistan has developed drugs for treating AIDS. A later correction and retraction of that statement by the reporter, who is fortunately not a Pakistani scientists, may not have been read by many around the world. A similar claim of the development of a unique gene probe for diagnosing tuberculosis by another Pakistani laboratory remains unfounded and no correction or retraction has appeared in the scientific press for almost a year. How the genuine, hard working Pakistani scientist feels about other similar claims and manipulations, I leave to your imagination and conscience.

By virtue of hard work or hollow words, we ourselves are responsible for earning the respect or ridicule of the rest of the world.

Ladies and Gentlemen, I take this opportunity to congratulate the Aga Khan University on many counts.

The Aga Khan University, and a few other institutions like the GIK Institute of Engineering Sciences & Technology at Topi, N.W.F.P., are becoming famous for their respect for merit and ability. This is the foundation-stone for establishing integrity and reliability and is a matter or pride for Pakistan.

The Aga Khan University symposia present a unique opportunity for serious research workers in the health sciences to present their work to a constructively critical audience of experts, to exchange views and to establish meaningful collaborations between laboratories.

The revolutionary modernization of the medical curriculum of this University should be followed by others as an example. The graduates of this University are making their mark at the national and international level both in medicine and nursing.

The emphasis on patient care through modern and innovative nursing practices, instituted at the AKU, will also help in providing comfort and in inspiring confidence in the patients.

Perhaps I should mention that the former Rector of the Aga Khan University, Professor John Dirks took the trouble of coming to Islamabad to evaluate the work being done at my

Biomedical and Genetic Engineering Division Laboratories in Islamabad. It was gratifying for me to know that he spoke to each young scientist individually. The words of praise he wrote for the excellence, expertise and dedication of my staff was a source of renewed excitement and enthusiasm for my young scientists. His generosity reflected, once again, the tradition of the Aga Khan University in recognizing and honouring merit and excellence.

Professor Dirks was quite enthusiastic about having collaborative projects with my staff. The offer still stands and I am glad that some faculty members here are working together with us. The number of qualified scientists, relative to Pakistan's population of almost one hundred and thirty million, is a very small one and I hope that with cooperation, exchange of ideas and technology you will be able to build a critical mass of experts in every field.

The scientific programme of this symposium is an impressive one. I hope that the 200 papers being presented at this meeting will meet the international standards that are expected of the Aga Khan University. I am confident that they will be excellent.

I congratulate the Aga Khan University for promoting education and research in Pakistan and the Muslim World and for their services for introducing and familiarizing Islamic Civilizations to other nations for the world.

Finally, I wish all the participants a productive and enjoyable symposium. My hopes and prayers are with you for your success and continued efforts in the service of humanity. I congratulate the organizers for their efforts and wish you all kinds of good luck.

And now with great pleasure, I inaugurate this Third Annual National Symposium of The Aga Khan University and declare it open with my best wishes for its unqualified success.

Thank you for remembering and inviting me on this very special occasion.

APPENDIX

PROPAGANDA AGAINST PAKISTAN'S PEACEFUL NUCLEAR PROGRAMME*

The first and the only nuclear weapons used against Japan in 1945 were those dropped by the so-called most civilised country, the USA, killing almost 150,000 people. Since then, though luckily, no atomic bombing has taken place the arms race has continued unabated. The wishful thinking of the USA to be alone to dominate the world, with an arsenal of nuclear weapons was shattered, within four years of testing the first nuclear weapon, by the Russians. Production of atomic bombs was followed by hydrogen bombs. The nuclear arms race was not confined to the USA and the USSR. Within a short span of time the United Kingdom and France joined the exclusive club and mastered the technology of making nuclear weapons. Peoples Republic of China, feeling threatened by the USSR and the USA, also embarked upon this programme and surprise was pulled by the exponent of non-violence policy, India, by exploding a nuclear device, purportedly for peaceful purpose. The plutonium was obtained from irradiated local fuel clandestinely using the Canadian Cirus Reactor and reprocessing it. Since May 18, 1974, when India exploded her nuclear bomb for all practical purposes, no new state has joined openly the nuclear club consisting of the USA, UK, France, USSR, China (and India). There have, however, been persistent reports, to the extent of surety, that Israel has also

---

* This article was originally pulished under the title, "An Analysis of Propaganda against Pakistan's Peaceful Nuclear Programme" in daily `The Muslim', Islamabad on March 16, 1984.

manufactured and stored a large number of nuclear weapons. In this context the statement of the Israeli President and the CIA report, given below are of great importance:

> "It has always been our intention to develop a nuclear potential. We now have that potential". E. Katzir President of Israel - Dec. 1974

> "We believe that Israel has produced nuclear weapons" CIA (USA) Sep. 1974

The main nuclear rivals, the USA and the USSR, (and to a lesser extent the UK, France and China) have stockpiled hundreds of thousands of nuclear weapons of various size and strength. They can destroy the whole world many a time over. They are still engaged in mass production of these weapons and also of regular testing of them. According to a recent report the Americans are producing eight nuclear weapons a day and have more than 26000 warheads deployed. A great variety of circumstances, created intentionally or arising unintentionally, may trigger the use of nuclear weapons. The probability of such an occurrence, though may be very small, it is not zero and still follows "Murphys' Law".

The hypocrisy of this whole exercise is the attitude of the nuclear giants towards developing countries. By forming an exclusive club, they are monopolizing the transfer of nuclear technology to energy starved Third World countries under the pretext of containment of nuclear weapons or non-proliferation. The control or restriction is relative; when it relates to Israel, India, South Africa, Brazil and Argentina, all out assistance is provided at government level and no stories or leakages are provided to the national or international press.

The situation is quite different when it concerns the Islamic countries. The world wide propaganda organized by the Western lobby in general, and the Jewish lobby in particular, against Pakistan, Libya and Iraq has put to shame the campaign carried out against Hitler in war days. The BBC panorama film, "Project 786 - The Islamic Bomb", the book entitled, "The Islamic Bomb" and thousands of articles and TV programmes have all been aimed against the Muslims. And the villain is of course, Pakistan. In spite of all our support and association with the Western countries, we are still the naughty horse to be whipped. Why this hypocrisy and double standard with us? The answer is simple. The Crusade is still on. Islam is the only religion which tore apart the ignorance of the West and threatened to finish it once for all. The Muslims spreading from Morocco to Indonesia, are a formidable force (if properly organized and industrialized) with unlimited wealth and manpower at their disposal. To perpetuate their backwardness and dependence on the Western world exactly fits in the well thought out strategy carved out by the Western countries.

Since of all the Islamic countries, Pakistan has been marked singularly and is on the hit list, let us analyse the whole matter systematically.

To start with, we are always rubbed against our face with the statement of the late Prime Minister, Mr Bhutto, who in the heat of the then existing circumstances in 1965, emotionally had said: "If India builds the bomb, we will eat grass or leaves, even go hungry. But we will get one of our own. We have no alternative".

It was easier to make the statement than to make the bomb. Pakistan did not have the technology, the resources or the manpower to do the job. It still has a very limited option but for the last 5 years lot of prophecies have been made of the impending detonation of a nuclear bomb by Pakistan. Let us look at what is involved to be able to make a nuclear bomb, a simple atomic bomb.

Only two fissile materials, viz uranium 235 (U-235) and plutonium 239 (Pu-239) are capable of being used for the construction of nuclear bomb. The technology to obtain U-235 or Pu-239 in sufficient quantity is a Herculean task. It is an extremely complicated and well guarded secret. And when the fissile material is available it is still a Herculean task to design and manufacture a workable nuclear weapon. The basic principles of an atomic bomb are given in the box but it is not as simple as it looks in the sketches. Let us now have a look at the ways and means of obtaining the fissile materials, viz U-235 and Pu-239.

1. Production of U-235

Natural uranium is only 0.7% U-235 and the rest is U-238. That means out of 140 atoms of natural uranium only one atom is of U-235. The identical chemical properties and miniscule difference in molecular weights of the two isotopes makes it very difficult to separate U-238 from U-235. The well known methods are the diffusion method and the centrifuge method. Diffusion method has been used by the USA, USSR, England, France and China to produce weapons grade material. The centrifuge method is a newcomer but is well-established and though plants producing reactor grade material (3-3.5% enriched) are openly operational, there is no information if this technology is being used for weapon's grade material by any country.

a. Gas Diffusion Process :

In diffusion process, gaseous uranium hexafluoride (UF_6) is compressed in axial compressors and fed to the so called converters which contain a cooler, to remove compression heat, and a large number of porous tubes. A vacuum, maintained by the compressor or the separation stage, causes some of the UF_6 to diffuse through the porous tube walls. In this way the lighter molecules become enriched in the diffuser because of their higher average gas velocity. This occurs due to collision of molecules with the wall when migrating through the pores of the membrane. Collision among the particles does not occur as otherwise it would cause the heavier and lighter molecules to push each other in the pores rendering the separation impossible. While the gas enriched in U-235 is fed to the converter of the next stage after compression, the depleted residue flows to the compressor of a preceding stage. Since the residual fraction is at a higher pressure level than the fraction that penetrated through the porous tube wall, the compressors are provided with two suction converters maintained at different pressure levels. The diagram shows the principle of this process. Some 1500-2000 diffusion stages are required in series to produce 3.5% - 4% enriched material used in light water reactors. More than 1500 stages are required to produce 90% enriched material, needed for nuclear weapons. Only the USA, USSR, England, France and China have diffusion plants to produce bomb reactor mode and weapon grade materials. The process is highly complicated and expensive requiring many years of hard work and billions of dollars. Naturally Pakistan is nowhere in this field and that is why nobody has ever accused Pakistan of even trying to put up a diffusion plant for the enrichment of uranium.

b. Gas Centrifuge Process :

The gas centrifuge process was first used in the USA by Prof. Beans and in Germany by Profs. Martin, Beyerie and Hartek during the Second World War on a laboratory scale but had to be stopped because expertise in metallurgical science was not able to cope with the demands of the centrifuge rotors. Work was started in the sixties and now the UK, Germany and Holland have operational plants with Japan joining recently with a small pilot plant. The USA is putting up a $ 10 billion plant at Portsmouth, Ohio.

The schematic diagram given shows a design of an ultra centrifuge machine. The rotor of the centrifuge is supported on a steel ball and is held at the top end by two axially opposed ring magnets so that there is no contact and thus no bearing friction. The rotor is driven eddy current motor at 75000 to 80000 rpm using a high frequency inventor. The interior of the rotor is connected to the ambient space at its top end through the circular hole between the ring magnets. The UF_6 is fed from the top to the centre of the machine when the pressure is very low. However, in order to restrict the gas friction of the rotor to minimum, the UF_6 is kept away from the bottom section of the rotor by a molecular pump or a seal. The removal lines for the enriched and the depleted frictions are designed as stationary tubes. The upper system of the feed and collection tubes is used at the same time to generate a convection flow in the axial direction which multiplies the elementary separation effect.

A centrifuge plant has many advantages over a diffusion plant and needs only about 15-30 stages to prepare reactor grade material and about 70-80 stages for weapons grade material. Moreover, a centrifuge plant can be built stepwise and expanded as and when desired. It is these advantages that make the centrifuge process so attractive. However, the design and production of centrifuge, and then to put up a functional industrial plant is a Herculean task. The work started in Pakistan by our own engineers and scientists is monumental. Even though the Western countries and news media have been engaged in the most ferocious and mischievous propaganda against Pakistan's peaceful nuclear programme and are talking as though Pakistan has already manufactured and stockpiled a huge nuclear arsenal we must take it with a pinch of salt. No doubt we have done an excellent work but, knowing the extreme sophistication and complication of a centrifuge plant, it will probably take some time before we can produce enough quantities of 3% (reactor-grade) material, not to talk of the 90% (weapon grade) material, if the Government decides to go ahead at all. So far, the authorities have categorically denied any attempt or intention of making nuclear weapons. The fact, however, remains that once the hard nut of low enrichment is cracked, the harder nut of weapon grade material will be available in a short time if the Government so desired. The capability is thus available once a low enriched facility is made operational. It is because of this capability created by Dr. Khan that the International Herald Tribune recently referred to him as the real father of Pakistan's nuclear programme.

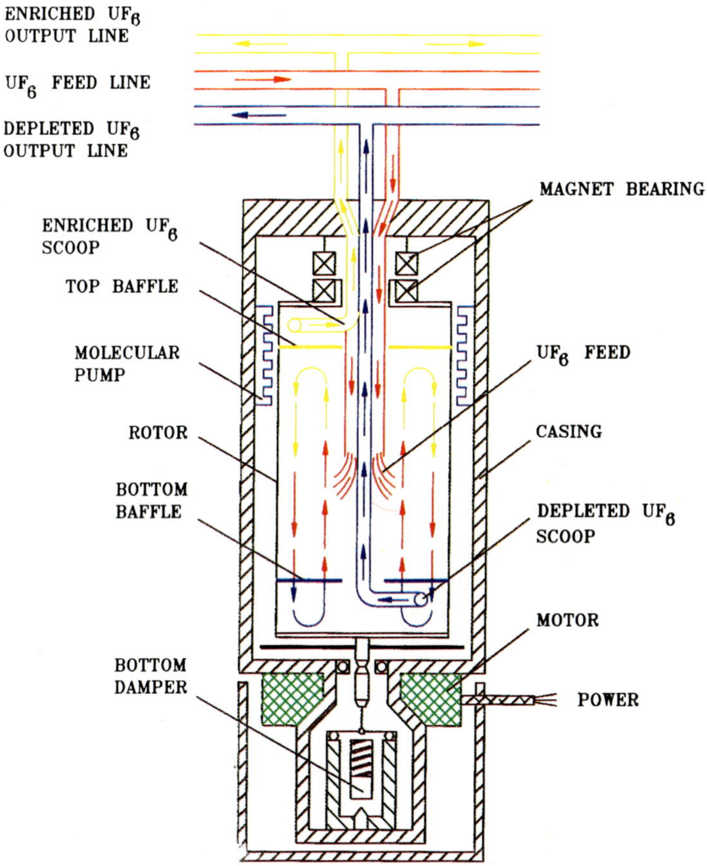

SCHEMATIC DIAGRAM OF AN ULTRA-CENTRIFUGE

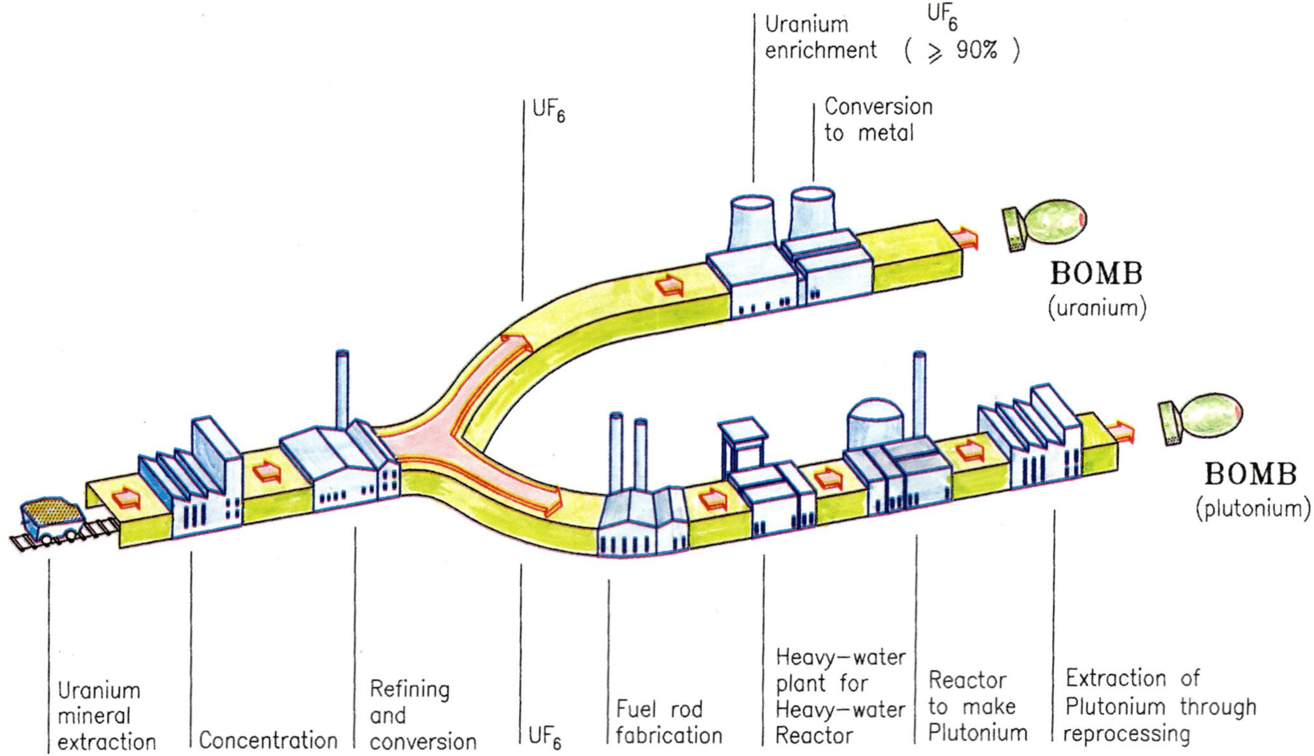

Uranium enrichment
UF6 (≥ 90%)
Conversion to metal
UF6
BOMB (uranium)
BOMB (plutonium)
Uranium mineral extraction
Concentration
Refining and conversion
UF6
Fuel rod fabrication
Heavy-water plant for Heavy-water Reactor
Reactor to make Plutonium
Extraction of Plutonium through reprocessing

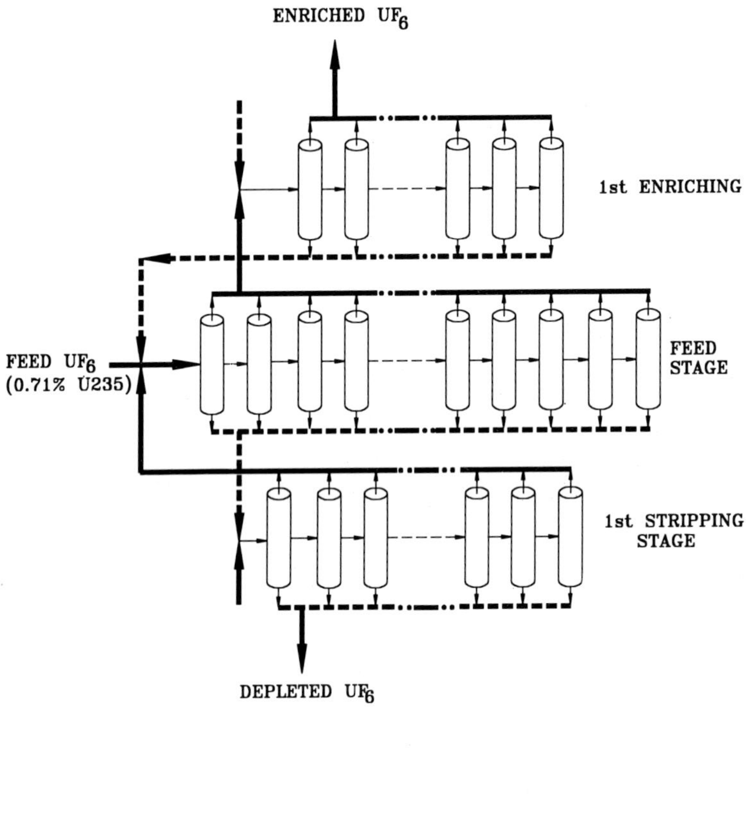

Schematic Diagram of a Cascade

2. Plutonium (PU - 239) Production

Pu-239 is not a natural element. Heavy isotopes like U-235 undergo fission after capturing either a slow or a fast neutron and are called fissile materials. Pu-239 is produced when U-238 nuclei (in reactor fuel) absorb slow neutrons. The U-239 nuclei so formed do not undergo fission but are ultimately transformed into Pu-239 with an atomic mass number 94. Actually U-239 nucleus decays by emitting an electron. The emission of an electron occurs when one of the neutrons in the radioactive nucleus spontaneously changes into a porton. A new element is formed by this fascinating event since the new nucleus contains an additional proton. Thus, when U-239 decays, an isotope with an atomic number of 93 is produced, namely Neptunium-239 (Np-239). And Np-239 is also radioactive undergoing beta decay (electron emission) to produce Pu-239.

$$^{238}_{92}U + ^{1}_{0}n \xrightarrow[23\ min]{\beta} {}^{239}_{93}Np \xrightarrow[2\text{-}3\ days]{\beta} {}^{239}_{94}Pu \xrightarrow[24000\ yrs]{\alpha} {}^{235}_{92}U\ (stable)$$

Radioactive nuclides are characterized by their half lives, the time taken for half of a number of radioactive atoms to decay. Pu-239 is radioactive with a half life of 24000 years while U-239 and Np-239 have short lives of only 13 months and 2-3 days respectively. Pu-239 decays in a different manner to U-239. Instead of emitting a beta particle it shoots out two protons and two neutrons tightly bound together and this entity is known as alpha particle. The nucleus left after this decay in this manner it will undergo fission and it is this property which has made Pu-239 the most sought after and dangerous material for the manufacture of nuclear weapons.

The Pu-239 required for the Manhattan Project was produced by uranium graphite reactors built at Oak Ridge and Hanford. Slightly burnt irradiated fuel from these reactors was reprocessed in a reprocessing plant to obtain the fissile Pu-239 for `The Fat Man'. The reprocessing technique is a rather sophisticated process and is well guarded because of the weapons implications.

The composition of the burnt fuel depends on the burn up time, the heat generated in the fuel (power rating) and the time elapsed since the end of irradiation etc. The reprocessing plant is meant for recovery of unburnt uranium and plutonium.

There are number of techniques (viz Bismuth Phosphate Process, Redox Process, Trigly Process, Butex Process, Purex process etc) for reprocessing the spent fuel to obtain pure uranium and plutonium. The purified plutonium can either be converted to plutonium oxide for fuel in a reactor or as metallic material for nuclear weapons.

Following India's secret development of an atomic bomb in 1974 explosion (on May 18,1974) the US Government spearheaded a campaign to stop the delivery of the reprocessing plant by France to Pakistan. We were forced to pay for India's misdeeds.

3. Reprocessing Plant For Pakistan

After almost 3 years of hectic and lengthy discussions on the part of Pakistan, a protocol was signed on 16.7.1976 between SGM of France and Pakistan, under IAEA supervision, under which France was to provide Pakistan with an industrial reprocessing plant. Till today one is at a loss to understand the logic behind the advice given to the then Prime Minister about purchasing this white elephant for about $ 300 millions projected cost on completion). We did not have any power reactors except KANUPP or enough fuel to reprocess and if someone was giving the impression that the reprocessing plant was a magic wand for making nuclear weapons he was taking the government for a ride. The basic fallacy and limitation of the deal was immediately obvious to the Americans that the reprocessing plant made no sense technically or economically in Pakistan's still limited nuclear power programme but had seeds of a decisive military option. Under constant, severe pressure from the USA, the French backed down finally from the deal on June 15,1978. In the history of nuclear energy one never saw such a sustained and vehement propaganda against anything as against Pakistan's reprocessing plant. The Western World, spearheaded by the USA, the Israelis and the Indians, went for our blood even though they knew fully well that the said plant did not pose the slightest threat to anybody, and was not able to give Pakistan any benefit or capability of making a nuclear device even a hypothetical one. To put the last nail in the coffin, President Carter cut off $ 40 million development aid to Pakistan in August 1978.

WHAT IS AN ATOM BOMB?

An Atom Bomb is a basic nuclear weapon which derives its energy or destructive power from the splitting or fission of the nuclides (nuclide = species of an atom characterized by the number of protons and the number of neutrons in its nucleus) of very heavy atoms, such as uranium or plutonium, by the impact or bombardment of neutron. The three nuclides of interest are U-233 and Pu-239 but only U-235 and Pu-239 have been used so far in nuclear weapons. The main steps in fission process are (a) large amount of energy released at each fission, (b) the radioactivity of nuclides resulting from the fission of the original nuclide (c) release of serval neutrons. It is the release of neutrons at fission that make a chain reaction possible. There exists a critical mass in which a self sustained chain reaction can take place. If an amount of fissionable material larger than the critical mass is put together an explosion takes place, because only one neutron is needed to start the chain reaction and the cosmic radiation can always provide this very easily. For this reason the bomb consists of 2 pieces of fissionable material are known to be used, viz (1) the Gun Method, in which the fissile material is in two parts, placed at the extreme ends of the barrel of the gun. The pieces are brought together by shooting one part into the other using ordinary explosives, and (2) the Implosion Method, in which a sphere of the fissile material smaller than a critical mass is surrounded by segments of suitably shaped plastic explosives. These are known as lenses and serve to focus the shock wave at the centre of the sphere where a neutron source is put to ensure availability of neutron at the right moment. The principle is roughly similar to focusing of light rays at a point by an optical lens.

Table 1. Critical masses (for materials of normal density)

Nuclide	Reflector	Thickness (mm)	Critical mass (kg)
Uranium-235	None		49
Uranium-235	Beryllium	100	14
Uranium-235	Nat. Uranium	100	18
Plutonium-239	None		12.5
Plutonium-239	Beryllium	52	5.4
Plutonium-239	?	320	2.5
Plutonium-239	? Uranium	50	6.4
Plutonium-239	? Uranium	240	4.4

According to available literature about 15-20 kg of U-235 or 5-7 kg of Pu-239 is needed for making an atomic bomb. The bomb dropped on Nagasaki was the implosion type with Pu 239 and was known as the Fat Man whereas that dropped on Hiroshima was the gun-type using U-235 and was known as the Little Boy.

The explosive yield of the bomb depends on the amount of fissile material that undergoes fission before the whole assembly is blown apart by the force of explosion. The neutron reflector, usually U-238, plays an important role in this respect by acting as a temper to hold the material just a little longer for the last important fission to take place. For this reason high density of U-238 is used which also acts as reflector for neutrons emitting from the fissile core. The schematic diagrams

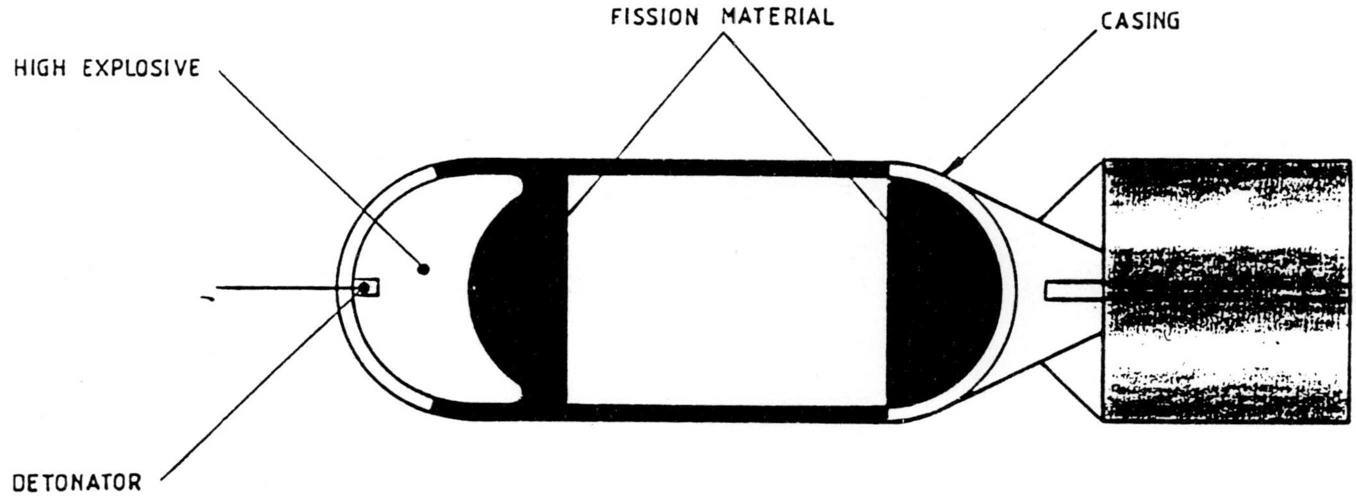

Gun barrel fission weapon

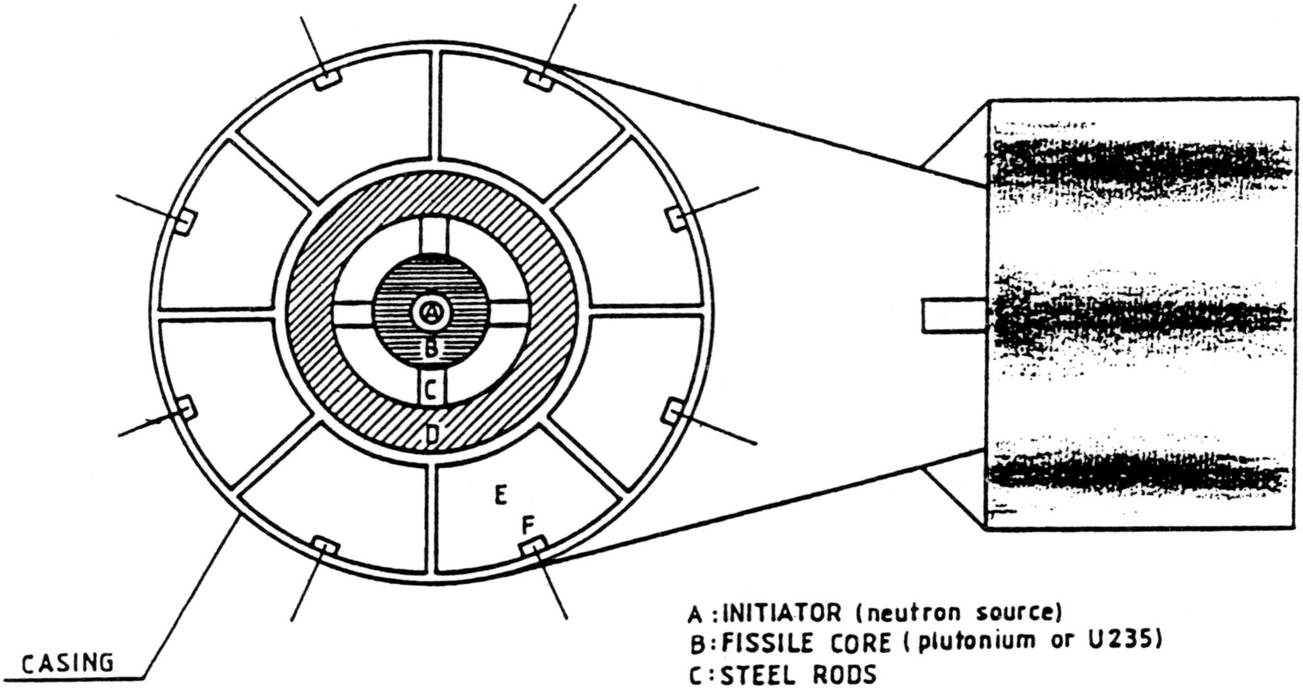

A : INITIATOR (neutron source)
B : FISSILE CORE (plutonium or U235)
C : STEEL RODS
D : TEMPER CUM REFLECTOR (natural uranium)
E : HIGH EXPLOSIVE LENS (shaped plastic charge)
F : DETONATOR (connected to power supply)

Configuration of components of an implosion type fission bomb

show the configuration of components of an atomic bomb, both for the implosion and the gun-types. The Table shows the critical masses for fissile materials. Both the Nagasaki and Hiroshima bombs were of about 20 Kg (20000 kg TNT explosive power) utilizing only about 1 kg of the fissile material. The size of an atomic bomb varies from 1 foot to 3 feet in diameter.

Index

A

B

C

D

E

F

G

H

I

Q

R

S

T

U

V

W

Y

Z